A DICTIONARY
OF
MODERN SLANG, CANT,
AND
VULGAR WORDS

A DICTIONARY

OF

MODERN SLANG, CANT,

AND

VULGAR WORDS,

USED AT THE PRESENT DAY IN THE STREETS OF LONDON; THE UNIVERSITIES OF OXFORD AND CAMBRIDGE; THE HOUSES OF PARLIAMENT, THE DENS OF ST. GILES; AND THE PALACES OF ST. JAMES.

PRECEDED BY A

HISTORY OF CANT AND VULGAR LANGUAGE;

WITH

GLOSSARIES OF TWO SECRET LANGUAGES,

SPOKEN BY THE WANDERING TRIBES OF LONDON, THE COSTERMONGERS, AND THE PATTERERS.

BY JOHN CAMDEN HOTTEN

GYAN

Published by

GYAN

Gyan Publishing House
5, Ansari Road
Daryaganj, New Delhi-110002
Phone: 011-47034999, 9811692060
E-mail: books@gyanbooks.com

Distribution Network
gyanbooks.com
India, USA, Canada, UK, Australia

ISBN: 978-93-6280-529-4 (PB)
First Published, 1860

2nd Impression 2024

Printed at: Gyan Press, Delhi.

A DICTIONARY OF MODERN SLANG, CANT, AND VULGAR WORDS

Author: JOHN CAMDEN HOTTEN

A DICTIONARY

OF

MODERN SLANG, CANT,

AND

VULGAR WORDS,

USED AT THE PRESENT DAY IN THE STREETS OF LONDON; THE UNIVERSITIES OF OXFORD AND CAMBRIDGE; THE HOUSES OF PARLIAMENT; THE DENS OF ST. GILES; AND THE PALACES OF ST. JAMES.

PRECEDED BY A

HISTORY OF CANT AND VULGAR LANGUAGE;

WITH

GLOSSARIES OF TWO SECRET LANGUAGES,

SPOKEN BY THE WANDERING TRIBES OF LONDON, THE COSTERMONGERS, AND THE PATTERERS.

By A LONDON ANTIQUARY.

"Rabble-charming words, which carry so much wild-fire wrapt up in them."—South.

SECOND EDITION,

REVISED, WITH TWO THOUSAND ADDITIONAL WORDS.

LONDON:

JOHN CAMDEN HOTTEN, PICCADILLY.

1860.

PREFACE TO THE SECOND EDITION.

THE First Edition of this work had a rapid sale, and within a few weeks after it was published the entire issue passed from the publisher's shelves into the hands of the public. A Second Edition, although urgently called for, was not immediately attempted. The First had been found incomplete and faulty in many respects, and the author determined to thoroughly revise and recast before again going to press. The present edition, therefore, will be found much more complete than the First; indeed, I may say that it has been entirely rewritten, and that, whereas the First contained but 3,000 words, this gives nearly 5,000, with a mass of fresh illustrations, and extended articles on the more important slang terms—HUMBUG, for instance. The notices of a *Lingua Franca* element in the language of London vagabonds is peculiar to this edition.

My best thanks are due to several correspondents for valuable hints and suggestions as to the probable etymologies of various colloquial expressions.

One literary journal of high repute recommended a

division of cant from slang; but the annoyance of two indices in a small work appeared to me to more than counterbalance the benefit of a stricter philological classification, so I have for the present adhered to the old arrangement; indeed, to separate cant from slang would be almost impossible.

Respecting the HIEROGLYPHICS OF VAGABONDS, I have been unable to obtain further information; but the following extract from a popular manual which I have just met with is worth recording, although, perhaps, somewhat out of place in a Preface.

"Gipseys follow their brethren by numerous marks, such as strewing handfuls of grass in the day time at a four lane or cross roads; the grass being strewn down the road the gang have taken; also, by a cross being made on the ground with a stick or knife, the longest end of the cross denotes the route taken. In the night time a cleft stick is placed in the fence at the cross roads, with an arm pointing down the road their comrades have taken. The marks are always placed on the left-hand side, so that the stragglers can easily and readily find them."—*Snowden's Magistrate's Assistant,* 1852, p. 444.

Piccadilly, March 15*th,* 1860.

PREFACE TO THE FIRST EDITION.

IF any gentleman of a studious turn of mind, who may have acquired the habit of carrying pencils and note-books, would for one year reside in Monmouth Court, Seven Dials; six months in Orchard Street, Westminster; three months in Mint Street, Borough; and consent to undergo another three months on the extremely popular, but very much disliked treadmill (*vulgo* the "Everlasting Staircase"), finishing, I will propose, by a six months' tramp, in the character of a cadger and beggar, over England, I have not the least doubt but that he would be able to write an interesting work on the languages, secret and vulgar, of the lower orders.

In the matter of SLANG, our studious friend would have to divide his time betwixt observation and research. Conversations on the outsides of omnibuses, on steamboat piers, or at railway termini, would demand his most attentive hearing, so would the knots of semi-decayed cabmen, standing about in bundles of worn-out great-coats and haybands, betwixt watering pails, and conversing in a dialect every third word of which is without home or respectable relations. He would also have to station himself for hours near gatherings of ragged boys playing or fighting, but ever and anon contributing to the note-book a pure street term. He would have to "hang about" lobbies, mark the refined word-droppings of magniloquent flunkies, "run after" all the popular preachers, go to the Inns of Court, be up all night and about all day—in fact, be a ubiquitarian, with a note-book and pencil in hand.

As for research, he would have to turn over each page of our popular literature, wander through all the weekly serials, wade through the newspapers, fashionable and unfashionable, and subscribe to Mudie's, and scour the novels. This done, and if he has been an observant man, I will engage to say, that he has made a choice gathering, and that we may reasonably expect an interesting little book.

I give this outline of preparatory study to show the reason the task has never been undertaken before. People in the present chase after respectability don't care to turn blackguards, and exchange cards with the Whitechapel Pecker or the Sharp's-alley Chicken, for the sake of a few vulgar, although curious words; and we may rest assured that it is quite impossible to write any account of vulgar or low language, and remain seated on damask in one's own drawing room. But a fortunate circumstance attended the compiler of the present work, and he has neither been required to reside in Seven Dials, visit the treadmill, or wander over the country in the character of a vagabond or a cadger.

In collecting old ballads, penny histories, and other printed street narratives, as materials for a *History of Cheap or Popular Literature*, he frequently had occasion to purchase in Seven Dials and the Borough a few old songs or dying speeches, from the chaunters and patterers who abound in those neighbourhoods. With some of these men (their names would not in the least interest the reader, and would only serve the purpose of making this Preface look like a vulgar page from the London Directory) an arrangement was made, that they should collect the cant and slang words used by the different wandering tribes of London and the country. Some of these chaunters are men of respectable education (although filling a vagabond's calling), and can write good hands, and express themselves fluently, if not with orthographical correctness. To prevent deception and mistakes, the words and phrases sent in were checked off by other chaunters and tramps. Assistance was also sought and obtained, through an intelligent printer in Seven Dials, from the costermongers in London, and the pedlars and hucksters who traverse the country. In this manner the greater number of cant words were procured, very valuable help being continually derived from *Mayhew's*

London Labour and London Poor, a work which had gone over much of the same ground. The slang and vulgar expressions were gleaned from every source which appeared to offer any materials; indeed the references attached to words in the Dictionary frequently indicate the channels which afforded them.

Although in the Introduction I have divided cant from slang, and treated the subjects separately, yet in the Dictionary I have only, in a few instances, pointed out which are slang, or which are cant terms. The task would have been a difficult one. Many words which were once cant are slang now. The words PRIG and COVE are instances in point. Once cant and secret terms, they are now only street vulgarisms.

The etymologies attempted are only given as contributions to the subject, and the derivation of no vulgar term is guaranteed. The origin of many street words will, perhaps, never be discovered, having commenced with a knot of illiterate persons, and spread amongst a public that cared not a fig for the history of the word, so long as it came to their tongues to give a vulgar piquancy to a joke, or relish to an exceedingly familiar conversation. The references and authorities given in italics frequently show only the direction or probable source of the etymology. The author, to avoid tedious verbiage, was obliged, in so small a work, to be curt in his notes and suggestions.

He has to explain also that a few words wiil, probably, be noticed in the Slang and Cant Dictionary that are questionable as coming under either of those designations. These have been admitted because they were originally either vulgar terms, or the compiler had something novel to say concerning them. The makers of our large dictionaries have been exceedingly crotchety in their choice of what they considered respectable words. It is amusing to know that Richardson used the word HUMBUG to explain the sense of other words, but omitted it in the alphabetical arrangement as not sufficiently respectable and ancient. The word SLANG, too, he served in the same way.

Filthy and obscene words have been carefully excluded, although street-talk, unlicensed and unwritten, abounds in these.

> "Immodest words admit of no defence,
> For want of decency is want of sense."

It appears from the calculations of philologists, that there are 38,000 words in the English language, including derivations. I believe I have, for the first time, in consecutive order, added at least 3,000 words to the previous stock,—vulgar and often very objectionable, but still terms in every-day use, and employed by thousands. It is not generally known, that the polite Lord Chesterfield once desired Dr. Johnson to compile a Slang Dictionary; indeed, it was Chesterfield, some say, who first used the word HUMBUG.

Words, like peculiar styles of dress, get into public favour, and come and go in fashion. When great favourites and universal they truly become household words, although generally considered slang, when their origin or antecedents are inquired into.

A few errors of the press, I am sorry to say, may be noticed; but, considering the novelty of the subject, and the fact that no fixed orthography of vulgar speech exists, it will, I hope, be deemed a not uninteresting essay on a new and very singular branch of human inquiry; for, as Mayhew remarks, "the whole subject of cant and slang is, to the philologist, replete with interest of the most profound character."

THE COMPILER WILL BE MUCH OBLIGED BY THE RECEIPT, THROUGH MR. CAMDEN HOTTEN, THE PUBLISHER, OF ANY CANT, SLANG, OR VULGAR WORDS NOT MENTIONED IN THE DICTIONARY. THE PROBABLE ORIGIN, OR ETYMOLOGY, OF ANY FASHIONABLE OR UNFASHIONABLE VULGARISM, WILL ALSO BE RECEIVED BY HIM WITH THANKS.

Piccadilly, June 30th, 1859.

CONTENTS.

THE HISTORY OF CANT, OR THE SECRET LANGUAGE OF VAGABONDS.

ACCOUNT OF THE HIEROGLYPHICS USED BY VAGABONDS.

THE HISTORY OF SLANG, OR THE VULGAR LANGUAGE OF FAST LIFE.

THE HISTORY OF CANT,

OR, THE

SECRET LANGUAGE OF VAGABONDS.

CANT and SLANG are universal and world-wide. Nearly every nation on the face of the globe, polite and barbarous, may be divided into two portions, the stationary and the wandering, the civilised and the uncivilised, the respectable and the scoundrel,—those who have fixed abodes and avail themselves of the refinements of civilisation, and those who go from place to place picking up a precarious livelihood by petty sales, begging, or theft. This peculiarity is to be observed amongst the heathen tribes of the southern hemisphere, as well as the oldest and most refined countries of Europe. As Mayhew very pertinently remarks, "it would appear, that not only are all races divisible into wanderers and settlers, but that each civilised or settled tribe has generally some wandering horde intermingled with, and in a measure preying upon it." In South Africa, the naked and miserable Hottentots are pestered by the still more abject *Sonquas;* and it may be some satisfaction for us to know that our old enemies at the Cape, the Kafirs, are troubled with a tribe of rascals called *Fingoes*,—the former term, we are informed by travellers, signifying beggars, and the latter wanderers and outcasts. In South America, and among the islands of the Pacific, matters are pretty much the same. Sleek and fat rascals, with not much inclination towards honesty, fatten, or rather fasten, like body insects, upon other rascals, who would be equally sleek and fat but for their vagabond dependents. Luckily for respectable persons, however, vagabonds, both at home and abroad, show certain outward peculiarities which distinguish them from the great mass of lawful people off whom they feed and fatten. Personal observation, and a little research into books, enable me to mark these external traits. The wandering races are remarkable for the development of the bones of the face, as the jaws, cheek-bones, &c., high crowned, stubborn-shaped heads, quick restless eyes,* and hands nervously

* "Swarms of vagabonds, whose eyes were so sharp as Lynx." —*Bullein's Simples and Surgery,* 1562.

itching to be doing;* for their love of gambling, —staking their very existence upon a single cast; for sensuality of all kinds; *and for their use of a* CANT *language with which to conceal their designs and plunderings.*

The secret jargon, or rude speech, of the vagabonds who hang upon the Hottentots is termed *cuze-cat.* In Finland, the fellows who steal seal skins, pick the pockets of bear-skin overcoats, and talk Cant, are termed Lappes. In France, the secret language of highwaymen, housebreakers, and pickpockets is named *Argot.* The brigands and more romantic rascals of Spain, term their private tongue *Germania*, or Robbers' Language. *Rothwalsch*, or Red Italian, is synonymous with Cant and thieves' talk in Germany. The vulgar dialect of Malta, and the Scala towns of the Levant—imported into this country and incorporated with English cant—is known as the *Lingua Franca*, or bastard Italian. And the crowds of lazy beggars that infest the streets of Naples and Rome, and the brigands that Albert Smith used to describe near Pompeii—stopping a railway train, and deliberately rifling the pockets and baggage of the passengers—their secret language is termed *Gergo.* In England, as we all know, it is called *Cant*—often improperly *Slang.*

Most nations, then, may boast, or rather lament,

* *Mayhew* has a curious idea upon the habitual restlessness of the nomadic tribes, *i.e.*, "Whether it be that in the mere act of wandering, there is a greater determination of blood to the

a vulgar tongue, formed principally from the national language, the hereditary property of thieves, tramps, and beggars,—the pests of civilised communities. The formation of these secret tongues vary, of course, with the circumstances surrounding the speakers. A writer in *Notes and Queries*,* has well remarked, that "the investigation of the origin and principles of Cant and Slang language opens a curious field of enquiry, replete with considerable interest to the philologist and the philosopher. It affords a remarkable instance of lingual contrivance, which, without the introduction of much arbitrary matter, has developed a system of communicating ideas, having all the advantages of a foreign language."

An inquiry into the etymology of foreign vulgar secret tongues, and their analogy with that spoken in England, would be curious and interesting in the extreme, but neither present space nor personal acquirements permit of the task, and therefore the writer confines himself to a short account of the origin of English Cant.

The terms CANT and CANTING were doubtless derived from *chaunt* or *chaunting*,—the "whining tone, or modulation of voice adopted by beggars, with intent to coax, wheedle, or cajole by pre-

surface of the body, and consequently a less quantity sent to the brain."—*London Labour*, vol. i., p. 2.

* Mr. Thos. Lawrence, who promised an *Etymological, Cant, and Slang Dictionary*. Where is the book?

tensions of wretchedness."* For the origin of the other application of the word CANT, pulpit hypocrisy, we are indebted to a pleasant page in the Spectator (No. 147):—"*Cant* is by some people derived from one Andrew Cant, who, they say, was a Presbyterian minister in some illiterate part of Scotland, who by exercise and use had obtained the faculty, alias gift, of talking in the pulpit in such a dialect that 'tis said he was understood by none but his own congregation,—and not by all of them. Since Master *Cant's* time it has been understood in a larger sense, and signifies all exclamations, whinings, unusual tones, and, in fine, all praying and preaching like the unlearned of the Presbyterians." This anecdote is curious, if it is not correct. It was the custom in Addison's time to have a fling at the blue Presbyterians, and the mention made by *Whitelocke* of Andrew Cant, a fanatical Scotch preacher, and the squib upon the same worthy, in *Scotch Presbyterian Eloquence Displayed*, may probably have started the whimsical etymology. As far as we are concerned, however, in the present inquiry, CANT was derived from *chaunt*, a beggar's whine; CHAUNTING being the recognised term amongst beggars to this day for begging orations and street whinings; and CHAUNTER, a street talker and tramp, the very term still used by strollers and patterers. The use

* *Richardson's Dictionary.*

of the word CANT, amongst beggars, must certainly have commenced at a very early date, for we find "TO CANTE, to speake," in Harman's list of Rogues' Words in the year 1566; and Harrison about the same time,* in speaking of beggars and Gipseys, says, "they have devised a language among themselves which they name CANTING, but others Pedlars' Frenche."

Now the word CANT in its old sense, and SLANG† in its modern application, although used by good writers and persons of education as synonymes, are in reality quite distinct and separate terms. CANT, apart from religious hypocrisy, refers to the old secret language, by allegory or distinct terms, of Gipseys, thieves, tramps, and beggars. SLANG represents that evanescent, vulgar language, ever changing with fashion and taste, which has principally come into vogue during the last seventy or eighty years, spoken by persons in every grade of life, rich and poor, honest and dishonest.‡ CANT

* *Description of England*, prefixed to *Holinshed's Chronicle*.

† The word SLANG, as will be seen in the chapter upon that subject, is purely a Gipsey term, although now-a-days it refers to low or vulgar language of any kind,—other than cant. SLANG and GIBBERISH in the Gipsey language are synonymous; but, as English adoptions, have meanings very different from that given to them in their original.

‡ The vulgar tongue consists of two parts: the first is the CANT Language; the second, those burlesque phrases, quaint allusions, and nick names for persons, things, and places, which, from long uninterrupted usage, are made classical by prescription.—*Grose's Dictionary of the Vulgar Tongue*, 1st edition, 1785.

is old; SLANG is always modern and changing. To illustrate the difference: a thief in *Cant* language would term a horse a PRANCER or a PRAD,—while in *slang*, a man of fashion would speak of it as a BIT OF BLOOD, or a SPANKER, or a NEAT TIT. A handkerchief, too, would be a BILLY, a FOGLE, or a KENT RAG, in the secret language of low characters,—whilst amongst vulgar persons, or those who aped their speech, it would be called a RAG, a WIPE, or a CLOUT. CANT was formed for purposes of secrecy. SLANG is indulged in from a desire to appear familiar with life, gaiety, town-humour, and with the transient nick names and street jokes of the day. Both Cant and Slang, I am aware, are often huddled together as synonymes, but they are distinct terms, and as such should be used.

To the Gipseys, beggars and thieves are undoubtedly indebted for their Cant language. The Gipseys landed in this country early in the reign of Henry the Eighth. They were at first treated as conjurors and magicians,—indeed they were hailed by the populace with as much applause as a company of English theatricals usually receive on arriving in a distant colony. They came here with all their old Eastern arts of palmistry, fortune-telling, doubling money by incantation and burial,—shreds of pagan idolatry; and they brought with them, also, the dishonesty of the lower caste of Asiatics, and the vagabondism they had acquired since leaving their ancient dwelling places in the East, many centuries before. They possessed, also, a *language* quite distinct from anything that had been heard in England, and they claimed the title of Egyptians, and as such, when their thievish wandering propensities became a public nuisance, were cautioned and proscribed in a royal proclamation by Henry VIII.* The Gipseys were not long in the country before they found native imitators. Vagabondism is peculiarly catching. The idle, the vagrant, and the criminal outcasts of society, caught an idea from the so called Egyptians—soon corrupted to Gipseys. They learned from them how to tramp, sleep under hedges and trees, to tell fortunes, and find stolen property for a consideration—frequently, as the saying runs, before it was lost. They also learned the value and application of a *secret tongue*, indeed all the accompaniments of maunding and imposture, except thieving and begging, which were well known in this country long before the Gipseys paid it a visit,—perhaps the only negative good that can be said in their favour.

Harman, in the year 1566, wrote a singular, not to say droll book, entitled, *A Caveat for commen Cvrsetors, vulgarley called Vagabones, newly augmented and inlarged*, wherein the history and various descriptions of rogues and vagabonds are given, together with their canting tongue. This book,

* "Outlandish people calling themselves *Egyptians*." 1530.

the earliest of the kind, gives the singular fact that within a dozen years after the landing of the Gipseys, companies of English vagrants were formed, places of meeting appointed, districts for plunder and begging operations marked out, and rules agreed to for their common management. In some cases Gipseys joined the English gangs, in others English vagrants joined the Gipseys. The fellowship was found convenient and profitable, as both parties were aliens to the laws and customs of the country, living in a great measure in the open air, apart from the lawful public, and often meeting each other on the same bye-path, or in the same retired valley;—but seldom intermarrying, and entirely adopting each other's habits. The common people, too, soon began to consider them as of one family,—all rogues, and from Egypt. The secret language spoken by the Gipseys, principally Hindoo and extremely barbarous to English ears, was found incomprehensible and very difficult to learn. The Gipseys, also, found the same difficulty with the English language. A rude, rough, and most singular compromise was made, and a mixture of Gipsey, Old English, newly-coined words, and cribbings from any foreign, and therefore secret language, mixed and jumbled together, formed what has ever since been known as the CANTING LANGUAGE, or PEDLER'S FRENCH; or, during the past century, ST. GILES' GREEK.

Such was the origin of CANT; and in illustration of its blending with the Gipsey or Cingari tongue, dusky and Oriental from the sunny plains of Central Asia, I am enabled to give the accompanying list of Gipsey, and often Hindoo words, with, in many instances, their English adoptions.

Gipsey.	*English.*
BAMBOOZLE, to perplex or mislead by hiding. *Mod Gip.*	BAMBOOZLE, to delude, cheat, or make a fool of any one.
BOSH, rubbish, nonsense, offal. *Gipsey and Persian.*	BOSH, stupidity, foolishness.
CHEESE, thing or article, "that's the CHEESE," or thing. *Gipsey and Hindoo.*	CHEESE, or CHEESY, a first-rate or very good article.
CHIVE, the tongue. *Gipsey.*	CHIVE, or CHIVEY, a shout, or loud-tongued.
DADE, or DADI, a father. *Gipsey.*	DADDY, nursery term for father.*
DISTARABIN, a prison. *Gipsey.*	STURABIN, a prison.
GAD, or GADSI, a wife. *Gipsey.*	GAD, a female scold; a woman who tramps over the country with a beggar or hawker.
GIBBERISH, the language of Gipseys, synonymous with SLANG. *Gipsey.*	GIBBERISH, rapid and unmeaning speech.
ISCHUR, SCHUR, or CHUR, a thief. *Gipsey and Hindoo.*	CUR, a mean or dishonest man.
LAB, a word. *Gipsey.*	LOBS, words.
LOWE, or LOWR, money. *Gipsey and Wallachian.*	LOWRE, money. *Ancient Cant.*

* In those instances, indicated by a *, it is impossible to say whether or not we are indebted to the Gipseys for the terms. DAD, in *Welsh*, also signifies a father. CUR is stated to be a mere term of reproach, like "Dog," which in all European languages has been applied in an abusive sense. Objections may also be raised against GAD and MAUND.

Gipsey.	*English.*
MAMI, a grandmother. *Gipsey.*	MAMMY, or MAMMA, a mother, formerly sometimes used for grandmother.
MANG, or MAUNG, to beg. *Gipsey and Hindoo.*	MAUND, to beg.
MORT, a free woman,—one for common use amongst the male Gipseys, so appointed by Gipsey custom. *Gipsey.*	MORT, or MOTT, a prostitute.
MU, the mouth. *Gipsey and Hindoo.*	MOO, or MUN, the mouth.
MULL, to spoil or destroy. *Gipsey.*	MULL, to spoil, or bungle.
PAL, a brother. *Gipsey.*	PAL, a partner, or relation.
PANÉ, water. *Gipsey. Hindoo,* PAWNEE.	PARNEY, rain.
RIG, a performance. *Gipsey.*	RIG, a frolic, or "spree."
ROMANY, speech or language. *Spanish Gipsey.*	ROMANY, the Gipsey language.
ROME, or ROMM, a man. *Gipsey and Coptick.*	RUM, a good man, or thing. In the Robbers' language of Spain (partly Gipsey) RUM signifies a harlot.
ROMEE, a woman. *Gipsey.*	RUMY, a good woman or girl.
SLANG, the language spoken by Gipseys. *Gipsey.*	SLANG, low, vulgar, unauthorised language.
TAWNO, little. *Gipsey.*	TANNY, TEENY, little.
TSCHIB, or JIBB, the tongue. *Gipsey and Hindoo.*	JIBB, the tongue; JABBER,* quick-tongued, or fast talk.

Here then we have the remarkable fact of several words of pure Gipsey and Asiatic origin going the round of Europe, passing into this country before the Reformation, and coming down to

* JABBER, I am reminded, may be only another form of GABBER, GAB, very common in Old English, from the *Anglo-Saxon*, GÆBBAN.

us through numerous generations purely in the mouths of the people. They have seldom been written or used in books, and simply as vulgarisms have they reached our time. Only a few are now cant, and some are household words. The word JOCKEY, as applied to a dealer or rider of horses, came from the Gipsey, and means in that language a whip. Our standard dictionaries give, of course, none but conjectural etymologies. Another word, BAMBOOZLE, has been a sore difficulty with lexicographers. It is not in the old dictionaries, although extensively used in familiar or popular language for the last two centuries ; in fact, the very word that Swift, Butler, L'Estrange, and Arbuthnot would pick out at once as a telling and most serviceable term. It is, as we have seen, from the Gipsey ; and here I must state that it was Boucher who first drew attention to the fact, although in his remarks on the dusky tongue, he has made a ridiculous mistake by concluding it to be identical with its offspring, CANT. Other parallel instances, with but slight variations from the old Gipsey meanings, could be mentioned, but sufficient examples have been adduced to show that Marsden, the great Oriental scholar in the last century, when he declared before the Society of Antiquaries that the Cant of English thieves and beggars had nothing to do with the language spoken by the despised Gipseys, was in error. Had the Gipsey tongue been analysed and committed to writing three centuries ago, there is every probability that many scores of words now in common use could be at once traced to its source. Instances continually occur now-a-days of street vulgarisms ascending to the drawing-rooms of respectable society. Why, then, may not the Gipsey-vagabond alliance three centuries ago have contributed its quota of common words to popular speech ?

I feel confident there is a Gipsey element in the English language hitherto unrecognised; slender it may be, but not, therefore, unimportant.

"Indeed," says Moore the poet, in a humorous little book, *Tom Crib's Memorial to Congress,* 1819, "the Gipsey language, with the exception of such terms as relate to their own peculiar customs, differs but little from the regular Flash or Cant language." But this was magnifying the importance of the alliance. Moore knew nothing of the Gipsey tongue other than the few Cant words put into the mouths of the beggars, in *Beaumont and Fletcher's Comedy of the Beggar's Bush,* and *Ben Jonson's Masque of the Gipseys Metamorphosed,*—hence his confounding Cant with Gipsey speech, and appealing to the Glossary of Cant for so called "Gipsey" words at the end of the *Life of Bamfylde Moore Carew,* to bear him out in his assertion. Still his remark bears much truth, and proof would have been found long ago if any scholar had taken the trouble to examine the "barbarous jargon of Cant," and to have compared it with Gipsey speech. As George Borrow, in his *Account of the Gipseys in Spain*, eloquently concludes his second volume, speaking of the connection of the Gipseys with Europeans :—"Yet from this temporary association were produced two results: European fraud became sharpened by coming into contact with Asiatic craft ; whilst European tongues, by imperceptible degrees, became recruited with various words (some of them wonderfully expressive), many of which have long been stumbling-blocks to the philologist, who, whilst stigmatising them as words of mere vulgar invention, or of unknown origin, has been far from dreaming that a little more research or reflection would have proved their affinity to the Sclavonic, Persian, or Romaic, or perhaps to the mysterious object of his veneration, the Sanscrit, the sacred tongue of the palm-covered regions of Ind; words originally introduced into Europe by objects too miserable to occupy for a moment his lettered attention,—the despised denizens of the tents of Roma."

But the Gipseys, their speech, their character—bad enough as all the world testifies—their history and their religious belief, have been totally disregarded, and their poor persons buffeted and jostled about until it is a wonder that any trace of origin or national speech exists in them. On the continent they received better attention at the hands of learned men. Their language was taken down, their history traced, and their extraordinary customs and practice of living in the open air, and eating raw or putrid meat, explained. They ate reptiles and told fortunes, because they had learnt it through their forefathers centuries back in Hindostan, and they devoured carrion because the Hindoo proverb—"*that which God kills is better than that killed by man*,"*—was still in their remembrance. Grellman, a learned German, was their principal historian, and to him we are almost entirely indebted for the little we know of their language.†

GIPSEY then started, and partially merged into CANT, and the old story told by Harrison and others, that the first inventor of canting was hanged for his pains, would seem to be a fable, for jargon as it is, it was, doubtless, of gradual formation, like all other languages or systems of speech. The Gipseys at the present day all know the *old cant* words, as well as their own tongue,—or rather what remains of it. As Borrow states, "the dialect of the English Gipseys is mixed with English words."‡ Those of the tribe who frequent fairs,

* This very proverb was mentioned by a young Gipsey to *Crabb*, a few years ago.—*Gipseys' Advocate*, p. 14.

† I except, of course, the numerous writers who have followed Grellman, and based their researches upon his labours.

‡ *Gipseys of Spain*, vol. i., p. 18.

and mix with English tramps, readily learn the new words, as they are adopted by what Harman calls, "the fraternity of vagabonds." Indeed, the old CANT is a common language to vagrants of all descriptions and origin scattered over the British Isles.

Ancient English CANT has considerably altered since the first dictionary was compiled by Harman, in 1566. A great many words are unknown in the present tramps' and thieves' vernacular. Some of them, however, bear still their old definitions, while others have adopted fresh meanings,—to escape detection, I suppose. "ABRAHAM MAN" is yet seen in our modern SHAM ABRAHAM, or PLAY THE OLD SOLDIER, *i.e.*, to feign sickness or distress. "AUTUM" is still a church or chapel amongst Gipseys; and "BECK," a constable, is our modern cant and slang BEEK, a policeman or magistrate. "BENE," or BONE, stands for *good* in Seven Dials, and the back streets of Westminster; and "BOWSE" is our modern BOOZE, to drink or fuddle. A "BOWSING KEN" was the old cant term for a public house, and BOOZING KEN, in modern cant, has precisely the same meaning. "BUFE" was then the term for a dog, now it is BUFFER,—frequently applied to men. "CASSAN" is both old and modern cant for cheese; the same may be said of "CHATTES" or CHATTS, the gallows. "COFE," or COVE, is still the vulgar synonyme for a man. "DRAWERS" was hose, or "hosen,"—now applied to the lining for trousers. "DUDES" was cant for clothes, we now say DUDDS. "FLAG" is still a fourpenny piece; and "FYLCHE" means to rob. "KEN" is a house, and "LICK" means to thrash; "PRANCER" is yet known amongst rogues as a horse; and "to PRIG," amongst high and low, is to steal. Three centuries ago, if one beggar said anything disagreeable to another, the person annoyed would say "STOW YOU," or hold your peace; low people now say STOW IT, equivalent to "be quiet." "TRINE" is still to hang; "WYN" yet stands for a penny. And many other words, as will be seen in the glossary, still retain their ancient meaning.

As specimens of those words which have altered their original cant signification, I may instance "CHETE," now written CHEAT. CHETE was in ancient cant what *chop* is in the Canton-Chinese, —an almost inseparable adjunct. Everything was termed a CHETE, and qualified by a substantive-adjective, which showed what kind of a CHETE was meant; for instance, "CRASHING CHETES" were teeth; a "MOFFLING CHETE," a napkin; a "GRUNTING CHETE," a pig, &c. &c. CHEAT now-a-days means to defraud or swindle, and lexicographers have tortured etymology for an original—but without success. *Escheats* and *escheatours* have been named, but with great doubts;

indeed, Stevens, the learned commentator on Shakespere, acknowledged that he "did not recollect to have met with the word *cheat* in our ancient writers."* CHEAT, to defraud, then, is no other than an old Cant term, somewhat altered in its meaning,† and as such it should be described in the next Etymological Dictionary. Another instance of a change in the meaning of the old Cant, but the retention of the word is seen in "CLY," formerly to take or steal, now a pocket;—remembering a certain class of low characters, a curious connection between the two meanings will be discovered. "MAKE" was a halfpenny, we now say MAG,—MAKE being modern Cant for appropriating,—"convey the wise it call." "MILLING" stood for stealing, it is now a pugilistic term for fighting or beating. "NAB" was a head,—low people now say NOB, the former meaning, in modern Cant, to steal or seize. "PEK" was meat,—we still say PECKISH, when hungry. "PRYGGES, *dronken Tinkers or beastly people*," as old Harman wrote, would scarcely be understood now; a PRIG, in the 19th century, is a pickpocket or thief. "QUIER," or QUEER, like *cheat*, was a very common prefix, and meant bad or

* *Shakes.* Hen. IV., part 2, act ii, scene 4.

† It is easy to see how *cheat* became synonymous with "fraud," when we remember that it was one of the most common words of the greatest class of cheats in the country.

wicked,—it now means odd, curious, or strange; but to the ancient cant we are indebted for the word, which etymologists should remember.* "ROME," or RUM, formerly meant good, or of the first quality, and was extensively used like *cheat* and *queer*,—indeed as an adjective it was the opposite of the latter. RUM now means curious, and is synonymous with queer, thus,—a "RUMMY old fellow," or a "QUEER old man." Here again we see the origin of an every day word, scouted by lexicographers and snubbed by respectable persons, but still a word of frequent and popular use. "YANNAM" meant bread, PANNUM is the word now. Other instances could be pointed out, but they will be observed in the dictionary.

Several words are entirely obsolete. "ALYBBEG" no longer means a bed, nor "ASKEW" a cup. "BOOGET,"† now-a-days, would not be understood for a basket; neither would "GAN" pass current for mouth. "FULLAMS" was the old cant term for false or loaded dice, and although used by Shake-

* I am reminded by an eminent philologist that the origin of QUEER is seen in the *German*, QUER, crooked,—hence "odd." I agree with this etymology, but still have reason to believe that the word was *first* used in this country in a cant sense. Is it mentioned any where as a respectable term before 1500? If not, it had a vulgar or cant introduction into this country.

† BOOGET properly signifies a leathern wallet, and is probably derived from the *low Latin*, BULGA. A tinker's budget is from the same source.

spere in this sense, is now unknown and obsolete. Indeed, as Tom Moore somewhere remarks, the present Greeks of St. Giles, themselves, would be thoroughly puzzled by many of the ancient canting songs,—taking for example, the first verse of an old favourite:

Bing out, bien Morts, and toure and toure,
Bing out, bien Morts, and toure;
For all your duds are bing'd awast;
The bien cove hath the loure.*

But I think I cannot do better than present to the reader at once an entire copy of the first Canting Dictionary ever compiled. As before mentioned, it was the work of one Thos. Harman, a gentleman who lived in the days of Queen Elizabeth. Some writers have remarked that Decker† was the first to compile a Dictionary of the vagabonds' tongue; whilst Borrow,‡ and Moore, the poet, stated that Richard Head performed that

* Which, literally translated, means:

Go out, good girls, and look and see,
Go out, good girls, and see;
For all your clothes are carried away,
And the good man has the money.

† Who wrote about the year 1610.

‡ *Gipseys of Spain*, vol. i., p. 18. Borrow further commits himself by remarking that "Head's Vocabulary has always been accepted as the speech of the English Gipseys." Nothing of the kind. Head professed to have lived with the Gipseys, but in reality filched his words from *Decker* and *Brome*.

service in his *Life of an English Rogue*, published in the year 1680. All these statements are equally incorrect, for the first attempt was made more than a century before the latter work was issued. The quaint spelling and old-fashioned phraseology are preserved, and the reader will quickly detect many vulgar street words, old acquaintances, dressed in antique garb.*

ABRAHAM-MEN, be those that fayn themselves to have beene mad, and have bene kept either in Bethelem, or in some other pryson a good time.

ALYBBEG, a bedde.

ASKEW, a cuppe.

AUTEM, a churche.

AUTEM MORTES, married wemen as chaste as a cowe.

BAUDYE BASKETS, bee women who goe with baskets and capcases on their armes, wherein they have laces, pinnes, nedles, whyte inkel, and round sylke gyrdels of all colours.

BECK [Beek], a constable.

BELLY-CHETE, apron.

BENE, good. *Benar*, better.

BENSHIP, very good.

BLETING CHETE, a calfe or sheepe.

BOOGET, a travelling tinker's baskete.

BORDE, a shilling.

BOUNG, a purse [*Friesic*, pong].

BOWSE, drink.

BOWSING-KEN, a alehouse.

BUFE [buffer, a man], a dogge.

BYNGE A WASTE, go you hence.

CACKLING-CHETE, a coke [cock], or capon.

CASSAN [cassam], cheese.

CASTERS, a cloake.

* The *modern* meanings of a few of the old cant words are given in brackets.

CATETH, "the vpright Cofe *cateth* to the Roge" [probably a shortening or misprint of *Canteth*].

CHATTES, the gallowes.

CHETE [see what has been previously said about this word].

CLY [a pocket], to take, receive, or have.

COFE [cove], a person.

COMMISSION [mish], a shirt.

COUNTERFET CRANKE, these that do counterfet the Cranke be yong knaves and yonge harlots, that deeply dissemble the falling sicknes.

CRANKE [cranky, foolish], falling evil [or wasting sickness].

CRASHING-CHETES, teeth.

CUFFEN, a manne [a *cuif* in Northumberland and Scotland signifies a lout or awkward fellow].

DARKEMANS, the night.

DELL, a yonge wench.

DEWSE-A-VYLE, the countrey.

DOCK, to deflower.

DOXES, harlots.

DRAWERS, hosen.

DUDES [or dudds], clothes.

FAMBLES, handes.

FAMBLING-CHETE, a ring on one's hand.

FLAGG, a groat.

FRATER, a beggar wyth a false paper.

FRESHE-WATER-MARINERS, these kind of caterpillers counterfet great losses on the sea:—their shippes were drowned in the playne of Salisbury.

FYLCHE, to robbe: *Fylch-man* [a robber].

GAGE, a quart pot.

GAN, a mouth.

GENTRY COFE, a noble or gentle man.

GENTRY-COFES-KEN, a noble or gentle man's house.

GENTRY MORT, a noble or gentle woman.

GERRY, excrement.

GLASYERS, eyes.

GLYMMAR, fyer.

GRANNAM, corne.

GRUNTING-CHETE, a pygge.

GYB, a writing.

GYGER [jigger], a dore.

HEARING-CHETES, eares.

JARKE, a seale.

JARKEMAN, one who make writings and set seales for [counterfeit] licences and pasports.

KEN, a house.

KYNCHEN CO [or *cove*], a young boye trained up like a "*Kynching Morte.*" [From the German diminutive *Kindschen.*]

KYNCHING MORTE, is a little gyrle, carried at their mothers' backe in a slate, or sheete, who brings them up sauagely.

LAG, water.

LAG OF DUDES, a bucke [or basket] of clothes.

LAGE, to washe.

LAP, butter, mylke, or whey.

LIGHTMANS, the day.

LOWING-CHETE, a cowe.

LOWRE, money.

LUBBARES,—"sturdy *Lubbares*," country bumpkins, or men of a low degree.

LYB-BEG, a bed.

LYCKE [lick], to beate.

LYP, to lie down.

LYPKEN, a house to lye in.

MAKE [mag], a halfpenny.

MARGERI PRATER, a hen.

MILLING, to steale [by sending a child in at the window].

MOFLING-CHETE, a napkin.

MORTES [motts], harlots.

MYLL, to robbe.

MYNT, gold.

NAB [nob], a heade.

NABCHET, a hat or cap.

NASE, dronken.

NOSEGENT, a nunne.

PALLYARD, a borne beggar [who counterfeits sickness, or incurable sores. They are mostly Welshmen, Harman says].

PARAM, mylke.

PATRICO, a priest.

PATRICOS KINCHEN, a pygge [a satirical hit at the church, *Patrico* meaning a parson or priest, and *Kinchen* his little boy or girl].

PEK [peckish], meat.

POPPELARS, porrage.

PRAT, a buttocke.

PRATLING-CHETE, a toung.

PRAUNCER, a horse.

PRIGGER OF PRAUNCERS, be horse stealers, for to prigge signifieth in their language to steale, and a Prauncer is a horse, so being put together, the matter was playn. [Thus writes old Thomas Harman, who concludes his description of this order of "pryggers," by very quietly saying, "I had the best gelding stolen out of my pasture, that I had amongst others, whyle this book was first a printing."]

PRYGGES, dronken Tinkers, or beastly people.

QUACKING-CHETE, a drake or duck.

QUAROMES, a body.

QUIER [queer], badde [see what has been previously said about this word].

QUYER CRAMP-RINGES, boltes or fetters.

QUIER CUFFIN, the iustice of peace.

QUYER-KYN, a pryson house.

RED SHANKE, a drake or ducke.

ROGER, a goose.

ROME, goode [now curious, noted, or remarkable in any way. *Rum* is the modern orthography].

ROME BOUSE [rum booze] wyne.

ROME MORT, the Queene [Elizabeth].

ROME VYLE [or Rum-ville], London.

RUFF PECK, baken [short bread, common in old times at farm houses].

RUFFMANS, the woods or bushes.

SALOMON, a alter or masse.

SKYPPER, a barne.

SLATE, a sheete or shetes.

SMELLING CHETE, a nose.

SMELLING CHETE, a garden or orchard.

SNOWT FAYRE [said of a woman who has a pretty face or is comely].

STALL [to initiate a beggar or rogue into the rights and privileges of the canting order. Harman relates, that when an upright-man, or initiated, first-class rogue, "mete any beggar, whether he be sturdy or impotent, he will demand of him whether ever he was '*stalled to the roge*' or no. If he say he was, he will know of whom, and his name yt stalled him. And if he be not learnedly able to show him the whole circumstance thereof, he will spoyle him of his money, either of his best garment, if it be worth any money, and haue him to the bowsing ken: which is, to some typpling house next adjoyninge, and layth there to gage the best thing that he hath for twenty pence or two shillings: this man obeyeth for feare of beatinge. Then dooth this upright man call for a gage of bowse, which is a quarte potte of drink, and powres the same vpon his peld pate, adding these words,—I, *G. P.* do stalle the, *W. T.* to the Roge, and that from henceforth it shall be lawfull for thee to cant, that is to aske or begge for thi liuing in al places." Something like this treatment is the popular idea of Freemasonry, and what schoolboys term "freeing."

STAMPES, legges.

STAMPERS, shoes.

STAULING KEN, a house that will receyue stollen wares.

STAWLINGE-KENS, tippling houses.

STOW YOU [stow it], hold your peace.

STRIKE, to steale.

STROMMELL, strawe.

SWADDER, or *Pedler* [a man who hawks goods].

THE HIGH PAD, the highway.

THE RUFFIAN CLY THEE, the devil take thee.

TOGEMANS [togg], a cloake.

TOGMAN, a coate.

TO BOWSE, to drinke.

TO CANTE, to speake.

TO CLY THE GERKE, to be whipped.

TO COUCH A HOGSHEAD, to lie down and slepe.

TO CUTTE, to say [*cut it* is modern slang for "be quiet"].

TO CUT BENE WHYDDES, to speake or give good words.

TO CUTTE QUYER WHYDDES, to giue euil words or euil language.

TO CUT BENLE, to speak gentle.

TO DUP YE GYGER [jigger], to open the dore.

TO FYLCHE, to robbe.

TO HEUE A BOUGH, to robbe or rifle a boweth [booth].

TO MAUNDE, to aske or require.

TO MILL A KEN, to robbe a house.

TO NYGLE [coition].

TO NYP A BOUNG [nip, to steal], to cut a purse.

TO SKOWER THE CRAMPRINGES, to weare boltes or fetters.

TO STALL, to make or ordain.

TO THE RUFFIAN, to the Devil.

TO TOWRE, to see.

TRYNING [trine], hanging.

TYB OF THE BUTERY, a goose.

WALKING MORTE, womene [who pass for widows].

WAPPING [coition].

WHYDDES, wordes.

WYN, a penny.

YANNAM, bread.

Turning our attention more to the Cant of modern times, in connection with the old, we find that words have been drawn into the thieves' vocabulary from every conceivable source. Hard or infrequent words, vulgarly termed *crack-jaw*, or *jaw-breakers*, were very often used and considered as cant terms. And here it should be mentioned that at the present day the most inconsistent and far-fetched terms are often used for secret purposes, when they are known to be caviare to the million.

It is really laughable to know that such words as *incongruous, insipid, interloper, intriguing, indecorum, forestal, equip, hush, grapple,* &c. &c., were current Cant words a century and a half ago; but such was the case, as any one may see in the *Dictionary of Canting Words,* at the end of *Bacchus and Venus,** 1737. They are inserted not as jokes or squibs, but as selections from the veritable pocket dictionaries of the Jack Sheppards and Dick Turpins of the day. If they were safely used as unknown and cabalistic terms amongst the commonalty, the fact would form a very curious illustration of the ignorance of our poor ancestors. One piece of information is conveyed to us, *i.e.*, that the "Knights" or "Gentlemen of the road," using these polite words in those days of highwaymen, were really well educated men, — which heretofore has always been a hard point of belief, notwithstanding old novels and operas.

Amongst those Cant words which have either altered their meaning, or have become extinct, I may cite LADY, formerly the Cant for "a very crooked, deformed, and ill-shapen woman;"† and

* This is a curious volume, and is worth from one to two guineas. The Canting Dictionary was afterwards reprinted, word for word, with the title of *The Scoundrel's Dictionary,* in 1751. It was originally published, without date, about the year 1710 by B. E., under the title of a *Dictionary of the Canting Crew.*

† *Bacchus and Venus,* 1737.

HARMAN, "a pair of stocks, or a constable." The former is a pleasant piece of satire, whilst the latter indicates a singular method of revenge. HARMAN was the first author who specially wrote against English vagabonds, and for his trouble his name became synonymous with a pair of stocks, and a policeman of the olden time.

Apart from the Gipsey element, we find that Cant abounds in terms from foreign languages, and that it exhibits the growth of most recognised and completely formed tongues,—the gathering of words from foreign sources. In the reign of Elizabeth and of King James I., several Dutch, Spanish, and Flemish words were introduced by soldiers who had served in the Low Countries, and sailors who had returned from the Spanish Main, who like "mine ancient Pistol" were fond of garnishing their speech with outlandish phrases. Many of these were soon picked up and adopted by vagabonds and tramps in their Cant language. The Anglo-Norman and the Anglo-Saxon, the Scotch, the French, the Italian, and even the classic languages of ancient Italy and Greece, have contributed to its list of words,—besides the various provincial dialects of England. Indeed, as Mayhew remarks, English Cant seems to be formed on the same basis as the *Argot* of the French, and the *Roth-Spræc* of the Germans,—partly metaphorical, and partly by the introduction of such corrupted foreign terms as are likely to be unknown to the society amid which the Cant speakers exist. ARGOT is the London thieves' word for their secret language,—it is, of course, from the French, but that matters not so long as it is incomprehensible to the police and the mob. BOOZE, or BOUSE, I am reminded by a friendly correspondent, comes from the Dutch, BUYSEN. DOMINE, a parson, is from the Latin; and DON, a clever fellow, has been filched from the Spanish. DONNA AND FEELES, a woman and children, is from the Lingua Franca, or bastard Italian, although it sounds like an odd mixture of Spanish and French; whilst DUDDS, the vulgar term for clothes, may have been pilfered either from the Gaelic or the Dutch. FEELE, a daughter, from the French; and FROW, a girl or wife, from the German—are common tramps' terms. So are GENT, silver, from the French, *Argent;* and VIAL, a country town, also from the French. HORRID-HORN, a fool, is believed to be from the Erse; and GLOAK, a man, from the Scotch. As stated before, the Dictionary will supply numerous other instances.

There is one source, however, of secret street terms, which, in the first edition of this work, was entirely overlooked,—indeed, it was unknown to the editor until pointed out by a friendly correspondent,—the *Lingua Franca*, or bastard Italian, spoken at Genoa, Trieste, Malta, Constantinople,

Smyrna, Alexandria, and all Mediterranean seaport towns. The ingredients of this imported Cant are many. Its foundation is Italian, with a mixture of modern Greek, German (from the Austrian ports), Spanish, Turkish, and French. It has been introduced to the notice of the London wandering tribes by the sailors, foreign and English, who trade to and from the Mediterranean seaports, by the swarms of organ players from all parts of Italy, and by the makers of images from Rome and Florence,—all of whom, in dense thoroughfares, mingle with our lower orders. It would occupy too much space here to give a list of these words. They are all noted in the Dictionary.

"There are several Hebrew terms in our Cant language, obtained, it would appear, from the intercourse of the thieves with the Jew *fences* (receivers of stolen goods); many of the Cant terms, again, are Sanscrit, got from the Gipseys; many Latin, got by the beggars from the Catholic prayers before the Reformation; and many, again, Italian, got from the wandering musicians and others; indeed the showmen have but lately introduced a number of Italian phrases into their Cant language."* The Hindostanèe also contributes several words, and these have been introduced by the Lascar sailors, who come over here in the East

* Mayhew's *London Labour and London Poor,* vol. iii., No. 43, Oct. 4th, 1851.

Indiamen, and lodge during their stay in the low tramps' lodging houses at the East end of London. Speaking of the learned tongues, I may mention that, precarious and abandoned as the vagabond's existence is, many persons of classical or refined education have from time to time joined the ranks, —occasionally from inclination, as in the popular instance of Bamfylde Moore Carew, but generally through indiscretion, and loss of character.* This will in some measure account for numerous classical and learned words figuring as Cant terms in the vulgar Dictionary.

In the early part of the last century, when highwaymen were by all accounts so plentiful, a great many new words were added to the canting vocabulary, whilst several old terms fell into disuse. CANT, for instance, as applied to thieves' talk, was supplanted by the word FLASH.

A singular feature, however, in vulgar language, is the retention and the revival of sterling old English words, long since laid up in ancient manuscripts, or the subject of dispute among learned antiquaries. Disraeli somewhere says, "the purest source of *neology* is in the revival of *old words*"—

"Words that wise Bacon or brave Rawleigh spake,"

---

* *Mayhew* (vol. i., p. 217), speaks of a low lodging-house, "in which there were at one time five university men, three surgeons, and several sorts of broken down clerks." But old Harman's saying, that "a wylde Roge is he that is *borne* a roge," will perhaps explain this seeming anomaly.

and Dr. Latham honours our subject by remarking that "the thieves of London are the conservators of Anglo-Saxonisms." Mayhew, too, in his interesting work, *London Labour and London Poor*, admits that many Cant and Slang phrases are merely old English terms, which have become obsolete through the caprices of fashion." And the reader who looks into the Dictionary of the vagabonds' lingo, will see at a glance that these gentlemen were quite correct, and that we are compelled to acknowledge the singular truth that a great many old words, once respectable, and in the mouths of kings and fine ladies, are now only so many signals for shrugs and shudders amongst exceedingly polite people. A Belgravian gentleman who had lost his watch or his pocket-handkerchief, would scarcely remark to his mamma that it had been BONED—yet BONE, in old times, meant to steal amongst high and low. And a young lady living in the precincts of dingy, but aristocratic May-Fair, although enraptured with a Jenny Lind or a Ristori, would hardly think of turning back in the box to inform papa that she, Ristori or Lind, "made no BONES of it"—yet the phrase was most respectable and well-to-do, before it met with a change of circumstances. "A CRACK article," however first-rate, would, as far as speech is concerned, have greatly displeased Dr. Johnson and Mr. Walker—yet both CRACK, in the sense of excellent, and CRACK UP, to boast or praise, were not considered vulgarisms in the time of Henry VIII. DODGE, a cunning trick, is from the Anglo-Saxon; and ancient nobles used to "get each other's DANDER UP" before appealing to their swords,—quite FLABERGASTING (also a respectable old word) the half score of lookers-on with the thumps and cuts of their heavy weapons. GALLAVANTING, waiting upon the ladies, was as polite in expression as in action; whilst a clergyman at Paule's Crosse, thought nothing of bidding a noisy hearer to "hold his GAB," or "shut up his GOB." GADDING, roaming about in an idle and trapesing manner, was used in an old translation of the Bible; and "to do anything GINGERLY" was to do it with great care. Persons of modern tastes will be shocked to know that the great Lord Bacon spoke of the lower part of a man's face as his GILLS.

Shakespere, or as the French say, "the divine William," also used many words which are now counted as dreadfully vulgar. "CLEAN gone," in the sense of out of sight, or entirely away; "you took me all A-MORT," or confounded me; "it won't FADGE," or suit, are phrases taken at random from the great dramatist's works. A London costermonger, or inhabitant of the streets, instead of saying "I'll make him yield," or "give in," in a fight or contest, would say, "I'll make him BUCKLE under." Shakespere, in his *Henry the*

Fourth (Part 2, Act i., Scene 1) has the word, and Mr. Halliwell, one of the greatest and most industrious of living antiquaries, informs us, that "the commentators do not supply another example." How strange, then, that the Bard of Avon, and the Cockney costermongers, should be joint partners and sole proprietors of the vulgarism. If Shakespere was not a pugilist, he certainly anticipated the terms of the prize ring—or they were respectable words before the prize ring was thought of—for he has PAY, to beat or thrash, and PEPPER, with a similar meaning; also FANCY, in the sense of pets and favourites,—pugilists are often termed *the* FANCY. The cant word PRIG, from the Saxon, *priccan*, to filch, is also Shakesperian; so indeed is PIECE, a contemptuous term for a young woman. Shakespere was not the only vulgar dramatist of his time. Ben Jonson, Beaumont and Fletcher, Brome, and other play-writers, occasionally put cant words into the mouths of their low characters, or employed old words which have since degenerated into vulgarisms. CRUSTY, poor tempered; "two of a KIDNEY," two of a sort; LARK, a piece of fun; LUG, to pull; BUNG, to give or pass; PICKLE, a sad plight; FRUMP, to mock, are a few specimens casually picked from the works of the old histrionic writers.

One old English mode of canting, simple and effective when familiarised by practice, was the inserting a consonant betwixt each syllable; thus, taking *g*, "How do you do?" would be "Hou*g* do*g* you*g* do*g*? The name very properly given to this disagreeable nonsense, we are informed by Grose, was *Gibberish*.

Another Cant has recently been attempted by transposing the initial letters of words, so that a mutton chop becomes a *c*utton *m*op, a pint of stout a *s*tint of *p*out; but it is satisfactory to know that it has gained no ground. This is called *Marrow-skying*, or *Medical Greek*, from its use by medical students at the hospitals. Albert Smith terms it the *Gower-street Dialect*.

The *Language of Ziph*, I may add, is another rude mode of disguising English, in use among the students at Winchester College.

ACCOUNT

OF THE

HIEROGLYPHICS USED BY VAGABONDS.

ONE of the most singular chapters in a *History of Vagabondism* would certainly be an account of the Hieroglyphic signs used by tramps and thieves. The reader may be startled to know that, in addition to a secret language, the wandering tribes of this country have private marks and symbolic signs with which to score their successes, failures, and advice to succeeding beggars; in fact, that the country is really dotted over with beggars' finger posts and guide stones. The assertion, however strange it may appear, is no fiction. The subject was not long since brought under the attention of the Government by Mr. Rawlinson.* "There is," he says in his report, "a sort of blackguards' literature, and the initiated understand each other by

* *Mr. Rawlinson's Report to the General Board of Health, Parish of Havant, Hampshire.*

slang [cant] terms, by pantomimic signs, *and by* HIEROGLYPHICS. *The vagrant's mark may be seen in Havant, on corners of streets, on door posts, and on house steps. Simple as these chalk lines appear, they inform the succeeding vagrants of all they require to know; and a few white scratches may say, 'be importunate,' or 'pass on.'*"

Another very curious account was taken from a provincial newspaper, published in 1849, and forwarded to *Notes and Queries*,* under the head of MENDICANT FREEMASONRY. "Persons," remarks the writer, "indiscreet enough to open their purses to the relief of the beggar tribe, would do well to take a readily learned lesson as to the folly of that misguided benevolence which encourages and perpetuates vagabondism. Every door or passage is pregnant with instruction as to the error committed by the patron of beggars, as the beggar-marks show that a system of freemasonry is followed, by which a beggar knows whether it will be worth his while to call into a passage or knock at a door. Let any one examine the entrances to the passages in any town, and there he will find chalk marks, unintelligible to him, but significant enough to beggars. If a thousand towns are examined, the same marks will be found at every passage entrance. The passage mark is a cypher with a twisted tail: in some cases the tail projects

* Vol. v., p. 210.

into the passage, in others outwardly; thus seeming to indicate whether the houses down the passage are worth calling at or not. Almost every door has its marks: these are varied. In some cases there is a cross on the brick work, in others a cypher: the figures 1, 2, 3, are also used. Every person may for himself test the accuracy of these statements by the examination of the brick work near his own doorway—thus demonstrating that mendicity is a regular trade, carried out upon a system calculated to save time, and realise the largest profits." These remarks refer mainly to provincial towns, London being looked upon as the tramps' home, and therefore too FLY, or experienced, to be duped by such means.

The only other notice of the hieroglyphics of vagabonds that I have met with, is in *Mayhew's London Labour and London Poor.** Mayhew obtained his information from two tramps, who stated that hawkers employ these signs as well as beggars. One tramp thus described the method of WORKING† a small town. "Two hawkers (PALS†) go together, but separate when they enter a village, one taking one side of the road, and selling different things; and so as to inform each other as to the character of the people at whose houses they call, *they chalk certain marks on their door posts.*" Another informant stated that "if a PATTERER†

* Vol. i., pages 218 and 247.] [† See Dictionary.

has been CRABBED (that is, offended) at any of the CRIBS (houses), *he mostly chalks a signal at or near the door.*"

Another use is also made of these hieroglyphics. Charts of successful begging neighbourhoods are rudely drawn, and symbolical signs attached to each house to show whether benevolent or adverse.* "In many cases there is over the kitchen mantel-piece" of a tramps' lodging-house "*a map of the district*, dotted here and there with memorandums of failure or success."† A correct facsimile of one of these singular maps has been placed as a frontispiece. It

* Sometimes, as appears from the following, the names of persons and houses are written instead. "In almost every one of the padding-kens, or low lodging-houses in the country, there is a list of walks pasted up over the kitchen mantel piece. Now at St. Albans, for instance, at the ——, and at other places, there is a paper stuck up in each of the kitchens. This paper is headed "WALKS OUT OF THIS TOWN," and underneath it is set down the names of the villages in the neighbourhood at which a beggar may call when out on his walk, and they are so arranged as to allow the cadger to make a round of about six miles each day, and return the same night. In many of these papers there are sometimes twenty walks set down. No villages that are in any way "gammy" [bad] are ever mentioned in these papers, and the cadger, if he feels inclined to stop for a few days in the town, will be told by the lodging-house keeper, or the other cadgers that he may meet there, what gentlemen's seats or private houses are of any account on the walk that he means to take. The names of the good houses are not set down in the paper for fear of the police."—*Mayhew*, vol. i., p. 418.

† *Mayhew*, vol. i., p. 218.

was obtained from the patterers and tramps who supplied a great many words for this work, and who have been employed by me for some time in collecting Old Ballads, Christmas Carols, Dying Speeches, and Last Lamentations, as materials for a *History of Popular Literature.* The reader will no doubt be amused with the drawing. The locality depicted is near Maidstone, in Kent, and I am informed that it was probably sketched by a wandering SCREEVER* in payment for a night's lodging. The English practice of marking everything, and scratching names on public property, extends itself to the tribe of vagabonds. On the map, as may be seen in the left hand corner, some TRAVELLER* has drawn a favourite or noted female, singularly nick-named *Three-quarter Sarah.* What were the peculiar accomplishments of this lady to demand so uncommon a name, the reader will be at a loss to discover, but a patterer says it probably refers to a shuffling dance of that name, common in tramps' lodging-houses, and in which "¾ Sarah" may have been a proficient. Above her, three beggars or hawkers have reckoned their day's earnings, amounting to 13s.; and on the right a tolerably correct sketch of a low hawker, or costermonger, is drawn. "To Dover, the *nigh* way," is the exact phraseology; and "hup here," a fair specimen of the self-acquired education of the tribe

* See Dictionary.

of cadgers. No key or explanation to the hieroglyphics was given in the original, because it would have been superfluous, when every inmate of the lodging-house knew the marks from their cradle—or rather their mother's back.

Should there be no map, "in most lodging-houses there is an old man who is guide to every 'walk' in the vicinity, and who can tell each house on every round, that is 'good for a cold tatur.'"* The hieroglyphics that are used are:—

X NO GOOD; too poor, and know too much.

 STOP,—If you have what they want, they will buy. They are pretty "*fly*" (knowing).

 GO IN THIS DIRECTION, it is better than the other road. Nothing that way.

◇ *BONE* (good). Safe for a "cold tatur," if for nothing else. "*Cheese your patter*" (don't talk much) here.

▽ *COOPER'D* (spoilt), by too many tramps calling there.

□ *GAMMY* (unfavourable), likely to have you taken up. Mind the dog.

⊙ *FLUMMUXED* (dangerous), sure of a month in "*quod*" (prison).

⊕ RELIGIOUS, but tidy on the whole.

Where did these signs come from, and when were they first used? are questions which I have asked myself again and again, whilst endeavouring to discover their history. Knowing the character of the Gipseys, and ascertaining from a tramp that they are well acquainted with the hieroglyphics,

* *Mayhew*, vol. i., p. 218.

"and have been as long ago as ever he could remember," I have little hesitation in ascribing the invention to them. And strange it would be if some modern Belzoni, or Champollion, discovered in these beggars' marks fragments of ancient Egyptian or Hindoo hieroglyphical writing! But this, of course, is a simple vagary of the imagination.

That the Gipseys were in the habit of leaving memorials of the road they had taken, and the successes that had befallen them, there can be no doubt. In an old book, *The Triumph of Wit*, 1724, there is a passage which appears to have been copied from some older work, and it runs thus:—"The Gipseys set out twice a year, and scatter all over England, each parcel having their appointed stages, that they may not interfere, nor hinder each other; and for that purpose, when they set forward in the country, *they stick up boughs in the way of divers kinds, according as it is agreed among them, that one company may know which way another is gone, and so take a different road.*" The works of *Hoyland* and *Borrow* supply other instances.

I cannot close this subject without drawing attention to the extraordinary fact, that actually on the threshold of the gibbet the sign of the vagabond is to be met with! "The murderer's signal is even exhibited from the gallows; as a red handkerchief held in the hand of the felon about to be executed is a token that he dies without having betrayed any professional secrets."*

Since the first edition of this work was published the author has received from various parts of England numerous evidences of the still active use of beggars' marks, and mendicant hieroglyphics. One gentleman writes from Great Yarmouth to say that only a short time since, whilst residing in Norwich, he used frequently to see them on the houses and street corners. From another gentleman, a clergyman, I learn that he has so far made himself acquainted with the meanings of the signs employed, that by himself marking the characters □ (*Gammy*) or ⊙ (*Flummuxed*) on the gate posts of his parsonage, he enjoys a singular immunity from alms-seekers of all orders.

* *Mr. Rawlinson's Report to the General Board of Health,—Parish of Havant, Hampshire.*

THE HISTORY OF SLANG,

OR THE

VULGAR LANGUAGE OF FAST LIFE.

SLANG is the language of street humour, of fast, high, and low life. CANT, as was stated in the chapter upon that subject, is the vulgar language of secrecy. They are both universal and ancient, and appear to have been the peculiar concomitants of gay, vulgar, or worthless persons in every part of the world, at every period of time. Indeed, if we are to believe implicitly the saying of *the* wise man, that "there is nothing new under the sun," the "fast" men of buried Nineveh, with their knotty and door-matty looking beards, may have cracked Slang jokes on the steps of Sennacherib's palace; and the stocks and stones of Ancient Egypt, and the bricks of venerable and used-up Babylon, may, for aught we know, be covered with Slang hieroglyphics unknown to modern antiquarians, and which have long been stumbling-blocks to the philologist; so impossible is it at this day to say what was then authorised, or what then vulgar language. Slang is as old as speech and the congregating together of people in cities. It is the result of crowding, and excitement, and artificial life. Even to the classics it was not unknown, as witness the pages of Aristophanes and Plautus, Terence and Athenæus. Martial, the epigrammatist, is full of Slang. When an uninvited guest accompanied his friend, the Slang of the day styled him his UMBRA; when a man was trussed, neck and heels, it called him jocosely QUADRUPUS.

Old English Slang was coarser, and depended more upon downright vulgarity than our modern Slang. It was a jesting speech, or humorous indulgence for the thoughtless moment, or the drunken hour, and it acted as a vent-peg for a fit of temper or irritability; but it did not interlard and permeate every description of conversation as now. It was confined to nick-names and improper subjects, and encroached but to a very small extent upon the domain of authorised speech. Indeed, it was exceedingly limited when compared with the vast territory of Slang in such general favour and complete circulation at the present day. Still, although not an alarming encumbrance, as in our time, Slang certainly did exist in this country centuries ago, as we may see if we look down the page of any respectable History of England. Cromwell was familiarly called OLD NOLL,—just the same as Buonaparte was termed BONEY, and Wellington CONKEY, or NOSEY, only a few years ago. His Legislature, too, was spoken of in a high-flavoured way as the BAREBONES, or RUMP Parliament, and his followers were nicknamed ROUNDHEADS, and the peculiar religious sects of his protectorate were styled PURITANS and QUAKERS.* The Civil War pamphlets, and the satirical hits of the Cavaliers and the Commonwealth men, originated numerous Slang words and vulgar similes, in full use at the present moment. Here is a field of inquiry for the Philological Society, indeed I may say a territory, for there are thirty thousand of these partisan tracts. Later still, in the court of Charles the Second, the naughty ladies and the gay lords, with Rochester at their head, talked Slang; and very naughty Slang it was too! Fops, in those days, when "over head and ears" in debt, and in continual fear of arrest, termed their enemies, the bailiffs, PHILISTINES† or MOABITES. At a later period, when collars were worn detached from shirts, in order to save the expense of washing—an object it would seem with needy "swells" in all ages—they obtained the name of JACOBITES. One half of the coarse wit in

* This term, with a singular literal downrightness, which would be remarkable in any other people than the French, is translated by them as the sect of *Trembleurs*.

† Swift alludes to this term in his *Art of Polite Conversation*, p. 14. 1738.

Butler's Hudibras lurks in the vulgar words and phrases which he was so fond of employing. They were more homely and forcible than the mild and elegant sentences of Cowley, and the people, therefore, hurrah'd them, and pronounced Butler one of themselves,—or, as we should say, in a joyful moment, a jolly good fellow. Orator Henley preached and prayed in Slang, and first charmed and then swayed the dirty mobs in Lincoln's Inn Fields by vulgarisms. Burly Grose mentions Henley, with the remark that we owe a great many Slang phrases to him. Swift, and old Sir Roger L'Estrange, and Arbuthnot, were all fond of vulgar or Slang language; indeed, we may see from a Slang word used by the latter how curious is the gradual adoption of vulgar terms in our standard dictionaries. The worthy doctor, in order to annihilate (or, as we should say with a fitting respect to the subject under consideration, SMASH) an opponent, thought proper on an occasion to use the word CABBAGE, not in the ancient and esculentary sense of a flatulent vegetable of the kitchen garden, but in the at once Slang sense of purloining or cribbing. Johnson soon met with the word, looked at it, examined it, weighed it, and shook his head, but out of respect to a brother doctor inserted it in his dictionary, labelling it, however, prominently "*Cant;*" whilst Walker and Webster, years after, when *to cabbage* was *to pilfer* all over England, placed the term in their dictionaries as an ancient and very respectable word. Another Slang term, GULL, to cheat, or delude, sometimes varied to GULLY, is stated to be connected with the Dean of St. Patrick. GULL, a dupe, or a fool, is often used by our old dramatists, and is generally believed to have given rise to the verb; but a curious little edition of *Bamfylde Moore Carew*, published in 1827, says that TO GULL, or GULLY, is derived from the well known *Gulliver*, the hero of the famous *Travels*. How crammed with Slang are the dramatic works of the last century! The writers of the comedies and farces in those days must have lived in the streets, and written their plays in the public-houses, so filled are they with vulgarisms and unauthorised words. The popular phrases, "I owe you one," "that's one for his nob," and "keep moving, dad," arose in this way.* The second of these sayings was, doubtless, taken from the card table, for at cribbage the player who holds the knave of the suit turned up counts "one for his nob," and the dealer who turns up a knave counts "two for his heels."

In Mrs. Centlivre's admirable comedy of *A Bold Stroke for a Wife*, we see the origin of that popular street phrase, THE REAL SIMON PURE. Simon Pure is the Quaker name adopted by Colonel Feignwell as a trick to obtain the hand of

* See *Notes and Queries*, vol. i., p. 185. 1850.

Mistress Anne Lovely in marriage. The veritable Quaker, the "real Simon Pure," recommended by Aminadab Holdfast, of Bristol, as a fit sojourner with Obadiah Prim, arrives at last to the discomfiture of the Colonel, who, to maintain his position and gain time, concocts a letter in which the real Quaker is spoken of as a housebreaker who had travelled in the "leather conveniency" from Bristol, and adopted the garb and name of the Western Quaker in order to pass off as the "REAL SIMON PURE," but only for the purpose of robbing the house and cutting the throat of the perplexed Obadiah. The scene in which the two Simon Pures, the *real* and the *counterfeit*, meet, is one of the best in the comedy.

Tom Brown, of "facetious memory," as his friends were wont to say, and Ned Ward, who wrote humorous books, and when tired drew beer for his customers at his ale-house in Long Acre,* were both great producers of Slang in the last century, and to them we owe many popular current phrases and household words.

Written Slang was checked rather than advanced by the pens of Addison, Johnson, and Goldsmith, although John Bee, the bottle-holder and historiographer of the pugilistic band of brothers in the youthful days of flat-nosed Tom Crib, has gravely

* He afterwards kept a tavern at Wapping, mentioned by Pope in the *Dunciad*.

stated that Johnson, when young and rakish, contributed to an early volume of the *Gentleman's Magazine* a few pages, by way of specimen, of a Slang dictionary, the result, Mr. Bee says, "of his midnight ramblings!"* And Goldsmith, I must not forget to remark, certainly coined a few words, although, as a rule, his pen was pure and graceful, and adverse to neologisms. The word FUDGE, it has been stated, was first used by him in literary composition, although it originated with one Captain Fudge, a notorious fibber, nearly a century before. Street-phrases, nick-names, and vulgar words were continually being added to the great stock of popular Slang up to the commencement of the present century, when it received numerous additions from pugilism, horse-racing, and "fast" life generally, which suddenly came into great public favour, and was at its height when the Prince Regent was in his rakish minority. Slang in those days was generally termed FLASH language. So popular was it with the "bloods" of high life that it constituted the best paying literary capital for certain authors and dramatists. Pierce Egan issued *Boxiana*, and *Life in London*, six portly octavo volumes, crammed with Slang; and Moncrieff wrote the most popular farce of the day, *Tom and Jerry* (adapted from the latter work), which, to use newspaper Slang, "took

* *Sportsman's Dictionary*, 1825, p. 15. I have searched the venerable magazine in vain for this Slang glossary.

the town by storm," and, with its then fashionable vulgarisms, made the fortune of the old Adelphi Theatre, and was, without exception, the most wonderful instance of a continuous theatrical RUN in ancient or modern times. This, also, was brimful of Slang. Other authors helped to popularise and extend Slang down to our own time, when it has taken a somewhat different turn, dropping many of the Cant and old vulgar words, and assuming a certain quaint and fashionable phraseology—Frenchy, familiar, utilitarian, and jovial. There can be no doubt but that common speech is greatly influenced by fashion, fresh manners, and that general change of ideas which steals over a people once in a generation. But before I proceed further into the region of *Slang*, it will be well to say something on the etymology of the word.

The word SLANG is only mentioned by two lexicographers—Webster and Ogilvie. Johnson, Walker, and the older compilers of dictionaries, give *slang* the preterite of *sling*, but not a word about SLANG in the sense of low, vulgar, or unrecognised language. The origin of the word has often been asked for in literary journals and books, but only one man, as far as I can learn, has ever hazarded an etymology—Jonathan Bee, the vulgar chronicler of the prize-ring.* With a recklessness peculiar to pugilism, Bee stated that SLANG was

* Introduction to *Bee's Sportsman's Dictionary*, 1825.

derived from "the *slangs* or fetters worn by prisoners, having acquired that name from the manner in which they were worn, as they required a sling of string to keep them off the ground." Bee had just been nettled at Pierce Egan producing a new edition of *Grose's Dictionary of the Vulgar Tongue*, and was determined to excel him in a vulgar dictionary of his own, which should be more racy, more pugilistic, and more original. How far he succeeded in this latter particular his ridiculous etymology of Slang will show. SLANG is not an English word, it is the Gipsey term for their secret language, and its synonyme is GIBBERISH—another word which was believed to have had no distinct origin.* Grose—stout and burly Captain Grose—who we may characterise as the greatest antiquary, joker, and drinker of porter of his day, was the first author who put the word SLANG into print. It occurs in his *Classical Dictionary of the Vulgar Tongue*, of 1785, with the signification that it implies "Cant or vulgar language." Grose, I

* The Gipseys use the word Slang as the Anglican synonyme for Romany, the continental (or rather Spanish) term for the Cingari or Gipsey tongue. *Crabb*, who wrote the *Gipsies' Advocate* in 1831, thus mentions the word :—"This language [Gipsey] *called by themselves* SLANG, or GIBBERISH, invented, as they think, by their forefathers for secret purposes, is not merely the language of one or a few of these wandering tribes, which are found in the European nations, but is adopted by the vast numbers who inhabit the earth."

may remark in passing, was a great favourite with the poet Burns, and so pleased by his extensive powers of story-telling and grog-imbibing, that the companionable and humour-loving Scotch bard wrote for his fat friend—or, to use his own words, "the fine, fat, fodgel wight"—the immortal poem of "Tam O'Shanter."

Without troubling the reader with a long account of the transformation into an English term of the word SLANG, I may remark in passing that it is easily seen how we obtained it from the Gipseys. Hucksters and beggars on tramp, or at fairs and races, associate and frequently join in any rough enterprise with the Gipseys. The word would be continually heard by them, and would in this manner soon become CANT;* and, when carried by "fast" or vulgar fashionables from the society of thieves and low characters to their own drawing-rooms, would as quickly become SLANG, and the representative term for all vulgar or Slang language.

Any sudden excitement, peculiar circumstance, or popular literary production, is quite sufficient to originate and set going a score of Slang words. Nearly every election or public agitation throws out offshoots of the excitement, or scintillations of the

* The word SLANG assumed various meanings amongst costermongers, beggars, and vagabonds of all orders. It was, and is still, used to express cheating by false weights, a raree show, for retiring by a back door, for a watch-chain, and for their secret language.

humour in the shape of Slang terms—vulgar at first, but at length adopted as semi-respectable from the force of habit and custom. There is scarcely a condition or calling in life that does not possess its own peculiar Slang. The professions, legal and medical, have each familiar and unauthorised terms for peculiar circumstances and things, and I am quite certain that the clerical calling, or "*the cloth*," is not entirely free from this peculiarity. Every workshop, warehouse, factory, and mill throughout the country has its Slang, and so have the public schools of Eton, Harrow, and Westminster, and the great Universities of Oxford and Cambridge. Sea Slang constitutes the principal charm of a sailor's "yarn," and our soldiers and officers have each their peculiar nicknames and terms for things and subjects proper and improper. A writer in *Household Words* (No. 183) has gone so far as to remark, that a person "shall not read one single parliamentary debate, as reported in a first-class newspaper, without meeting scores of Slang words;" and "that from Mr. Speaker in his chair, to the Cabinet Ministers whispering behind it—from mover to seconder, from true blue Protectionist to extremest Radical—Mr. Barry's New House echoes and re-echoes with Slang." Really it seems as if our boasted English tongue was a very paltry and ill-provided contrivance after all; or can it be that we are the most vulgar of people?

The universality of Slang is extraordinary. Let any person for a short time narrowly examine the conversation of their dearest and nearest friends, aye, censor-like, even slice and analyse their own supposed correct talk, and they shall be amazed at the numerous unauthorised, and what we can only call vulgar, words they continually employ. It is not the number of new words that we are ever introducing that is so reprehensible, there is not so much harm in this practice (frequently termed in books "the license of expression") if neologisms are really required, but it is the continually encumbering of *old* words with fresh and strange meanings. Look at those simple and useful verbs, *do, cut, go,* and *take*, and see how they are hampered and overloaded, and then let us ask ourselves how it is that a French or German gentleman, be he ever so well educated, is continually blundering and floundering amongst our *little* words when trying to make himself understood in an ordinary conversation. He may have studied our language the required time, and have gone through the usual amount of "grinding," and practised the common allotment of patience, but all to no purpose as far as accuracy is concerned. I am aware that most new words are generally regarded as Slang, although afterwards they may become useful and respectable additions to our standard dictionaries. JABBER and HOAX were

Slang and Cant terms in Swift's time; so indeed were MOB and SHAM.* Words directly from the Latin and Greek, and Carlyleisms, are allowed by an indulgent public to pass and take their places in books. Sound contributes many Slang words—a source that etymologists too frequently overlook. Nothing pleases an ignorant person more than a high-sounding term "full of fury." How melodious and drum-like are those vulgar coruscations RUMBUMPTIOUS, SLANTINGDICULAR, SPLENDIFEROUS, RUMBUSTIOUS, and FERRICADOUZER. What a "pull" the sharp-nosed lodging-house keeper thinks she has over her victims if she can but hurl such testimonies of a liberal education at them when they are disputing her charges, and threatening to ABSQUATULATE! In the United States the vulgar-genteel even excel the poor "stuck-up" Cockneys in their formation of a native fashionable language. How charming to a refined ear are ABSKIZE, CATAWAMPOUSLY, EXFLUNCTIFY, OBSCUTE, KESLOSH, KESOUSE, KESWOLLOP, and KEWHOLLUX! Vulgar words representing action and brisk movement

* *North*, in his *Examen*, p. 574, says, "I may note that the rabble first changed their title, and were called the MOB in the assemblies of this [Green Ribbon] club. It was their beast of burden, and called first *mobile vulgus*, but fell naturally into the contraction of one syllable, and ever since is become proper English." In the same work, p. 231, the disgraceful origin of SHAM is given.

often owe their origin to sound. Mispronunciation, too, is another great source of vulgar or slang words—RAMSHACKLE, SHACKLY, NARY-ONE for neither, or neither one, OTTOMY for anatomy, RENCH for rinse, are specimens. The commonalty dislike frequently occurring words difficult of pronunciation, and so we have the street abridgments of BIMEBY for by and by, CAZE for because, GIN for given, HANKERCHER for handkerchief, RUMATIZ for rheumatism, BACKY for tobacco, and many others, not perhaps Slang, but certainly all vulgarisms. Archbishop Whately, in his interesting *Remains of Bishop Copleston*, has inserted a leaf from the Bishop's note-book on the popular corruption of names, mentioning among others KICKSHAWS, as from the French, *quelques choses*; BEEFEATER, the lubberly guardian of royalty in a procession, and the supposed devourer of enormous beefsteaks, as but a vulgar pronunciation of the French, *buffetier*; and GEORGE and CANNON, the sign of a public-house, as nothing but a corruption (although so soon!) of the popular premier of the last generation, *George Canning*. Literature has its Slang terms; and the desire on the part of writers to say funny and startling things in a novel and curious way (the late *Household Words*,* for instance), contributes many unauthorised words to the great stock of Slang.

* It is rather singular that this popular journal should have contained a long article on *Slang* a short time ago.

Fashionable, or *Upper-class Slang*, is of several varieties. There is the Belgravian, military and naval, parliamentary, dandy, and the reunion and visiting Slang. Concerning the Slang of the fashionable world, a writer in *Household Words* curiously, but not altogether truthfully, remarks, that it is mostly imported from France; and that an unmeaning gibberish of Gallicisms runs through English fashionable conversation, and fashionable novels, and accounts of fashionable parties in the fashionable newspapers. Yet, ludicrously enough, immediately the fashionable magnates of England seize on any French idiom, the French themselves not only universally abandon it to us, but positively repudiate it altogether from their idiomatic vocabulary. If you were to tell a well-bred Frenchman that such and such an aristocratic marriage was on the *tapis*, he would stare with astonishment, and look down on the carpet in the startled endeavour to find a marriage in so unusual a place. If you were to talk to him of the *beau monde*, he would imagine you meant the world which God made, not half-a-dozen streets and squares between Hyde Park Corner and Chelsea Bun House. The *thé dansante** would be completely inexplicable to him. If you were to point out to him the Dow-

* The writer is quite correct in instancing this piece of fashionable twaddle. The mongrel formation is exceedingly amusing to a polite Parisian.

ager Lady Grimguffin acting as *chaperon* to Lady Amanda Creamville, he would imagine you were referring to the *petit Chaperon rouge* — to little Red Riding Hood. He might just understand what was meant by *vis-a-vis*, *entremets*, and some others of the flying horde of frivolous little foreign slangisms hovering about fashionable cookery and fashionable furniture; but three-fourths of them would seem to him as barbarous French provincialisms, or, at best, but as antiquated and obsolete expressions, picked out of the letters of Mademoiselle Scuderi, or the tales of Crebillon the "younger." Servants, too, appropriate the scraps of French conversation which fall from their masters' guests at the dinner table, and forthwith in the world of flunkeydom the word "know" is disused, and the lady's maid, in doubt on a particular point, asks John whether or no he SAVEYS it?* What, too, can be more abominable than that heartless piece of fashionable newspaper Slang, regularly employed when speaking of the successful courtship of young people in the fashionable world:—

MARRIAGE IN HIGH LIFE.—We understand that a marriage is ARRANGED (!) betwixt the Lady, &c. &c., and the Honourable, &c. &c.

ARRANGED! Is that cold-blooded Smithfield or Mark-lane term for a sale or a purchase the proper

* Savez vous cela?

word to express the hopeful, joyous, golden union of young and trustful hearts? Which is the proper way to pronounce the names of great people, and what the correct authority? Lord Cowper, we are often assured, is Lord *Cooper*—on this principle Lord Cowley would certainly be Lord *Cooley*—and Mr. Carew, we are told, should be Mr. *Carey*, Ponsonby should be ***Punsunby***, Eyre should be ***Aire***, Cholmondeley should be ***Chumley***, St. John ***Singen***, Majoribanks ***Marshbanks***, Derby ***Darby*** (its ancient pronunciation), and Powell should always be ***Poel.*** I don't know that these lofty persons have as much cause to complain of the illiberality of fate in giving them disagreeable names as did the celebrated Psyche (as she was termed by Tom Moore), whose original name, through her husband, was *Teague*, but which was afterwards altered to Tighe.

Parliamentary Slang, excepting a few peculiar terms connected with "*the* House" (scarcely Slang, I suppose), is mainly composed of fashionable, literary, and learned Slang. When members, however, get excited and wish to be forcible, they are often not very particular which of the street terms they select, providing it carries, as good old Dr. South said, plenty of wild-fire in it. Sir Hugh Cairns very lately spoke of "that homely but expressive phrase, DODGE." Out of "the House," several Slang terms are used in connection with Parliament or members of Parliament. If Lord

Palmerston is known by name to the tribes of the Caucasus and Asia Minor as a great foreign diplomatist, when the name of our Queen Victoria is an unknown title to the inhabitants of those parts—as was stated in the *Times* a short time ago,—I have only to remark that amongst the costers and the wild inhabitants of the streets he is better known as PAM. I have often heard the cabmen on the "ranks" in Piccadilly remark of the late Chancellor of the Exchequer, when he has been going from his residence at Grosvenor Gate, to Derby House in St. James's Square,—"hollo, there! de yer see old DIZZY doing a stump?" A PLUMPER is a single vote at an election,—not a SPLIT-TICKET; and electors who have occupied a house, no matter how small, and boiled a pot in it, thus qualifying themselves for voting, are termed POT-WOLLOPERS. A quiet WALK OVER is a re-election without opposition and much cost. A CAUCUS meeting refers to the private assembling of politicians before an election, when candidates are chosen and measures of action agreed upon. The term comes from America. A JOB, in political phraseology, is a government office or contract obtained by secret influence or favouritism. Only the other day the *Times* spoke of "the patriotic member of Parliament POTTED OUT in a dusty little lodging somewhere about Bury-street." The term QUOCKERWODGER, although referring to a wooden toy figure which jerks its limbs about when pulled by a string, has been supplemented with a political meaning. A pseudo-politician, one whose strings of action are pulled by somebody else, is now often termed a QUOCKERWODGER. The term RAT, too, in allusion to rats deserting vessels about to sink, has long been employed towards those turncoat politicians who change their party for interest. Who that occasionally passes near the Houses of Parliament has not often noticed stout or careful M.P.s walk briskly through the Hall and on the curb-stone in front, with umbrella or walking cane uplifted, shout to the cabmen on the rank, FOUR-WHEELER! The term is a useful one, but I am afraid we must consider it Slang, until it is stamped with the mint mark of lexicographical authority.*

Military, or *Officers' Slang* is on a par, and of a character with *Dandy Slang*. Inconvenient friends, or elderly and lecturing relatives, are pronounced DREADFUL BORES. Four-wheel cabs are called BOUNDERS; and a member of the Four-in-hand

* From an early period politics and partyism have attracted unto themselves quaint Slang terms. Horace Walpole quotes a party nickname of February, 1742, as a Slang word of the day:—"The Tories declare against any further prosecution, if Tories there are, for now one hears of nothing but the BROAD-BOTTOM; it is the reigning Cant word, and means the taking all parties and people, indifferently, into the ministry." Thus BROAD-BOTTOM in those days was Slang for *coalition*.

Club, driving to Epsom on the Derby day, would, using fashionable slang phraseology, speak of it as TOOLING HIS DRAG DOWN TO THE DERBY. A vehicle, if not a DRAG (or dwag) is a TRAP, or a CASK; and if the TURN OUT happens to be in other than a trim condition, it is pronounced at once as not DOWN THE ROAD. Your city swell would say it is not UP TO THE MARK; whilst the costermonger would call it WERY DICKEY. In the army a barrack or military station is known as a LOBSTER-BOX; to "cram" for an examination is to MUG-UP; to reject from the examination is to SPIN; and that part of the barrack occupied by subalterns is frequently spoken of as the ROOKERY. In dandy or swell Slang, any celebrity, from Robson of the Olympic, to the Pope of Rome, is a SWELL. Wrinkled faced old professors, who hold dress and fashionable tailors in abhorrence, are called AWFUL SWELLS,—if they happen to be very learned or clever. I may remark that in this upper class Slang a title is termed a HANDLE; trousers, INEXPRESSIBLES; or when of a large pattern, or the inflated Zouave cut, HOWLING BAGS; a superior appearance, EXTENSIVE; a four-wheeled cab, a BIRDCAGE; a dance, a HOP; dining at another man's table, "sitting under his MAHOGANY;" anything flashy or showy, LOUD; the peculiar make or cut of a coat, its BUILD; full dress, FULL-FIG; wearing clothes which represent the very extreme of fashion, "dressing to DEATH;" a reunion, a SPREAD; a friend (or a "good fellow"), a TRUMP; a difficulty, a SCREW LOOSE; and everything that is unpleasant, "from bad sherry to a writ from a tailor," JEUCED INFERNAL. The military phrase, "to send a man to COVENTRY," or permit no person to speak to him, although an ancient saying, must still be considered Slang.

The *Universities of Oxford and Cambridge*, and the great public schools, are the hotbeds of fashionable Slang. Growing boys and high-spirited young fellows detest restraint of all kinds, and prefer making a dash at life in a Slang phraseology of their own, to all the set forms and syntactical rules of *Alma Mater*. Many of the most expressive words in a common chit-chat, or free-and-easy conversation, are old University vulgarisms. CUT, in the sense of dropping an acquaintance, was originally a Cambridge form of speech; and HOAX, to deceive or ridicule, we are informed by Grose, was many years since an Oxford term. Among the words that fast society has borrowed from our great scholastic [I was going to say *establishments*, but I remembered the linen drapers' horrid and habitual use of the word] institutions, I find CRIB, a house or apartments; DEAD-MEN, empty wine bottles; DRAWING TEETH,* wrenching off knockers;

* This is more especially an amusement with medical students, and is comparatively unknown out of London.

FIZZING, first-rate, or splendid; GOVERNOR, or RELIEVING OFFICER, the general term for a male parent; PLUCKED, defeated or turned back; QUIZ, to scrutinise, or a prying old fellow; and ROW, a noisy disturbance. The Slang words in use at Oxford and Cambridge would alone fill a volume. As examples I may instance SCOUT, which at Oxford refers to an undergraduate's valet, whilst the same menial at Cambridge is termed a GYP,—popularly derived by the Cantabs from the Greek, GYPS (γυψ), a vulture; SCULL, the head, or master of a college; BATTLES, the Oxford term for rations, changed at Cambridge into COMMONS. The term DICKEY, a half shirt, I am told, originated with the students of Trinity College, Dublin, who at first styled it a TOMMY, from the Greek, *τομη*, a section. CRIB, a literal translation, is now universal; GRIND refers to a walk, or "constitutional;" HIVITE is a student of St. Begh's (St. Bee's) College, Cumberland; to JAPAN, in this Slang speech, is to ordain; MORTAR-BOARD is a square college cap; SIM a student of a Methodistical turn,—in allusion to the Rev. Charles Simeon; SLOGGERS, at Cambridge, refers to the second division of race boats, known at Oxford as TORPIDS; SPORT is to show or exhibit; TROTTER is the jocose term for a tailor's man who goes round for orders; and TUFTS are wealthy students who dine with the DONS, and are distinguished by golden *tufts*, or tassels, in their caps. There are many terms in use at Oxford not known at Cambridge; and such Slang names as COACH, GULF, HARRY-SOPH, POKER, or POST-MORTEM, common enough at Cambridge, are seldom or never heard at the great sister University. For numerous other examples of college Slang, the reader is referred to the Dictionary.

Religious Slang, strange as the compound may appear, exists with other descriptions of vulgar speech at the present day. *Punch*, a short time since, in one of those half-humorous, half-serious articles in which he is so fond of lecturing any national abuse or popular folly, remarked that Slang had "long since penetrated into the Forum, and now we meet it in the Senate, *and even the Pulpit itself is no longer free from its intrusion.*" I would not, for one moment, wish to infer that the practice is general. On the contrary, and in justice to the clergy, it must be said that the principal disseminators of pure English throughout the country are the ministers of our Established Church. Yet it cannot be denied but that a great deal of Slang phraseology and disagreeable vulgarism have gradually crept into the very pulpits which should give forth as pure speech as doctrine.

Dean Conybeare, in his able *Essay on Church Parties*,* has noticed this wretched addition to our pulpit speech. As stated in his Essay, the practice

* *Edinburgh Review*, October, 1853.

appears to confine itself mainly to the exaggerated forms of the High and Low Church—the Tractarians and the "Recordites."* By way of illustration, the Dean cites the evening parties, or social meetings, common amongst the wealthier lay members of the Recordite (exaggerated Evangelical) Churches, where the principal topics discussed—one or more favourite clergymen being present in a quasi-official manner—are "the merits and demerits of different preachers, the approaching restoration of the Jews, the date of the Millennium, the progress of the 'Tractarian heresy,' and the anticipated 'perversion' of High Church neighbours." These subjects are canvassed in a dialect differing considerably from common English. The words FAITHFUL, TAINTED, ACCEPTABLE, DECIDED, LEGAL, and many others, are used in a technical sense. We hear that Mr. A. has been more OWNED than Mr. B; and that Mr. C. has more SEALS† than Mr. D. Again, the word GRACIOUS is invested with a meaning as extensive as that attached by young ladies to *nice*. Thus, we hear of a "GRACIOUS sermon," a "GRACIOUS meeting," a "GRACIOUS child, and even a "GRACIOUS whipping." The word DARK

* A term derived from the *Record Newspaper*, the exponent of this singular section of the Low, or so called Evangelical Church.

† A preacher is said, in this phraseology, to be OWNED, when he makes many converts, and his converts are called his SEALS.

has also a new and peculiar usage. It is applied to every person, book, or place, not impregnated with Recordite principles. We once were witnesses of a ludicrous misunderstanding resulting from this phraseology. "What did you mean (said A. to B.) by telling me that —— was such a very DARK village? I rode over there to day, and found the street particularly broad and cheerful, and there is not a tree in the place." "*The Gospel is not preached there,*" was B.'s laconic reply. The conclusion of one of these singular evening parties is generally marked by an "*exposition*"—an unseasonable sermon of nearly one hour's duration, circumscribed by no text, and delivered from the table by one of the clerical visitors with a view to "improve the occasion." In the same Essay, the religious Slang terms for the two great divisions of the Established Church, receive some explanation. The old-fashioned High Church party, rich and "stagnant," noted for its "sluggish mediocrity, hatred of zeal, dread of innovation, abuse of dissent, blundering and languid utterance," is called the HIGH AND DRY; whilst the corresponding division, known as the Low Church, equally stagnant with the former, but poorer, and more lazily inclined (from absence of education), to dissent, receives the nickname of the LOW AND SLOW. Already have these terms become so familiar that they are shortened, in ordinary conversation, to the DRY and the SLOW. The so-called "Broad

Church," I should remark, is often spoken of as the BROAD AND SHALLOW.

What can be more objectionable than the irreverent and offensive manner in which many of the dissenting ministers continually pronounce the names of the Deity, God and Lord. God, instead of pronouncing in the plain and beautifully simple old English way, G-O-D, they drawl out into GORDE or GAUDE; and Lord, instead of speaking in the proper way, they desecrate into LOARD or LOERD,—lingering on the *u*, or the *r*, as the case may be, until an honest hearer feels disgusted, and almost inclined to run the gauntlet of beadles and deacons, and pull the vulgar preacher from his pulpit. I have observed that many young preachers strive hard to acquire this peculiar pronunciation, in imitation of the older ministers. What can more properly, then, be called Slang, or, indeed, the most objectionable of Slang, than this studious endeavour to pronounce the most sacred names in a uniformly vulgar and unbecoming manner. If the old-fashioned preacher whistled Cant through his nose, the modern vulgar reverend whines Slang from the more natural organ. These vagaries of speech will, perhaps, by an apologist, be termed "pulpit peculiarities," and the writer dared to intermeddle with a subject that is or should be removed from his criticisms. The terms used by the mob towards the Church, however illiberal and satirically vulgar, are within his province in such an inquiry as the present. A clergyman, in vulgar language, is spoken of as a CHOKER, a CUSHION THUMPER, a DOMINE, an EARWIG, a GOSPEL GRINDER, a GRAY COAT PARSON—if he is a lessee of the great tithes, ONE IN TEN, PADRE—if spoken of by an Anglo-Indian, a ROOK, a SPOUTER, a WHITE CHOKER, or a WARMING PAN RECTOR, if he only holds the living *pro tempore*, or is simply keeping the place warm for his successor. If a Tractarian, his outer garment is rudely spoken of as a PYGOSTOLE, or M.B. (MARK OF THE BEAST) COAT. His profession is termed THE CLOTH, and his practice TUB THUMPING. Should he belong to the dissenting body, he is probably styled a PANTILER, or a PSALM SMITER, or, perhaps, a SWADDLER. His chapel, too, is spoken of as a SCHISM SHOP. A Roman Catholic, I may remark, is coarsely named a BRISKET BEATER.

Particular as lawyers generally are about the meaning of words, they have not prevented an unauthorised phraseology from arising, which we may term *Legal Slang*. So forcibly did this truth impress a late writer, that he wrote in a popular journal, "You may hear Slang every day in term from barristers in their robes, at every mess-table, at every bar-mess, at every college commons, and in every club dining-room." Swift, in his *Art of Polite Conversation* (p. 15), published a century and a half ago, states that VARDI was the Slang in his time for "verdict." A few of the most common and well-known terms used out of doors, with reference to legal matters, are COOK, to hash or make up a balance-sheet; DIPPED, mortgaged; DUN, to solicit payment; FULLIED, to be "*fully* committed for trial;" LAND-SHARK, a sailor's definition of a lawyer; LIMB OF THE LAW, a milder term for the same "professional;" MONKEY WITH A LONG TAIL, a mortgage—phrase used in the well-known case for libel, Smith *v.* Jones; MOUTHPIECE, the coster's term for his counsel; "to go through the RING," to take advantage of the Insolvency Act; SMASH, to become bankrupt; SNIPE, an attorney with a long bill; and WHITEWASHED, said of any debtor who has taken the benefit of the Insolvent Act. Lawyers, from their connection with the police courts, and transactions with persons in every grade of society, have ample opportunities for acquiring street Slang, which in cross-questioning and wrangling they frequently avail themselves of.

It has been said there exists a *Literary Slang*, or "the *Slang of Criticism*—dramatic, artistic, and scientific. Such words as 'æsthetic,' 'transcendental,' the 'harmonies,' the 'unities,' a 'myth:' such phrases as 'an exquisite *morceau* on the big drum,' a 'scholarlike rendering of John the Baptist's great toe,' 'keeping harmony,' 'middle distance,' 'ærial perspective,' 'delicate handling,' 'nervous chiaroscuro,' and the like." More than one literary journal that I could name are fond of employing such terms in their art criticisms, but it is questionable, after all, whether they are not allowable as the generous inflections and bendings of a bountiful language, for the purpose of expressing fresh phases of thought, and ideas not yet provided with representative words.* The well-known and ever-acceptable *Punch*, with his fresh and choice little pictorial bits by Leech, often employs a Slang term to give point to a joke, or humour to a line of satire. A short time since (4th May, 1859) he gave an original etymology of the school-boy-ism SLOG. SLOG, said the classical and studious *Punch*, is derived from the Greek word SLOGO, to baste, to wallop, to slaughter. And it was not long ago that he amused his readers with two columns on *Slang* and *Sanscrit*:—

"The allegory which pervades the conversation of all Eastern nations," remarked the philosophical *Punch*, "is the foundation of Western Slang; and the increased number of students of the Oriental languages, especially since Sanscrit and Arabic have been made subjects for the Indian Civil Service Examinations, may have contributed to supply the English language with a

* "All our newspapers contain more or less colloquial words; in fact, there seems no other way of expressing certain ideas connected with passing events of every-day life, with the requisite force and piquancy. In the English newspapers the same thing is observable, and certain of them contain more of the class denominated Slang words than our own."—*Bartlett's Americanisms*, p. x., 1859.

large portion of its new dialect. While, however, the spirit of allegory comes from the East, there is so great a difference between the brevity of Western expression and the more cumbrous diction of the Oriental, that the origin of a phrase becomes difficult to trace. Thus, for instance, whilst the Turkish merchant might address his friend somewhat as follows—'That which seems good to my father is to his servant as the perfumed breath of the west wind in the calm night of the Arabian summer;' the Western negociator observes more briefly, 'ALL SERENE!'"

But the vulgar term, BRICK, *Punch* remarks in illustration,

"must be allowed to be an exception, its Greek derivation being universally admitted, corresponding so exactly as it does in its rectangular form and compactness to the perfection of manhood, according to the views of *Plato* and *Simonides;* but any deviation from the simple expression, in which locality is indicated,—as, for instance, 'a genuine Bath,'—decidedly breathes the Oriental spirit."

It is singular that what *Punch* says, unwittingly and in humour, respecting the Slang expression, BOSH, should be quite true. BOSH, remarks *Punch*, after speaking of it as belonging to the stock of words pilfered from the Turks, "is one whose innate force and beauty the slangographer is reluctantly compelled to admit. It is the only word which seems a proper appellation for a great deal which we are obliged to hear and to read every day of our life." BOSH, nonsense or stupidity, is derived from the *Gipsey* and the *Persian*. The universality of Slang, I may here remark, is proved by its continual use in the pages of *Punch.* Whoever thinks, unless belonging to a past generation, of asking a friend to explain the stray vulgar words employed by the *London Charivari?*

The *Athenæum,* the most learned and censor-like of all the "weeklies," often indulges in a Slang word, when force of expression or a little humour is desired, or when the writer wishes to say something which is better said in Slang, or so-called vulgar speech, than in the authorised language of Dr. Johnson or Lindley Murray. It was but the other day that a writer in its pages employed an old and favourite word, used always when we were highly pleased with any article at school,—STUNNING. *Bartlett*, the compiler of the *Dictionary of Americanisms*, continually cites the *Athenæum* as using Slang and vulgar expressions;—but the magazine the American refers to is not the excellent literary journal which is so esteemed at the present day, it was a smaller, and now defunct "weekly." Many other highly respectable journals often use Slang words and phrases. The *Times* (or, in Slang, the THUNDERER) frequently employs unauthorised terms; and, following a "leader"* of the purest and most eloquent English composition, may sometimes be seen another "article"* on a totally

* The terms *leader* and *article* can scarcely be called Slang, yet it would be desirable to know upon what authority they were first employed in their present peculiar sense.

different subject, containing, perhaps, a score or more of exceedingly questionable words. Among the words and phrases which may be included under the head of Literary Slang are,—BALAAM, matter kept constantly in type about monstrous productions of nature, to fill up spaces in newspapers; BALAAM BOX, the term given in *Blackwood* to the depository for rejected articles; and SLATE, to pelt with abuse, or CUT UP in a review. The Slang names given to newspapers are curious;—thus, the *Morning Advertiser* is known as the TAP-TUB, the TIZER, and the GIN AND GOSPEL GAZETTE. The *Morning Post* has obtained the suggestive *soubriquet* of JEAMES; whilst the *Morning Herald* has long been caricatured as MRS. HARRIS, and the *Standard* as MRS. GAMP.*

The *Stage*, of course, has its Slang—"both before and behind the curtain," as a journalist remarks. The stage manager is familiarly termed DADDY; and an actor by profession, or a "professional," is called a PRO. A man who is occasionally hired at a trifling remuneration to come upon the stage as one of a crowd, or when a number of actors are wanted to give effect, is named a SUP,—an abbreviation of "supernumerary." A SURF is a third-rate actor who frequently pursues another calling;

* For some account of the origin of these nicknames see under MRS. HARRIS in the Dictionary.

and the band, or orchestra between the pit and the stage, is generally spoken of as the MENAGERY. A BEN is a benefit; and SAL is the Slang abbreviation of "salary." Should no wages be forthcoming on the Saturday night, it is said that the GHOST DOESN'T WALK. The travelling or provincial theatricals, who perform in any large room that can be rented in a country village, are called BARN STORMERS. A LENGTH is forty-two lines of any dramatic composition; and a RUN is the good or bad success of a performance. A SADDLE is the additional charge made by a manager to an actor or actress upon their benefit night. To MUG UP is to paint one's face, or arrange the person to represent a particular character; to CORPSE, or to STICK, is to balk, or put the other actors out in their parts by forgetting yours. A performance is spoken of as either a GOOSER or a SCREAMER, should it be a failure or a great success;—if the latter, it is not infrequently termed a HIT. To STAR IT is to perform as the centre of attraction, with none but subordinates and indifferent actors in the same performance. The expressive term CLAP-TRAP, high-sounding nonsense, is nothing but an ancient theatrical term, and signified a TRAP to catch a CLAP by way of applause. "Up amongst the GODS," refers to being among the spectators in the gallery,—termed in French Slang PARADIS.

There exists, too, in the great territory of vulgar

speech what may not inappropriately be termed *Civic Slang*. It consists of mercantile and Stock Exchange terms, and the Slang of good living and wealth. A turkey hung with sausages is facetiously styled AN ALDERMAN IN CHAINS; and a half-crown, perhaps from its rotundity, is often termed an ALDERMAN. A BEAR is a speculator on the Exchange; and a BULL, although of another order, follows a like profession. There is something very humorous and applicable in the slang term LAME DUCK, a defaulter in stock-jobbing speculations. The allusion to his "waddling out of the Alley," as they say, is excellent. BREAKING SHINS, in City slang, is borrowing money; a rotten or unsound scheme is spoken of as FISHY; "RIGGING the market" means playing tricks with it; and STAG was a common term during the railway mania for a speculator without capital, a seller of "scrip" in "Diddlesex Junction" and other equally safe lines. In Lombard-street a MONKEY is £500, a PLUM £100,000, and a MARYGOLD is one million sterling. But before I proceed further in a sketch of the different kinds of Slang, I cannot do better than to speak here of the extraordinary number of Cant and Slang terms in use to represent money,—from farthings to bank notes the value of fortunes. *Her Majesty's coin, collectively or in the piece, is insulted by no less than one hundred and thirty distinct Slang words*, from the humble

BROWN (a halfpenny) to FLIMSIES, or LONG-TAILED ONES (bank notes).

"Money," it has been well remarked, "the bare, simple word itself, has a sonorous, significant ring in its sound," and might have sufficed, one would have imagined, for all ordinary purposes. But a vulgar or "fast" society has thought differently, and so we have the Slang synonymes BEANS, BLUNT, (*i.e.*, specie,—not *stiff* or *rags*, bank notes), BRADS, BRASS, BUSTLE, COPPERS (copper money, or mixed pence), CHINK, CHINKERS, CHIPS, CORKS, DIBBS, DINARLY, DIMMOCK, DUST, FEATHERS, GENT (silver,—from *argent*), HADDOCK (a purse of money), HORSE NAILS, LOAVER, LOUR (the oldest Cant term for money), MOPUSSES, NEEDFUL, NOBBINGS (money collected in a hat by street performers), OCHRE (gold), PEWTER, PALM OIL, QUEEN'S PICTURES, QUIDS, RAGS (bank notes), READY, or READY GILT, REDGE (gold), RHINO, ROWDY, SHINERS (sovereigns), SKIN (a purse of money), STIFF (paper, or bill of acceptance), STUFF, STUMPY, TIN (silver), WEDGE (silver), and YELLOW-BOYS (sovereigns);—just forty-two vulgar equivalents for the simple word *money*. So attentive is Slang speech to financial matters, that there are seven terms for bad, or "bogus" coin (as our friends, the Americans, call it): a CASE is a counterfeit five-shilling piece; HALF A CASE represents half that sum; GRAYS are halfpence made double for gambling purposes; QUEER-SOFT is counterfeit or lead coin; SCHOFEL refers to coated or spurious coin; SHEEN is bad money of any description; and SINKERS bears the same and not inappropriate meaning. FLYING THE KITE, or obtaining money on bills and promissory notes, is a curious allusion to children tossing about a paper kite; and RAISING THE WIND is a well-known phrase for procuring money by immediate sale, pledging, or a forced loan. In winter or in summer any elderly gentleman who may have prospered in life is pronounced WARM; whilst an equivalent is immediately at hand in the phrase "his pockets are well LINED." Each separate piece of money has its own Slang term, and often half a score of synonymes. To begin with that extremely humble coin, a *farthing:* first we have FADGE, then FIDDLER, then GIG, and lastly QUARTEREEN. A *halfpenny* is a BROWN or a MADZA SALTEE (Cant), or a MAG, or a POSH, or a RAP,—whence the popular phrase, "I don't care a *rap*." The useful and universal *penny* has for Slang equivalents a COPPER, a SALTEE (Cant), and a WINN. *Two-pence* is a DEUCE, and *three-pence* is either a THRUMS or a THRUPS. *Four-pence,* or a *groat,* may in vulgar speech be termed a BIT, a FLAG, or a JOEY. *Six-pence* is well represented in street talk, and some of the Slangisms are very comical, for instance, BANDY, BENDER, CRIPPLE, and DOWNER; then we have FYE-BUCK, HALF A

HOG, KICK (thus "two and a kick," or 2s. 6d.), LORD OF THE MANOR, PIG, POT (the price of a *pot* of beer), SNID, SPRAT, SOW'S BABY, TANNER, TESTER, TIZZY,—sixteen vulgar words to one coin. *Seven-pence* being an uncommon amount has only one Slang synonyme, SETTER. The same remark applies to *eight-pence* and *nine-pence*, the former being only represented by OTTER, and the latter by the Cant phrase, NOBBA-SALTEE. *Ten-pence* is DACHA-SALTEE, and *eleven-pence* DACHA-ONE,—both Cant expressions. *One shilling* boasts ten Slang equivalents; thus we have BEONG, BOB, BREAKY-LEG, DEANER, GEN (either from *argent*, silver, or the back slang), HOG, PEG, STAG, TEVISS, and TWELVER. *Half-a-crown* is known as an ALDERMAN, HALF A BULL, HALF A TUSHEROON, and a MADZA CAROON; whilst a *crown* piece, or *five shillings*, may be called either a BULL, or a CAROON, or a CARTWHEEL, or a COACHWHEEL, or a THICK-UN, or a TUSHEROON. The next advance in Slang money is *ten shillings*, or *half-a-sovereign*, which may be either pronounced as HALF A BEAN, HALF A COUTER, a MADZA POONA, or HALF A QUID. A *sovereign*, or *twenty shillings*, is a BEAN, CANARY, COUTER, FOONT, GOLDFINCH, JAMES, POONA, QUID, a THICK-UN, or a YELLOW-BOY. *Guineas* are nearly obsolete, yet the terms NEDS, and HALF NEDS, are still in use. Bank notes are FLIMSIES, LONG-TAILED ONES, or SOFT. A

FINUF is a five-pound note. One hundred pounds (or any other "round sum") quietly handed over as payment for services performed is curiously termed "a COOL hundred." Thus ends, with several omissions, this long list of Slang terms for the coins of the realm, which for copiousness, I will engage to say, is not equalled by any other vulgar or unauthorised language in Europe.

The antiquity of many of these Slang names is remarkable. WINN was the vulgar term for a penny in the days of Queen Elizabeth; and TESTER, a sixpence (formerly a shilling), was the correct name in the days of Henry the Eighth. The reader, too, will have remarked the frequency of animals' names as Slang terms for money. Little, as a modern writer has remarked, do the persons using these phrases know of their remote and somewhat classical origin, which may, indeed, be traced to the period antecedent to that when monarchs monopolised the surface of coined money with their own image and superscriptions. They are identical with the very name of money among the early Romans, which was *pecunia,* from *pecus,* a flock. The collections of coin dealers amply show that the figure of a HOG was anciently placed on a small silver coin; and that that of a BULL decorated larger ones of the same metal. These coins were frequently deeply crossed on the reverse; this was for the convenience of easily breaking them into two or more pieces, should the bargain for which they were employed require it, and the parties making it had no smaller change handy to complete the transaction. Thus we find that the HALF BULL of the itinerant street seller, or "traveller,"* so far from being a phrase of modern invention, as is generally supposed, is in point of fact referable to an era extremely remote. There are many other Cant words directly from a classic source, as will be seen in the Dictionary.

Shopkeepers' Slang is, perhaps, the most offensive of all Slang. It is not a casual eyesore, as newspaper Slang, neither is it an occasional discomfort to the ear, as in the case of some vulgar byeword of the street; but it is a perpetual nuisance, and stares you in the face on tradesmen's invoices, on labels in the shop-windows, and placards on the hoardings, in posters against the house next to your own door—if it happens to be empty for a few weeks,—and in bills thrust into your hand, as you peaceably walk through the streets. Under your doors, and down your area, Slang hand-bills are dropped by some PUSHING tradesman, and for the thousandth time you are called upon to learn that an ALARMING SACRIFICE is taking place in the next street, that prices are DOWN AGAIN, that in consequence of some other tradesman not DRIVING a ROARING TRADE, being in fact SOLD UP, and for the time being a resident in BURDON'S HOTEL

* See Dictionary.

(Whitecross-street Prison), the PUSHING tradesman wishes to sell out at AWFULLY LOW PRICES, "to the kind patrons, and numerous customers," &c. &c., "that have on every occasion," &c. &c. In this Slang any occupation or calling is termed a LINE,—thus the "Building-LINE." A tailor usurps to himself a good deal of Slang. Amongst operatives he is called a SNIP, or a STEEL BAR DRIVER; by the world, a NINTH PART OF A MAN; and by the young collegian, or "fast" man, a SUFFERER. If he takes army contracts, it is SANK WORK; if he is a SLOP tailor, he is a SPRINGER UP, and his garments are BLOWN TOGETHER. Perquisites with him are SPIFFS, and remnants of cloth, PEAKING. The percentage he allows to his assistants (or COUNTER JUMPERS) on the sale of old-fashioned articles, is termed TINGE. If he pays his workmen in goods, or gives them tickets upon other tradesmen, with whom he shares the profit, he is soon known as a TOMMY MASTER. If his business succeeds, it TAKES; if neglected, it becomes SHAKY, and GOES TO POT; if he is deceived by a creditor (a not by any means unusual circumstance) he is LET IN, or, as it is sometimes varied, TAKEN IN. I need scarcely remark that any credit he may give is termed TICK.

Operatives' or Workmen's Slang, in quality, is but slightly removed from tradesmen's Slang. When belonging to the same shop or factory, they GRAFT there, and are BROTHER CHIPS. They generally dine at SLAP BANG SHOPS, and are often paid at TOMMY SHOPS. At the nearest PUB, or public-house, they generally have a SCORE CHALKED UP against them, which has to be WIPED OFF regularly on the Saturday night. When out of work, they borrow a word from the flunkey vocabulary, and describe themselves as being OUT OF COLLAR. They term each other FLINTS and DUNGS, if they are "society" or "non-society" men. Their salary is a SCREW, and to be discharged is to GET THE SACK. When they quit work, they KNOCK OFF; and when out of employ, they ask if any HANDS are wanted. FAT is the vulgar synonyme for perquisites; ELBOW-GREASE signifies labour; and SAINT MONDAY is the favourite day of the week. Names of animals figure plentifully in the workman's vocabulary; thus we have GOOSE, a tailor's smoothing iron; SHEEP'S-FOOT, an iron hammer; SOW, a receptacle for molten iron, whilst the metal poured from it is termed PIG. I have often thought that many of the Slang terms for money originally came from the workshop, thus—BRADS, from the ironmonger; CHIPS, from the carpenter; DUST, from the goldsmith; FEATHERS, from the upholsterer; HORSE NAILS, from the farrier; HADDOCK, from the fishmonger; and TANNER, from the leather-dresser. The subject is curious. Allow me to call the attention of numismatists to it.

There yet remain several distinct divisions of Slang to be examined;—the Slang of the *stable*, or *jockey* Slang; the Slang of the *prize ring;* the Slang of *servitude*, or *flunkeydom;* vulgar, or *street* Slang; the Slang of *softened oaths;* and the Slang of *intoxication*. I shall only examine the last two. If society, as has been remarked, is a sham, from the vulgar foundation of commonalty to the crowning summit of royalty, especially do we perceive the justness of the remark in the Slang makeshifts for oaths, and sham exclamations for passion and temper. These apologies for feeling are a disgrace to our vernacular, although it is some satisfaction to know that they serve the purpose of reducing the stock of national profanity. "You BE BLOWED," or "I'll BE BLOWED IF," &c., is an exclamation often heard in the streets. BLAZES, or "like BLAZES," came probably from the army. BLAST, too, although in general vulgar use, may have had a like origin; so may the phrase, "I wish I may be SHOT, if," &c. BLOW ME TIGHT, is a very windy and common exclamation. The same may be said of STRIKE ME LUCKY, NEVER TRUST ME, and SO HELP ME DAVY; the latter derived from the truer old phrase, I'LL TAKE MY DAVY ON'T, *i.e.*, my *affidavit*, DAVY being a corruption of that word. BY GOLLY, GOL DARN IT, and SO HELP ME BOB, are evident shams for profane oaths. NATION is but a softening of *damnation;* and OD, whether used in OD DRAT IT, or OD'S BLOOD, is but an apology for the name of the Deity. The Irish phrase, BAD SCRAN TO YER! is equivalent to wishing a person bad food. "I'm SNIGGERED if you will," and "I'm JIGGERED," are other stupid forms of mild swearing,—fearful of committing an open profanity, yet slyly nibbling at the sin. Both DEUCE and DICKENS are vulgar old synonymes for the devil; and ZOUNDS is an abbreviation of GOD'S WOUNDS,—a very ancient catholic oath.

In a casual survey of the territory of Slang, it is curious to observe how well represented are the familiar wants and failings of life. First, there's money, with one hundred and twenty Slang terms and synonymes; then comes drink, from small beer to champagne; and next, as a very natural sequence, *intoxication*, and fuddlement generally, with some half a hundred vulgar terms, graduating the scale of drunkenness from a slight inebriation, to the soaky state of gutterdom and stretcherdom, —I pray the reader to forgive the expressions. The Slang synonymes for mild intoxication are certainly very choice,—they are BEERY, BEMUSED, BOOZY, BOSKY, BUFFY, CORNED, FOGGY, FOU, FRESH, HAZY, ELEVATED, KISKY, LUSHY, MOONY, MUGGY, MUZZY, ON, SCREWED, STEWED, TIGHT, and WINEY. A higher or more intense state of beastliness is represented by the expressions, PODGY, BEARGERED, BLUED, CUT, PRIMED,

LUMPY, PLOUGHED, MUDDLED, OBFUSCATED, SWIPEY, THREE SHEETS IN THE WIND, and TOP-HEAVY. But the climax of fuddlement is only obtained when the DISGUISED individual CAN'T SEE A HOLE IN A LADDER, or when he is all MOPS AND BROOMS, or OFF HIS NUT, or with his MAIN-BRACE WELL SPLICED, or with the SUN IN HIS EYES, or when he has LAPPED THE GUTTER, and got the GRAVEL RASH, or on the RAN-TAN, or on the RE-RAW, or when he is SEWED UP, or regularly SCAMMERED,—then, and not till then, is he entitled in vulgar society to the title of LUSHINGTON, or recommended to PUT IN THE PIN.

A

DICTIONARY OF MODERN SLANG, CANT, & VULGAR WORDS;

MANY WITH THEIR ETYMOLOGIES TRACED.

A 1, first rate, the very best; "she's a prime girl she is; she is A 1."—*Sam Slick*. The highest classification of ships at Lloyd's; common term in the United States, also at Liverpool and other English seaports. Another, even more intensitive form, is "first-class, letter A, No. 1."

ABOUT RIGHT, "to do the thing ABOUT RIGHT," *i.e.*, to do it properly, soundly, correctly; "he guv it 'im ABOUT RIGHT," *i.e.*, he beat him severely.

ABRAM-SHAM, or SHAM-ABRAHAM, to feign sickness or distress. From ABRAM MAN, the *ancient cant* term for a begging impostor, or one who pretended to have been mad.—*Burton's Anatomy of Melancholy*, part i., sec. 2, vol. i., p. 360. When Abraham Newland was Cashier of the Bank of England, and signed their notes, it was sung:—

"I have heard people say
That SHAM ABRAHAM you may,
But you mustn't SHAM ABRAHAM Newland."

ABSQUATULATE, to run away, or abscond; a hybrid *American* expression, from the Latin *ab*, and "squat," to settle.

ADAM'S ALE, water.—*English*. The *Scotch* term is ADAM'S WINE.

AGGERAWATORS (corruption of *Aggravators*), the greasy locks of hair in vogue among costermongers and other street folk, worn twisted from the temple back towards the ear. They are also, from a supposed resemblance in form, termed NEWGATE KNOCKERS, which see.—*Sala's Gas-light*, &c.

ALDERMAN, a half-crown—possibly from its rotundity.

ALDERMAN, a turkey.

ALDERMAN IN CHAINS, a turkey hung with sausages.

ALL OF A HUGH! all on one side, or with a thump; the word HUGH being pronounced with a grunt.—*Suffolk.*

ALL MY EYE, answer of astonishment to an improbable story; ALL MY EYE AND BETTY MARTIN, a vulgar phrase with similar meaning, said to be the commencement of a Popish prayer to St. Martin, "Oh mihi, beate Martine," and fallen into discredit at the Reformation.

ALL-OVERISH, neither sick nor well, the premonitory symptoms of illness.

ALL-ROUNDERS, the fashionable shirt collars of the present time worn meeting in front.

ALL-SERENE, an ejaculation of acquiescence.

ALLS, tap-droppings, refuse spirits sold at a cheap rate in gin-palaces.—*See* LOVEAGE.

ALL-THERE, in strict fashion, first-rate, "up to the mark;" a vulgar person would speak of a spruce, showily-dressed female as being ALL-THERE. An artizan would use the same phrase to express the capabilities of a skilful fellow workman.

ALL TO PIECES, utterly, excessively; "he beat him ALL TO PIECES," *i.e.*, excelled or surpassed him exceedingly.

ALL TO SMASH, or GONE TO PIECES, bankrupt, or smashed to pieces.—*Somersetshire.*

ALMIGHTY DOLLAR, an *American* expression for the "power of money," first introduced by Washington Irving in 1837.

AN'T, or AÏN'T, the vulgar abbreviation of "am not," or "are not."

ANOINTING, a good beating.

ANY HOW, in any way, or at any rate, bad; "he went on ANY HOW," *i.e.*, badly or indifferently.

APPLE CART, "down with his APPLE CART," *i.e.*, upset him.—*North.*

APPLE PIE ORDER, in exact or very nice order.

AREA-SNEAK, a boy thief who commits depredations upon kitchens and cellars.—*See* CROW.

ARGOT, a term used amongst London thieves for their secret or cant language. *French* term for slang.

ARTICLE, a man or boy, derisive term.

ARY, corruption of ever a, e'er a; ARY ONE, e'er a one.

ATTACK, to carve, or commence operations on; "ATTACK that beef, and oblige!"

ATTIC, the head; "queer in the ATTIC," intoxicated.—*Pugilistic.*

AUNT-SALLY, a favourite game on race-courses and at fairs, consisting of a wooden head mounted on a stick, firmly fixed in the ground; in the nose of which, or rather in that part of the facial arrangement of AUNT SALLY which is generally considered incomplete without a nasal projection, a tobacco pipe is inserted. The fun consists in standing at a distance and demolishing AUNT SALLY'S pipe-clay projection with short bludgeons, very similar to the half of a broom-handle. The Duke of Beaufort is a "crack hand" at smashing pipe noses, and his performances two years ago on Brighton race-course are yet fresh in remembrance. The noble Duke, in the summer months, frequently drives the old London and Brighton four-horse mail coach, "Age"—a whim singular enough now, but common forty years ago."

AUTUMN, a slang term for an execution by hanging. When the drop was introduced instead of the old gallows, cart, and ladder, and a man was for the first time "turned-off" in the present fashion, the mob were so pleased with the invention that they spoke of the operation as at AUTUMN, or the FALL OF THE LEAF (*sc.* the drop), with the man about to be hung.

AVAST, a sailor's phrase for stop, shut up, go away,—apparently connected with the *old cant,* BYNGE A WASTE.

AWAKE, or FLY, knowing, thoroughly understanding, not ignorant of. The phrase WIDE AWAKE carries the same meaning in ordinary conversation.

AWFUL (or, with the Cockneys, ORFUL), a senseless expletive, used to intensify a description of anything good or bad; "what an AWFUL fine woman!" *i.e.,* how handsome, or showy!

AXE, to ask.—*Saxon,* ACSIAN.

BABES, the lowest order of KNOCK-OUTS (which see), who are prevailed upon not to give opposing biddings at auctions, in consideration of their receiving a small sum (from one shilling to half-a-crown), and a certain quantity of beer. BABES exist in Baltimore, U.S., where they are known as blackguards and "rowdies."

BACK JUMP, a back window.

BACK SLANG IT, to go out the back way.

BACK OUT, to retreat from a difficulty; the reverse of GO AHEAD. Metaphor borrowed from the stables.

BACON, "to save one's BACON," to escape.

BAD, "to go to the BAD," to deteriorate in character, be ruined. *Virgil* has an exactly similar phrase, *in pejus ruere.*

BAGMAN, a commercial traveller.

BAGS, trowsers. Trowsers of an extensive pattern, or exaggerated fashionable cut, have lately been termed HOWLING-BAGS, but only when the style has been very "*loud.*" The word is probably an abbreviation for b–mbags. "To have the BAGS off," to be of age and one's own master, to have plenty of money.

BAKE, "he's only HALF BAKED," *i.e.*, soft, inexperienced.

BAKER'S DOZEN. This consists of thirteen or fourteen; the surplus number, called the *inbread*, being thrown in for fear of incurring the penalty for short weight. To "give a man a BAKER'S DOZEN," in a slang sense, means to give him an extra good beating or pummelling.

BALAAM, printers' slang for matter kept in type about monstrous productions of nature, &c., to fill up spaces in newspapers that would otherwise be vacant. The term BALAAM-BOX has long been used in *Blackwood* as the name of the depository for rejected articles.

BALL, prison allowance, viz., six ounces of meat.

BALLYRAG, to scold vehemently, to swindle one out of his money by intimidation and sheer abuse, as alleged in a late cab case (*Evans* v. *Robinson*).

BALMY, insane.

BAMBOOZLE, to deceive, make fun of, or cheat a person; abbreviated to BAM, which is used also as a substantive, a deception, a sham, a "sell." *Swift* says BAMBOOZLE was invented by a nobleman in the reign of Charles II.; but this I conceive to be an error. The probability is that a nobleman first *used* it in polite society. The term is derived from the *Gipseys.*

BANDED, hungry.

BANDY, or CRIPPLE, a sixpence, so called from this coin being generally bent or crooked; old term for flimsy or bad cloth, temp. Q. Elizabeth.

BANG, to excel or surpass; BANGING, great or thumping.

BANG-UP, first-rate.

BANTLING, a child; stated in *Bacchus and Venus*, 1737, and by *Grose*, to be a cant term.

BANYAN-DAY, a day on which no meat is served out for rations; probably derived from the BANIANS, a Hindoo caste, who abstain from animal food.—*Sea.*

BAR, or BARRING, excepting; in common use in the betting-ring; "I bet against the field BAR two." The Irish use of BARRIN' is very similar.

BARKER, a man employed to cry at the doors of "gaffs," shows, and puffing shops, to entice people inside.

BARKING IRONS, pistols.

BARNACLES, a pair of spectacles; corruption of BINOCULI?

BARNEY, a LARK, SPREE, rough enjoyment; "get up a BARNEY," to have a "lark."

BARNEY, a mob, a crowd.

BARN-STORMERS, theatrical performers who travel the country and act in barns, selecting short and frantic pieces to suit the rustic taste.—*Theatrical.*

BARRIKIN, jargon, speech, or discourse; "we can't tumble to that BARRIKIN," *i.e.*, we don't understand what he says. *Miege* calls it "a sort of stuff."

BASH, to beat, thrash; "BASHING a donna," beating a woman; originally a provincial word, and chiefly applied to the practice of beating walnut trees, when in bud, with long poles, to increase their productiveness. Hence the West country proverb—

> "A woman, a whelp, and a walnut tree,
> The more you BASH 'em, the better they be."

BAT, "on his own BAT," on his own account.—*See* HOOK.

BATS, a pair of bad boots.

BATTER, "on the BATTER," literally "on the streets," or given up to roistering and debauchery.

BATTLES, the students' term at Oxford for rations. At Cambridge, COMMONS.

BAWDYKEN, a brothel.—*See* KEN.

BAZAAR, a shop or counter. *Gipsey* and *Hindoo*, a market.

BEAK, a magistrate, judge, or policeman; "baffling the BEAK," to get remanded. *Ancient cant*, BECK. *Saxon*, BEAG, a necklace or gold collar—emblem of authority. Sir John Fielding was called the BLIND-BEAK in the last century

Query, if connected with the Italian BECCO, which means a (bird's) *beak*, and also a *blockhead*.

BEAKER-HUNTER, a stealer of poultry.

BEANS, money; "a haddock of BEANS," a purse of money; formerly BEAN meant a guinea; *French*, BIENS, property; also used as a synonyme for BRICK, which see.

BEAR, one who contracts to deliver or sell a certain quantity of stock in the public funds on a forthcoming day at a stated place, but who does not possess it, trusting to a decline in public securities to enable him to fulfil the agreement and realise a profit.—*See* BULL. Both words are slang terms on the Stock Exchange, and are frequently used in the business columns of newspapers.

> "He who sells that of which he is not possessed is proverbially said to sell the skin before he has caught the BEAR. It was the practice of stock-jobbers, in the year 1720, to enter into a contract for transferring South Sea Stock at a future time for a certain price; but he who contracted to sell had frequently no stock to transfer, nor did he who bought intend to receive any in consequence of his bargain; the seller was, therefore, called a BEAR, in allusion to the proverb, and the buyer a BULL, perhaps only as a similar distinction. The contract was merely a wager, to be determined by the rise or fall of stock; if it rose, the seller paid the difference to the buyer, proportioned to the sum determined by the same computation to the seller."—*Dr. Warton on Pope.*

BEARGERED, to be drunk.

BEAT, or BEAT-HOLLOW, to surpass or excel.

BEAT, the allotted range traversed by a policeman on duty.

BEAT-OUT, DEAD-BEAT, tired or fagged.

BEATER-CASES, boots: *Nearly obsolete.*

BEAVER, old street term for a hat; GOSS is the modern word, BEAVER, except in the country, having fallen into disuse.

BE-BLOWED, a windy exclamation equivalent to an oath.—*See* BLOW-ME.

BED-POST, "in the twinkling of a BED-POST," in a moment, or very quickly. Originally BED-STAFF, a stick placed vertically in the frame of a bed to keep the bedding in its place.—*Shadwell's Virtuoso*, 1676, act i., scene 1. This was used sometimes as a defensive weapon.

BEE, "to have a BEE in one's bonnet," *i.e.*, to be not exactly sane.

BEERY, intoxicated, or fuddled with beer.

BEESWAX, poor soft cheese.

BEETLE-CRUSHERS, or SQUASHERS, large flat feet.

BELCHER, a kind of handkerchief.—*See* BILLY.

BELL, a song.

BELLOWS, the lungs.

BELLOWSED, or LAGGED, transported.

BELLOWS-TO-MEND, out of breath.

BELLY-TIMBER, food, or "grub."

BELLY-VENGEANCE, small sour beer, apt to cause gastralgia.

BEMUSE, to fuddle one's self with drink, "BEMUSING himself with beer," &c.—*Sala's Gas-light and Day-light*, p. 308.

BEN, a benefit.—*Theatrical.*

BEND, "that's above my BEND," *i.e.*, beyond my power, too expensive, or too difficult for me to perform.

BENDER, a sixpence,—from its liability to bend.

BENDER, the arm; "over the BENDER," synonymous with "over the left."—*See* OVER. Also an ironical exclamation similar to WALKER.

BENE, good.—*Ancient cant;* BENAR was the comparative.—*See* BONE. *Latin.*

BENJAMIN, a coat. Formerly termed a JOSEPH, in allusion, perhaps, to Joseph's coat of many colours.—*See* UPPER-BENJAMIN.

BENJY, a waistcoat.

BEONG, a shilling.—*See* SALTEE.

BESTER, a low betting cheat.

BESTING, excelling, cheating. BESTED, taken in, or defrauded.

BETTER, more; "how far is it to town?" "oh, BETTER 'n a mile.—*Saxon* and *Old English*, now a vulgarism.

BETTY, a skeleton key, or picklock.—*Old cant.*

B. FLATS, bugs.

BIBLE CARRIER, a person who sells songs without singing them.

BIG, "to look BIG," to assume an inflated dress, or manner; "to talk BIG," *i e.*, boastingly, or with an "extensive" air.

BIG-HOUSE, the work-house.

BILBO, a sword; abbrev. of BILBOA blade. Spanish swords were anciently very celebrated, especially those of Toledo, Bilboa, &c.

BILK, a cheat, or a swindler. Formerly in frequent use, now confined to the streets, where it is very general. *Gothic*, BILAICAN.

BILK, to defraud, or obtain goods, &c. without paying for them; "to BILK the schoolmaster," to get information or experience without paying for it.

BILLINGSGATE (when applied to speech), foul and coarse language. Not many years since, one of the London notorieties was to hear the fishwomen at Billingsgate abuse each other. The anecdote of Dr. Johnson and the Billingsgate virago is well known.

BILLY, a silk pocket handkerchief.—*Scotch.*—*See* WIPE.

⁎ A list of the slang terms descriptive of the various patterns of handkerchiefs, pocket and neck, is here subjoined:—

BELCHER, close striped pattern, yellow silk, and intermixed with white and a little black; named from the pugilist, Jim Belcher.
BIRD'S EYE WIPE, diamond spots.
BLOOD-RED FANCY, red.
BLUE BILLY, blue ground with white spots.
CREAM FANCY, any pattern on a white ground.
GREEN KING'S MAN, any pattern on a green ground.
RANDAL'S MAN, green, with white spots; named after Jack Randal, pugilist.
WATER'S MAN, sky coloured.
YELLOW FANCY, yellow, with white spots.
YELLOW MAN, all yellow.

BILLY-BARLOW, a street clown; sometimes termed a JIM CROW, or SALTIMBANCO,—so called from the hero of a slang song.—*Bulwer's Paul Clifford.*

BILLY-HUNTING, buying old metal.

BIRD-CAGE, a four-wheeled cab.

BIT, fourpence; in America 12½ cents is called a BIT, and a defaced 20 cent piece is termed a LONG BIT. A BIT is the smallest coin in Jamaica, equal to 6d.

BIT, a purse, or any sum of money.

BIT-FAKER, or TURNER OUT, a coiner of bad money.

BITCH, tea; "a BITCH party," a tea-drinking.—*University.*

BITE, a cheat; "a Yorkshire BITE," a cheating fellow from that county.—*North;* also *old slang,* used by *Pope.* Swift says it originated with a nobleman in his day.

BITE, to cheat; "to be BITTEN," to be taken in or imposed upon. Originally a Gipsey term.—*See Bacchus and Venus.*

BIVVY, or GATTER, beer; "shant of BIVVY," a pot, or quart of beer. In Suffolk, the afternoon refreshment of reapers is called BEVER. It is also an old English term.

> "He is none of those same ordinary eaters, that will devour three breakfasts, and as many dinners, without any prejudice to their BEVERS, drinkings, or suppers."—*Beaumont and Fletcher's Woman Hater* 1—3.

Both words are probably from the Italian, *bevere, bere.* Latin, *bibere.* English, *beverage.*

BLACK AND WHITE, handwriting.

BLACKBERRY-SWAGGER, a person who hawks tapes, boot laces, &c.

BLACK-LEG, a rascal, swindler, or card cheat.

BLACK-SHEEP, a "bad lot," "*mauvais sujet;*" also a workman who refuses to join in a strike.

BLACK-STRAP, port wine.

BLADE, a man—in ancient times the term for a soldier; "knowing BLADE," a wide awake, sharp, or cunning man.

BLACKGUARD, a low, or dirty fellow.

> "A cant word amongst the vulgar, by which is implied a dirty fellow of the meanest kind. Dr. Johnson says, and he cites only the modern authority of Swift. But the introduction of this word into our language belongs not to the vulgar, and is more than a century prior to the time of Swift. Mr. Malone agrees with me in exhibiting the two first of the following examples. The *black-guard* is evidently designed to imply a fit attendant on the devil. Mr. Gifford, however, in his late edition of Ben Jonson's works, assigns an origin of the name different from what the old examples which I have cited seem to countenance. It has been formed, he says, from those 'mean and dirty dependants, in great houses, who were selected to carry coals to the kitchen, halls, &c. To this smutty regiment, who attended the progresses, and rode in the carts with the pots and kettles, which, with every other article of furniture, were then moved from palace to palace, the people, in derision, gave the name of *black guards;* a term since become sufficiently familiar, and never properly explained.'—Ben Jonson, ii. 169, vii. 250."—*Todd's Johnson's Dictionary.*

BLARNEY, flattery, exaggeration.—*Hibernicism.*

BLAST, to curse.

BLAZES, "like BLAZES," furious or desperate, a low comparison.

BLEST, a vow; "BLEST if I'll do it," *i.e.*, I am determined not to do it; euphemism for CURST.

BLEED, to victimise, or extract money from a person, to spunge on, to make suffer vindictively.

BLEW, or BLOW, to inform, or peach.

BLEWED, got rid of, disposed of, spent; "I BLEWED all my blunt last night," I spent all my money.

BLIND, a pretence, or make believe.

BLIND-HOOKEY, a gambling game at cards.

BLINKER, a blackened eye.—*Norwich slang.*

BLINK FENCER, a person who sells spectacles.

BLOAK, or BLOKE, a man; "the BLOAK with a jasey," the man with a wig, *i.e.*, the Judge. *Gipsey* and *Hindoo*, LOKE. *North*, BLOACHER, any large animal.

BLOB (from BLAB), to talk. Beggars are of two kinds,—those who SCREEVE (introduce themselves with a FAKEMENT, or false document), and those who BLOB, or state their case in their own truly "unvarnished" language.

BLOCK, the head.

BLOCK ORNAMENTS, the small dark coloured pieces of meat exposed on the cheap butchers' blocks or counters,—debateable points to all the sharp visaged argumentative old women in low neighbourhoods.

BLOOD, a fast or high-mettled man. Nearly obsolete in the sense in which it was used in George the Fourth's time.

BLOOD-RED FANCY, a kind of handkerchief worn by pugilists and frequenters of prize fights.—*See* BILLY.

BLOODY-JEMMY, a sheep's head.—*See* SANGUINARY JAMES.

BLOW, to expose, or inform; "BLOW the gaff," to inform against a person. In *America*, to BLOW is slang for to taunt.

BLOW A CLOUD, to smoke a cigar or pipe—a phrase in use two centuries ago.

BLOW ME, or BLOW ME TIGHT, a vow, a ridiculous and unmeaning ejaculation, inferring an appeal to the ejaculator; "I'm BLOWED if you will" is a common expression among the lower orders; "BLOW ME UP" was the term a century ago. —*See Parker's Adventures*, 1781.

BLOW OUT, or TUCK IN, a feast.

BLOW UP, to make a noise, or scold; formerly a cant expression used amongst thieves, now a recognised and respectable phrase. BLOWING UP, a jobation, a scolding.

BLOWEN, a showy or flaunting prostitute, a thief's paramour. In *Wilts*, a BLOWEN is a blossom. *Germ.* BLUHEN, to bloom.

"O du *bülhende* Mädchen viel schöne Willkomm!"—*German Song.*

Possibly, however, the street term BLOWEN may mean one whose reputation has been BLOWN UPON, or damaged.

BLOWER, a girl; a contemptuous name in opposition to JOMER.

BLUBBER, to cry in a childish manner.—*Ancient.*

BLUDGERS, low thieves, who use violence.

BLUE, a policeman; "disguised in BLUE and liquor."—*Boots at the Swan.*

BLUE, or BLEW, to pawn or pledge.

BLUE, confounded or surprised; "to look BLUE," to be astonished or disappointed.

BLUE BILLY, the handkerchief (blue ground with white spots) worn and used at prize fights. Before a SET TO, it is common to take it from the neck and tie it round the leg as a garter, or round the waist, to "keep in the wind." Also, the refuse ammoniacal lime from gas factories.

BLUE BLANKET, a rough over coat made of coarse pilot cloth.

BLUE-BOTTLE, a policeman. It is singular that this well known slang term for a London constable should have been used by Shakespere. In part ii. of King Henry IV., act v., scene 4, Doll Tearsheet calls the beadle, who is dragging her in, a "thin man in a censer, a BLUE-BOTTLE rogue."

BLUED, or BLEWED, tipsey or drunk.

BLUE DEVILS, the apparitions supposed to be seen by habitual drunkards.

BLUE MOON, an unlimited period.

BLUE MURDER, a desperate or alarming cry. *French*, MORT-BLEU.

BLUE RUIN, gin.

BLUE-PIGEON FLYERS, journeymen plumbers, glaziers, and others, who, under the plea of repairing houses, strip off the lead, and make way with it. Sometimes they get off with it by wrapping it round their bodies.

BLUES, a fit of despondency.—*See* BLUE DEVILS.

BLUEY, lead. *German*, BLEI.

BLUFF, an excuse.

BLUFF, to turn aside, stop, or excuse.

BLUNT, money. It has been said that this term is from the *French* BLOND, sandy or golden colour, and that a parallel may be found in BROWN or BROWNS, the slang for half-pence. The etymology seems far fetched, however.

BLURT OUT, to speak from impulse, and without reflection.—*Shakespere.*

BOB, a shilling. Formerly BOBSTICK, which may have been the original.

BOB, "s'help my BOB," a street oath, equivalent to "so help me God." Other words are used in street language for a similarly evasive purpose, *i.e.*, CAT, GREENS, TATUR, &c., all equally profane and disgusting.

BOBBISH, very well, clever, spruce; "how are you doing?" "oh! pretty BOBBISH."—*Old.*

BOBBY, a policeman. Both BOBBY and PEELER were nicknames given to the new police, in allusion to the christian and surnames of the late *Sir Robert Peel,* who was the prime mover in effecting their introduction and improvement. The term BOBBY is, however, older than the *Saturday Reviewer,* in his childish and petulant remarks, imagines. The official square-keeper, who is always armed with a cane to drive away idle and disorderly urchins, has, time out of mind, been called by the said urchins, BOBBY *the Beadle.* BOBBY is also, I may remark, an old English word for striking or hitting, a quality not unknown to policemen.—*See Halliwell's Dictionary.*

BODMINTON, blood.—*Pugilistic.*

BODY-SNATCHERS, bailiffs and runners: SNATCH, the trick by which the bailiff captures the delinquent.

BODY-SNATCHERS, cat stealers.

BOG or BOG-HOUSE, a water-closet.—*School term.* In the Inns of Court, I am informed, this term is very common.

BOG-TROTTER, satirical name for an Irishman.—*Miege. Camden,* however, speaking of the "debateable land" on the borders of England and Scotland, says "both these dales breed notable BOG-TROTTERS."

BOILERS, the slang name given to the New Kensington Museum and School of Art, in allusion to the peculiar form of the buildings, and the fact of their being mainly composed of, and covered with, sheet iron.—*See* PEPPER-BOXES.

BOLT, to run away, decamp, or abscond.

BOLT, to swallow without chewing.

BONE, good, excellent. ◊, the vagabond's hieroglyphic for BONE, or good, chalked by them on houses and street corners, as a hint to succeeding beggars. *French,* BON.

BONE, to steal or pilfer. BONED, seized, apprehended.—*Old.*

BONE-GRUBBERS, persons who hunt dust-holes, gutters, and all likely spots for refuse bones, which they sell at the rag-shops, or to the bone-grinders.

BONE-PICKER, a footman.

BONES, dice; also called ST. HUGH'S BONES.

BONES, "he made no BONES of it," he did not hesitate, *i.e.*, undertook and finished the work without difficulty, "found no BONES in the jelly."—*Ancient, vide Cotgrave.*

BONNET, a gambling cheat. "A man who sits at a gaming-table, and appears to be playing against the table; when a stranger enters, the BONNET generally wins."—*Times*, Nov. 17, 1856. Also, a pretence, or make-believe, a sham bidder at auctions.

BONNET, to strike a man's cap or hat over his eyes and nose.

BONNETTER, one who induces another to gamble.

BOOK, an arrangement of bets for and against, chronicled in a pocket-book made for that purpose; "making a BOOK upon it," common phrase to denote the general arrangement of a person's bets on a race. "That does not suit my BOOK," *i.e.*, does not accord with my other arrangements. *Shakespere* uses BOOK in the sense of "a paper of conditions."

BOOM, "to tip one's BOOM off," to be off, or start in a certain direction.—*Sea.*

BOOKED, caught, fixed, disposed of.—Term in *Book-keeping.*

BOOZE, drink. *Ancient cant,* BOWSE.

BOOZE, to drink, or more properly, to use another slang term, to "lush," viz., to drink continually, until drunk, or nearly so. The term is an old one. Harman, in Queen Elizabeth's days, speaks of "BOUSING (or boozing) and belly-cheere." The term was good English in the fourteenth century, and comes from the Dutch, BUYZEN, to tipple.

BOOZE, or SUCK-CASA, a public-house.

BOOZING-KEN, a beer-shop, a low public house.—*Ancient.*

BOOZY, intoxicated or fuddled.

BORE, a troublesome friend or acquaintance, a nuisance, anything which wearies or annoys. The *Gradus ad Cantabrigiam* suggests the derivation of BORE from the *Greek*, Βαρος, a burden. *Shakespere* uses it, King Henry VIII., i., 1—

> "——— at this instant
> He BORES me with some trick."

Grose speaks of this word as being much in fashion about the year 1780-81, and states that it vanished of a sudden, without leaving a trace behind. Not so, burly Grose, the term is still in favour, and is as piquant and expressive as ever. Of the modern sense of the word BORE, the Prince

Consort made an amusing and effective use in his masterly address to the British Association, at Aberdeen, September 14, 1859. He said (as reported by the *Times*):—

"I will not weary you by further examples, with which most of you are better acquainted than I am myself, but merely express my satisfaction that there should exist bodies of men who will bring the well-considered and understood wants of science before the public and the Government, who will even hand round the begging-box, and expose themselves to refusals and rebuffs, to which all beggars all liable, with the certainty besides of being considered great BORES. Please to recollect that this species of "bore" is a most useful animal, well adapted for the ends for which nature intended him. He alone, by constantly returning to the charge, and repeating the same truths and the same requests, succeeds in awakening attention to the cause which he advocates, and obtains that hearing which is granted him at last for self-protection, as the minor evil compared to his importunity, but which is requisite to make his cause understood."

BOSH, nonsense, stupidity.—*Gipsey* and *Persian*. Also pure *Turkish*, BOSH LAKERDI, empty talk. A person, in the *Saturday Review*, has stated that BOSH is coeval with Morier's novel, *Hadji Babi*, which was published in 1828; but this is a blunder. The term was used in this country as early as 1760, and may be found in the *Student*, vol. ii., p. 217.

BOSH, a fiddle.

BOSH-FAKER, a violin player.

BOS-KEN, a farm-house. *Ancient.—See* KEN.

BOSKY, inebriated —*Household Words*, No. 183.

BOSMAN, a farmer; "faking a BOSMAN on the main toby," robbing a farmer on the highway. Boss, a master.—*American*. Both terms from the *Dutch*, BOSCH-MAN, one who lives in the woods; otherwise *Boschjeman* or *Bushman*.

BOSS-EYED, a person with one eye, or rather with one eye injured.

BOTHER, to teaze, to annoy.

BOTHER (from the *Hibernicism* POTHER), trouble, or annoyance. *Grose* has a singular derivation, BOTHER, or BOTH-EARED, from two persons talking at the same time, or to both ears. BLOTHER, an old word, signifying to chatter idly.—*See Halliwell*.

BOTHERATION! trouble, annoyance; "BOTHERATION to it," confound it, or deuce take it, an exclamation when irritated.

BOTTLE-HOLDER, an assistant to a "Second,"—*Pugilistic*; an abettor; also, the bridegroom's man at a wedding.

BOTTY, conceited, swaggering.

BOUNCE, impudence.

BOUNCE, a showy swindler.

BOUNCE, to boast, cheat, or bully.—*Old cant.*

BOUNCER, a person who steals whilst bargaining with a tradesman; a lie.

BOUNDER, a four-wheel cab. *Lucus a non lucendo?*

BOUNETTER, a fortune-telling cheat.—*Gipsey.*

BOW-CATCHERS, or KISS-CURLS, small curls twisted on the cheeks or temples of young—and often old—girls, adhering to the face as if gummed or pasted. Evidently a corruption of BEAU-CATCHERS. In old times these were called *love-locks,* when they were the marks at which all the puritan and ranting preachers levelled their pulpit pop-guns, loaded with sharp and virulent abuse. Hall and Prynne looked upon all women as strumpets who dared to let the hair depart from a straight line upon their cheeks. The French prettily term them *accroche-cœurs,* whilst in the United States they are plainly and unpleasantly called SPIT-CURLS. Bartlett says:—"SPIT CURL, a detached lock of hair curled upon the temple; probably from having been at first filastered into shape by the saliva. It is now understood that the mucilage of quince seed is used by the ladies for this purpose."

> "You may prate of your lips, and your teeth of pearl,
> And your eyes so brightly flashing;
> My song shall be of that SALIVA CURL
> Which threatens my heart to smash in."
>
> *Boston Transcript,* October 30, 1858.

When men twist the hair on each side of their faces into ropes they are sometimes called BELL-ROPES, as being wherewith to *draw the belles.* Whether BELL-ROPES or BOW-CATCHERS, it is singular they should form part of the prisoner's paraphernalia, and that a jaunty little kiss-me-quick curl should, of all things in the world, ornament a gaol dock; yet such was formerly the case. Hunt, the murderer of Weare, on his trial, we are informed by the *Athenæum,* appeared at the bar with a highly pomatumed love-lock sticking tight to his forehead. Young ladies, think of this!

BOWL-OUT, to put out of the game, to remove out of one's way, to detect.—*Cricketing term.*

BOWLAS, round tarts made of sugar, apple, and bread, sold in the streets.

BOWLES, shoes.

BOX-HARRY, a term with bagmen or commercial travellers, implying dinner and tea at one meal; also dining with Humphrey, *i.e.*, going without.—*Lincolnshire.*

BRACE UP, to pawn stolen goods.

BRACELETS, handcuffs.

BRADS, money. Properly, a small kind of nails used by cobblers.—Compare HORSE NAILS.

BRAD-FAKING, playing at cards.

BRAGGADOCIO, three months' imprisonment as a reputed thief or old offender,—sometimes termed a DOSE, or a DOLLOP. —*Household Words*, vol. i., p. 579.

BRAN-NEW, quite new. Properly, *Brent*, BRAND, or *Fire-new*, *i.e.*, fresh from the anvil.

BRASS, money.

BREAD-BASKET, DUMPLING DEPOT, VICTUALLING OFFICE, &c., are terms given by the "*Fancy*" to the digestive organ.

BREAK-DOWN, a jovial, social gathering, a FLARE UP; in Ireland, a wedding.

BREAKING SHINS, borrowing money.

BREAKY-LEG, a shilling.

BREAKY-LEG, strong drink; "he's been to Bungay fair, and BROKE BOTH HIS LEGS," *i.e.*, got drunk. In the ancient Egyptian language the determinative character in the hieroglyphic verb "to be drunk," has the significant form of the leg of a man being amputated.

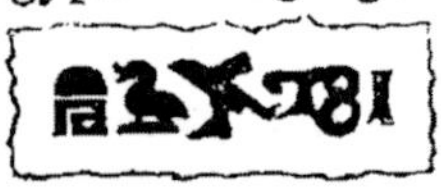

BREECHED, or TO HAVE THE BAGS OFF, to have plenty of money; "to be well BREECHED," to be in good circumstances.

BREECHES, "to wear the BREECHES," said of a wife who usurps the husband's prerogative.

BREEKS, breeches.—*Scotch*, now common.

BRICK, a "jolly good fellow;" "a regular BRICK," a staunch fellow.

> "I bonnetted Whewell, when we gave the Rads their gruel,
> And taught them to eschew all their addresses to the Queen.
> If again they try it on, why to floor them I'll make one,
> Spite of Peeler or of Don, like a BRICK and a *Bean.*"
> *The Jolly Bachelors*, Cambridge, 1840.

Said to be derived from an expression of Aristotle, τετραγωνος ἀνηρ.

BRIEF, a pawnbroker's duplicate.

BRISKET BEATER, a Roman Catholic.

BROADS, cards. BROADSMAN, a card sharper.

BROAD AND SHALLOW, an epithet applied to the so-called "Broad church," in contradistinction to the "High" and "Low" Church.—*See* HIGH AND DRY.

BROAD-FENCER, card seller at races.

BROSIER, a bankrupt.—*Cheshire.* BROSIER-MY-DAME, school term. implying a clearing of the housekeeper's larder of provisions, in revenge for stinginess.—*Eton.*

BROTHER-CHIP, fellow carpenter. Also, BROTHER-WHIP, a fellow coachman; and BROTHER-BLADE, of the same occupation or calling—originally a fellow soldier.

BROWN, a halfpenny.—*See* BLUNT.

BROWN, "to do BROWN," to do well or completely (in allusion to roasting); "doing it BROWN," prolonging the frolic, or exceeding sober bounds; "DONE BROWN," taken in, deceived, or surprised.

BROWN BESS, the old Government regulation musket.

BROWN PAPERMEN, low gamblers.

BROWN SALVE, a token of surprise at what is heard, and at the same time means "I understand you."

BROWN-STUDY, a reverie. Very common even in educated society, but hardly admissible in writing, and therefore must be considered a vulgarism. It is derived, by a writer in *Notes and Queries*, from BROW study, from the old German BRAUN, or AUG-BRAUN, an eye-brow.—*Ben Jonson.*

BROWN-TO, to understand, to comprehend.—*American.*

BRUISER, a fighting man, a pugilist.—*Pugilistic.* *Shakespere* uses the word BRUISING in a similar sense.

BRUMS, counterfeit coins. *Nearly obsolete.* Corruption of *Brummagem* (Bromwicham), the ancient name of *Birmingham*, the great emporium of plated goods and imitation jewellery.

BRUSH, or BRUSH-OFF, to run away, or move on.—*Old cant.*

BUB, drink of any kind.—*See* GRUB. *Middleton*, the dramatist, mentions BUBBER, a great drinker.

BUB, a teat, woman's breast.

BUCK, a gay or smart man, a cuckold.

BUCKHORSE, a smart blow or box on the ear; derived from the name of a celebrated "bruiser" of that name.

BUCKLE, to bend; "I can't BUCKLE to that," I don't understand it; to yield or give in to a person. *Shakespere* uses the word in the latter sense, Henry IV., i. 1; and *Halliwell* says that "the commentators do not supply another example." How strange that in our own streets the term should be used every day! Stop the first costermonger, and he will soon inform you the various meanings of BUCKLE.—*See Notes and Queries*, vols. vii., viii., and ix.

BUCKLE-TO, to bend to one's work, to begin at once, and with great energy.

BUDGE, to move, to inform, to SPLIT, or tell tales.

BUFF, to swear to, or accuse; to SPLIT, or peach upon. *Old* word for boasting, 1582.

BUFF, the bare skin; "stripped to the BUFF."

BUFFER, a dog. Their skins were formerly in great request—hence the term, BUFF meaning in old English *to skin*. It is still used in the ring, BUFFED meaning stripped to the skin. In Irish cant, BUFFER is a *boxer*. The BUFFER of a railway carriage doubtless received its very appropriate name from the old pugilistic application of this term.

BUFFER, a familiar expression for a jolly acquaintance, probably from the *French*, BOUFFARD, a fool or clown; a "jolly old BUFFER," said of a good humoured or liberal old man. In 1737, a BUFFER was a "rogue that killed good sound horses for the sake of their skins, by running a long wire into them."—*Bacchus and Venus*. The term was once applied to those who took false oaths for a consideration.

BUFFLE HEAD, a stupid or obtuse person.—*Miege*. *German*, BUFFEL-HAUPT, buffalo-headed.

BUFFY, intoxicated.—*Household Words*, No. 183.

BUGGY, a gig, or light chaise. Common term in America and in Ireland.

BUG-HUNTERS, low wretches who plunder drunken men.

BUILD, applied in fashionable slang to the make or style of dress, &c.; "it's a tidy BUILD, who made it?"

BULGER, large; synonymous with BUSTER.

BULL, term amongst prisoners for the meat served to them in jail.

BULL, one who agrees to purchase stock at a future day, at a stated price, but who does not possess money to pay for it, trusting to a rise in public securities to render the transaction a profitable one. Should stocks fall, the bull is then called upon to pay the difference.—*See* BEAR, who is the opposite of a BULL, the former selling, the latter purchasing—the one operating for a *fall* or a *pull down*, whilst the other operates for a *rise* or *toss up*.

BULL, a crown piece; formerly, BULL'S EYE.

BULL-THE-CASK, to pour hot water into an empty rum puncheon, and let it stand until it extracts the spirit from the wood. The result is drunk by sailors in default of something stronger.—*Sea.*

BULLY, a braggart; but in the language of the streets, a man of the most degraded morals, who protects prostitutes, and lives off their miserable earnings.—*Shakespere*, Midsummer Night's Dream, iii. 1; iv. 2.

BUM, the part on which we sit.—*Shakespere*. BUMBAGS, trowsers.

BUM-BAILIFF, a sheriff's officer,—a term, some say, derived from the proximity which this gentleman generally maintains to his victims. *Blackstone* says it is a corruption of "bound bailiff."

BUM-BOATS, shore boats which supply ships with provisions, and serve as means of communication between the sailors and the shore.

BUM-BRUSHER, a schoolmaster.

BUMMAREE. This term is given to a class of speculating salesmen at Billingsgate market, not recognised as such by the trade, but who get a living by buying large quantities of fish of the salesmen and re-selling it to smaller buyers. The word has been used in the statutes and bye-laws of the markets for upwards of 100 years. It has been variously derived, but is most probably from the *French*, BONNE MAREE, good fresh fish! "Marée signifie toute sorte de poisson de mer qûi n'est pas salé; bonne marée—*marée fraiche*, vendeur de marée."—*Dict. de l'Acad. Franc.* The BUMMAREES are accused of many trade tricks. One of them is to blow up cod-fish with a pipe until they look double their actual size. Of course when the fish come to table they are flabby, sunken, and half dwindled away. In Norwich, TO BUMMAREE ONE is to run up a score at a public house just open, and is equivalent to "running into debt with one."

BUNCH OF FIVES, the hand, or fist.

BUNDLE, "to BUNDLE a person off," *i.e.*, to pack him off, send him flying.

BUNG, the landlord of a public-house.

BUNG, to give, pass, hand over, drink, or indeed to perform any action; BUNG UP, to close up—*Pugilistic;* "BUNG over the rag," hand over the money—*Old*, used by *Beaumont and Fletcher*, and *Shakespere*. Also, to deceive one by a lie, to CRAM, which see.

BUNKER, beer.

BUNTS, costermonger's perquisites; the money obtained by giving light weight, &c.; costermongers' goods sold by boys on commission. Probably a corruption of *bonus*, BONE being the slang for good. BUNCE, *Grose* gives as the cant word for money.

BURDON'S HOTEL, Whitecross-street prison, of which the Governor is or was a Mr. Burdon.

BURERK, a lady. *Grose* gives BURICK, a prostitute.

BURKE, to kill, to murder, by pitch plaster or other foul means. From Burke, the notorious Whitechapel murderer, who with others used to waylay people, kill them, and sell their bodies for dissection at the hospitals.

BURYING A MOLL, running away from a mistress.

BUSKER, a man who sings or performs in a public house.—*Scotch.*

BUSK (or BUSKING), to sell obscene songs and books at the bars and in the tap-rooms of public houses. Sometimes implies selling any articles.

BUSS, an abbreviation of "omnibus," a public carriage. Also, a kiss.

BUST, or BURST, to tell tales, to SPLIT, to inform. BUSTING, informing against accomplices when in custody.

BUSTER (BURSTER), a small new loaf; "twopenny BUSTER," a twopenny loaf. "A pennorth o' BEES WAX (cheese) and a penny BUSTER," a common snack at beershops.

BUSTER, an extra size; "what a BUSTER," what a large one; "in for a BUSTER," determined on an extensive frolic or spree. *Scotch*, BUSTUOUS; *Icelandic*, BOSTRA.

BUSTLE, money; "to draw the BUSTLE."

BUTTER, or BATTER, praise or flattery. To BUTTER, to flatter, cajole.

BUTTER-FINGERED, apt to let things fall.

BUTTON, a decoy, sham purchaser, &c. At any mock or sham auction seedy specimens may be seen. Probably from the connection of *buttons* with *Brummagem*, which is often used as a synonyme for a sham.

BUTTONER, a man who entices another to play.—*See* BONNETTER.

BUTTONS, a page,—from the rows of gilt buttons which adorn his jacket.

BUTTONS, "not to have all one's BUTTONS," to be deficient in intellect.

BUZ, to pick pockets; BUZ-FAKING, robbing.

BUZ, to share equally the last of a bottle of wine, when there is not enough for a full glass for each of the party.

BUZZERS, pickpockets. *Grose* gives BUZ COVE and BUZ GLOAK, the latter is very ancient cant.

BUZ-BLOAK, a pickpocket, who principally confines his attention to purses and loose cash. *Grose* gives BUZ-GLOAK (or CLOAK ?), an ancient cant word. BUZ-NAPPER, a young pickpocket.

BUZ-NAPPER'S ACADEMY, a school in which young thieves are trained. Figures are dressed up, and experienced tutors stand in various difficult attitudes for the boys to practice upon. When clever enough they are sent on the streets. It is reported that a house of this nature is situated in a court near Hatton Garden. The system is well explained in *Dickens' Oliver Twist*.

BYE-BLOW, a bastard child.

BY GEORGE, an exclamation similar to BY JOVE. The term is older than is frequently imagined, vide *Bacchus and Venus* (p. 117), 1737. "Fore (or by) GEORGE, I'd knock him down." A street compliment to Saint George, the patron Saint of England, or possibly to the House of Hanover.

BY GOLLY, an ejaculation, or oath; a compromise for "by God." In the United States, small boys are permitted by their guardians to say GOL DARN anything, but they are on no account allowed to commit the profanity of G—d d——g anything. An effective ejaculation and moral waste-pipe for interior passion or wrath is seen in the exclamation—BY THE-EVER-LIVING-JUMPING-MOSES — a harmless phrase, that from its length expends a considerable quantity of fiery anger.

CAB, in statutory language, "a hackney carriage drawn by one horse." Abbreviated from CABRIOLET, *French;* originally meaning "a light low chaise." The wags of Paris playing upon the word (quasi *cabri* au lait) used to call a superior turn-out of the kind a *cabri au crême.* Our abbreviation, which certainly smacks of slang, has been stamped with the authority of "GEORGE, *Ranger.*" See the notices affixed to the carriage entrances of St. James's Park.

CAB, to stick together, to muck, or tumble up.—*Devonshire.*

CABBAGE, pieces of cloth said to be purloined by tailors.

CABBAGE, to pilfer or purloin. Termed by Johnson a cant word, but adopted by later lexicographers as a respectable term. Said to have been first used in this sense by *Arbuthnot.*

CABBY, the driver of a cab.

CAD, or CADGER (from which it is shortened), a mean or vulgar fellow; a beggar; one who would rather live on other people than work for himself; a man trying to worm something out of another, either money or information. *Johnson* uses the word, and gives *huckster* as the meaning, but I never heard it used in this sense. CAGER, or GAGER, the *old cant* term for a man. The exclusives in the Universities apply the term CAD to all non-members.

CAD, an omnibus conductor.

CADGE, to beg in an artful or wheedling manner.—*North.*

CADGING, begging of the lowest degree.

CAG-MAG, bad food, scraps, odds and ends; or that which no one could relish. *Grose* gives CAGG MAGGS, old and tough Lincolnshire geese, sent to London to feast the poor cockneys.

CAGE, a minor kind of prison.—*Shakespere,* part ii. of Henry IV., iv. 2.

CAKE, a flat, a soft or doughy person, a fool.

CAKEY-PANNUM-FENCER, a man who sells street pastry.

CALL-A-GO, in street "patter," is to remove to another spot, or address the public in different vein.

CAMESA, shirt or chemise.—*Span. Ancient cant,* COMMISSION.

CAMISTER, a preacher, clergyman, or master.

CANARY, a sovereign. This is stated by a correspondent to be a Norwich term, that city being famous for its breed of those birds.

CANISTER, the head.—*Pugilistic.*

CANISTER-CAP, a hat.—*Pugilistic.*

CANNIKEN, a small can, similar to PANNIKIN.—*Shakespere.*

CANT, a blow or toss; "a cant over the kisser," a blow on the mouth.—*Kentish.*

CANT OF TOGS, a gift of clothes.

CARDINAL, a lady's cloak. This, I am assured, is the *Seven Dials* cant term for a lady's garment, but curiously enough the same name is given to the most fashionable patterns of the article by Regent-street drapers. A cloak with this name was in fashion in the year 1760. It received its title from its similarity in shape to one of the vestments of a cardinal.

CARNEY, soft talk, nonsense, gammon.—*Hibernicism.*

CAROON, five shillings. *French,* COURONNE; Gipsey, COURNA, —PANSH COURNA, half-a-crown.

CARPET, "upon the CARPET," any subject or matter that is uppermost for discussion or conversation. Frequently quoted as *sur le tapis,* but it does not seem to be a correct Parisian phrase.

CARRIER PIGEONS, swindlers, who formerly used to cheat Lottery Office Keepers. *Nearly obsolete.*

CARROTS, the coarse and satirical term for red hair.

CARRY-ON, to joke a person to excess, to carry on a "spree" too far; "how we CARRIED ON, to be sure!" *i.e.,* what fun we had.

CART, a race-course.

CARTS, a pair of shoes. In Norfolk the carapace of a crab is called a *crab cart,* hence CARTS would be synonymous with CRAB SHELLS, which see.

CART WHEEL, a five shilling piece.

CASA, or CASE, a house, respectable or otherwise. Probably from the *Italian,* CASA.—*Old cant.* The *Dutch* use the word KAST in a vulgar sense for a house, *i.e.,* MOTTEKAST, a brothel. CASE sometimes means a water-closet.

CASCADING, vomiting.

CASE, a bad crown piece. HALF-A-CASE, a counterfeit half crown. There are two sources, either of which may have contributed this slang term. CASER is the Hebrew word for a crown; and silver coin is frequently counterfeited by coating or CASING pewter or iron imitations with silver.

CASE. A few years ago the term CASE was applied to persons and things; "what a CASE he is," *i.e.*, what a curious person; "a rum CASE that," or "you are a CASE," both synonymous with the phrase "odd fish," common half-a-century ago. Among young ladies at boarding schools a CASE means a love affair.

CASK, fashionable slang for a brougham, or other private carriage.—*Household Words*, No. 183.

CASSAM, cheese—not CAFFAN, which Egan, in his edition of *Grose*, has ridiculously inserted.—*Ancient cant. Latin*, CASEUS.

CASTING UP ONE'S ACCOUNTS, vomiting.—*Old.*

CASTOR, a hat. CASTOR was once the ancient word for a BEAVER; and strange to add, BEAVER was the slang for CASTOR, or hat, thirty years ago, before gossamer came into fashion.

CAT, to vomit like a cat.—*See* SHOOT THE CAT.

CAT, a lady's muff; "to free a CAT," *i.e.*, steal a muff.

CATARACT, a black satin scarf arranged for the display of jewellery, much in vogue among "commercial gents."

CATCH 'EM ALIVE, a trap, also a small-tooth comb.

CATCHY (similar formation to *touchy*), inclined to take an undue advantage.

CATEVER, a queer, or singular affair; anything poor, or very bad. From the *Lingua Franca*, and *Italian*, CATTIVO, bad. Variously spelled by the lower orders.—*See* KERTEVER.

CATGUT-SCRAPER, a fiddler.

CAT-LAP, a contemptuous expression for weak drink.

CAT'S WATER, old Tom, or Gin.

CAT AND KITTEN SNEAKING, stealing pint and quart pots from public-houses.

CATCH-PENNY, any temporary contrivance to obtain money from the public, penny shows, or cheap exhibitions.

CAT-IN-THE-PAN, a traitor, a turn-coat—derived by some from the *Greek*, καταπαν, altogether; or from *cake in pan*, a pan cake, which is frequently turned from side to side.

CAUCUS, a private meeting held for the purpose of concerting measures, agreeing upon candidates for office before an election, &c.—*See Pickering's Vocabulary.*

CAVAULTING, coition. *Lingua Franca*, CAVOLTA.

CAVE, or CAVE IN, to submit, shut up.—*American.* Metaphor taken from the sinking of an abandoned mining shaft.

CHAFF, to gammon, joke, quiz, or praise ironically. CHAFF-bone, the jaw-bone.—*Yorkshire.* CHAFF, jesting. In *Anglo Saxon,* CEAF is chaff; and CEAFL, bill, beak, or jaw. In the "Ancien Riwle," A.D. 1221, *ceafle* is used in the sense of idle discourse.

CHALK-OUT, or CHALK DOWN, to mark out a line of conduct or action; to make a rule, order. Phrase derived from the *Workshop.*

CHALK UP, to credit, make entry in account books of indebtedness; "I can't pay you now, but you can CHALK IT UP," *i.e.,* charge me with the article in your day-book. From the old practice of chalking one's score for drink behind the bar-doors of public houses.

CHALKS, "to walk one's CHALKS," to move off, or run away. An ordeal for drunkenness used on board ship, to see whether the suspected person can walk on a chalked line without overstepping it on either side.

CHAP, a fellow, a boy; "a low CHAP," a low fellow—abbreviation of CHAP-MAN, a huckster. Used by Byron in his *Critical Remarks.*

CHARIOT-BUZZING, picking pockets in an omnibus.

CHARLEY, a watchman, a beadle.

CHARLEY-PITCHERS, low, cheating gamblers.

CHATTER BASKET, common term for a prattling child amongst nurses.

CHATTER-BOX, an incessant talker or chatterer.

CHATTRY-FEEDER, a spoon.

CHATTS, dice,—formerly the gallows; a bunch of seals.

CHATTS, lice, or body vermin.

CHATTY, a filthy person, one whose clothes are not free from vermin; CHATTY DOSS, a lousy bed.

CHAUNTER-CULLS, a singular body of men who used to haunt certain well known public-houses, and write satirical or libellous ballads on any person, or body of persons, for a consideration. 7s. 6d. was the usual fee, and in three hours the ballad might be heard in St. Paul's Churchyard, or other public spot. There are two men in London at the present day who gain their living in this way.

CHAUNTERS, those street sellers of ballads, last copies of verses, and other broadsheets, who sing or bawl the contents of their papers. They often term themselves PAPER WORKERS. *A. N.*—*See* HORSE CHAUNTERS.

CHAUNT, to sing the contents of any paper in the streets. CANT, as applied to vulgar language, was derived from CHAUNT.—*See Introduction.*

CHEAP, "doing it on the CHEAP," living economically, or keeping up a showy appearance with very little means.

CHEAP JACKS, or JOHNS, oratorical hucksters and patterers of hardware, &c., at fairs and races. They put an article up at a high price, and then cheapen it by degrees, indulging in volleys of coarse wit, until it becomes to all appearance a bargain, and as such it is bought by one of the crowd. The popular idea is that the inverse method of auctioneering saves them paying for the auction license.

CHEEK, share or portion; "where's my CHEEK?" where is my allowance?

CHEEK, impudence, assurance; CHEEKY, saucy or forward. *Lincolnshire,* CHEEK, to accuse.

CHEEK, to irritate by impudence.

CHEEK BY JOWL, side by side,—said often of persons in such close confabulation as almost to have their faces touch.

CHEESE, anything good, first-rate in quality, genuine, pleasant, or advantageous, is termed THE CHEESE. *Mayhew* thinks CHEESE, in this sense, is from the *Saxon,* CEOSAN, to choose, and quotes *Chaucer,* who uses CHESE in the sense of choice. The *London Guide,* 1818, says it was from some young fellows translating "c'est une autre CHOSE" into "that is another CHEESE." CHEESE is also *Gipsey* and *Hindoo* (*see Introduction*); and *Persian,* CHIZ, a thing.—*See* STILTON.

CHEESE, or CHEESE IT (evidently a corruption of *cease*), leave off, or have done; "CHEESE your barrikin," hold your noise.

CHEESY, fine or showy.

CHERUBS, or CHERUBIMS, the chorister boys who chaunt in the services at the abbeys.

CHESHIRE CAT, "to grin like a CHESHIRE CAT," to display the teeth and gums when laughing. Formerly the phrase was "to grin like a CHESHIRE CAT *eating* CHEESE." A *hardly satisfactory* explanation has been given of this phrase—that Cheshire is a county palatine, and the cats, when they think of it, are so tickled with the notion that they can't help grinning.

CHICKEN, a young girl.

CHICKEN-HEARTED, cowardly, fearful.

CHI-IKE, a hurrah, a good word, or hearty praise.

CHINK, money.—*Ancient.*—See FLORIO.

CHINKERS, money.

CHIP OF THE OLD BLOCK, a child who resembles its father. BROTHER CHIP, one of the same trade or profession.

CHIPS, money.

CHISEL, to cheat.

CHITTERLINGS, the shirt frills worn still by ancient beaux; properly, the *entrails of a pig*, to which they are supposed to bear some resemblance. *Belgian,* SCHYTERLINGH.

CHIVARLY, coition. Probably a corruption from the *Lingua Franca.*

CHIVE, a knife; a sharp tool of any kind.—*Old cant.* This term is particularly applied to the tin knives used in gaols.

CHIVE, to cut, saw, or file.

CHIVE, or CHIVEY, a shout; a halloo, or cheer, loud tongued. From CHEVY-CHASE, a boy's game, in which the word CHEVY is bawled aloud; or from the *Gipsey?—See Introduction.*

CHIVE-FENCER, a street hawker of cutlery.

CHIVEY, to chase round, or hunt about.

CHOCK-FULL, full till the scale comes down with a shock. *French,* CHOC. A correspondent suggests CHOKED-FULL.

CHOKE OFF, to get rid of. Bull dogs can only be made to loose their hold by choking them.

CHOKER, a cravat, a neckerchief. WHITE-CHOKER, the white neckerchief worn by mutes at a funeral, and waiters at a tavern. Clergymen are frequently termed WHITE-CHOKERS.

CHOKER, or WIND-STOPPER, a garrotter.

CHONKEYS, a kind of mince meat baked in a crust, and sold in the streets.

CHOP, to change.—*Old.*

CHOPS, properly CHAPS, the mouth, or cheeks; "down in the CHOPS," or "down in the mouth," *i.e.*, sad or melancholy.

CHOUSE, to cheat out of one's share or portion. Hackluyt, CHAUS; Massinger, CHIAUS. From the Turkish, in which language it signifies an interpreter. Gifford gives a curious story as to its origin :—

> In the year 1609 there was attached to the Turkish embassy in England an interpreter, or CHIAOUS, who by cunning, aided by his official position, managed to cheat the Turkish and Persian merchants then in London out of the large sum of £4,000, then deemed an enormous amount. From the notoriety which attended the fraud, and the magnitude of the swindle, any one who cheated or defrauded was said to *chiaous*, or *chause*, or CHOUSE; to do, that is, as this *Chiaous* had done.—*See Trench, Eng. Past and Present, p.* 87.

CHOUT, an entertainment.

CHOVEY, a shop.

CHRISTENING, erasing the name of the maker from a stolen watch, and inserting a fictitious one in its place.

CHUBBY, round-faced, plump.

CHUCK, a schoolboy's treat.—*Westminster school.* Food, provision for an entertainment.—*Norwich.*

CHUCK, to throw or pitch.

CHUCKING A JOLLY, when a costermonger praises the inferior article his mate or partner is trying to sell.

CHUCKING A STALL, where one rogue walks in front of a person while another picks his pockets.

CHUCKLE-HEAD, a fool.—*Devonshire.*

CHUFF IT, *i.e.*, be off, or take it away, in answer to a street seller who is importuning you to purchase. *Halliwell* mentions CHUFF as a "term of reproach," surly, &c.

CHUM, an acquaintance. A recognised term, but in such frequent use with the lower orders that it demanded a place in this glossary.

CHUM, to occupy a joint lodging with another person.

CHUMMING-UP, an old custom amongst prisoners when a fresh culprit is admitted to their number, consisting of a noisy welcome—rough music made with pokers, tongs, sticks, and saucepans. For this ovation the initiated prisoner has to pay, or FORK OVER, half a crown—or submit to a loss of coat and waistcoat. The practice is ancient.

CHUMMY, a chimney sweep; also a low-crowned felt hat.

CHUNK, a thick or dumpy piece of any substance.—*Kentish.*

CHURCH A YACK (or watch), to take the works of a watch from its original case and put them into another one, to avoid detection.—*See* CHRISTEN.

CHURCHWARDEN, a long pipe, "A YARD OF CLAY."

CLAGGUM, boiled treacle in a hardened state, *Hardbake.*—*See* CLIGGY.

CLAP, to place; "do you think you can CLAP your hand on him?" *i.e.*, find him out.

CLAPPER, the tongue.

CLAP-TRAP, high-sounding nonsense. An ancient *Theatrical* term for a "TRAP to catch a CLAP by way of applause from the spectators at a play."—*Bailey's Dictionary.*

CLARET, blood.—*Pugilistic.*

CLEAN, quite, or entirely; "CLEAN gone," entirely out of sight, or away.—*Old, see Cotgrave.*—*Shakespere.*

CLEAN OUT, to thrash, or beat; to ruin, or bankrupt any one; to take all they have got, by purchase, or force. *De Quincey*, in his article on "Richard Bentley," speaking of the law-suit between that great scholar and Dr. Colbatch, remarks that the latter "must have been pretty well CLEANED OUT."

CLICK, knock, or blow. CLICK-HANDED, left-handed.—*Cornish.*

CLICK, to snatch.

CLIFT, to steal.

CLIGGY, or CLIDGY, sticky.—*Anglo Saxon*, CLÆG, clay.—*See* CLAGGUM.

CLINCHER, that which rivets or confirms an argument, an incontrovertible position. Metaphor from the workshop.

CLINK-RIG, stealing tankards from public-houses, taverns, &c.

CLIPPING, excellent, very good.

CLOCK, "to know what's O'CLOCK," a definition of knowingness in general.—*See* TIME O'DAY.

CLOD-HOPPER, a country clown.

CLOUT, or RAG, a cotton pocket handkerchief.—*Old cant.*

CLOUT, a blow, or intentional strike.—*Ancient.*

CLOVER, happiness, or luck.

CLUMP, to strike.

CLY, a pocket.—*Old cant* for to steal. A correspondent derives this word from the *Old English*, CLEYES, claws; *Anglo Saxon*, CLEA. This pronunciation is still retained in Norfolk; thus, to CLY would mean to pounce upon, snatch.—*See* FRISK.

CLY-FAKER, a pickpocket.

COACH, a Cambridge term for a private tutor.

COACH WHEEL, or TUSHEROON, a crown piece, or five shillings.

COALS, "to call (or pull) over the COALS," to take to task, to scold.

COCK, or more frequently now a days, COCK-E-E, a vulgar street salutation—corruption of COCK-EYE. The latter is frequently heard as a shout or street cry after a man or boy.

COCK AND A BULL STORY, a long, rambling anecdote.—*See Notes and Queries*, vol. iv., p. 313.

COCKCHAFER, the treadmill.

COCK-EYE, one that squints.

COCKLES, "to rejoice the COCKLES of one's heart," a vulgar phrase implying great pleasure.—*See* PLUCK.

COCKNEY, a native of London. Originally, a spoilt or effeminate boy, derived from COCKERING, or foolishly petting a person, rendering them of soft or luxurious manners. Halliwell states, in his admirable essay upon the word, that "some writers trace the word with much probability to the imaginary land of COCKAYGNE, the lubber land of the olden times." *Grose* gives Minsheu's absurd but comical derivation:—A citizen of London being in the country, and hearing a horse neigh, exclaimed, "*Lord! how that horse laughs.*" A bystander informed him that that noise was called neighing. The next morning, when the cock crowed, the citizen, to show that he had not forgotten what was told him, cried out, "*do you hear how the* COCK NEIGHS?"

COCK OF THE WALK, a master spirit, head of a party. Places where poultry are fed are called WALKS, and the barn-door cocks invariably fight for the supremacy till one has obtained it.

COCKS, fictitious narratives, in verse or prose, of murders, fires, and terrible accidents, sold in the streets as true accounts. The man who hawks them, a patterer, often changes the scene of the awful event to suit the taste of the neighbourhood he is trying to delude. Possibly a corruption of *cook*, a cooked statement, or, as a correspondent suggests, the COCK LANE Ghost may have given rise to the term. This had a great run, and was a rich harvest to the running stationers.

COCK ONE'S TOES, to die.

COCK ROBIN SHOP, a small printer's office, where low wages are paid to journeymen who have never served a regular apprenticeship.

COCKSHY, a game at fairs and races, where trinkets are set upon sticks, and for one penny three throws at them are accorded, the thrower keeping whatever he knocks off. From the ancient game of throwing or "shying" at live cocks.

COCKSURE, certain.

COCKY, pert, saucy.

COCKYOLY BIRDS, little birds, frequently called "dickey birds."—*Kingsley's Two Years Ago.*

COCK, "to COCK your eye," to shut or wink one eye.

COCUM, advantage, luck, cunning, or sly, "to fight COCUM," to be wily and cautious.

CODDS, the "poor brethren" of the Charter house. At p. 133 of the *Newcomes*, Mr. Thackeray writes, "The Cistercian lads call these old gentlemen CODDS, I know not wherefore." An abbreviation of CODGER.

CODGER, an old man; "a rum old CODGER," a curious old fellow. CODGER is sometimes used synonymous with CADGER, and then signifies a person who gets his living in a questionable manner. CAGER, or GAGER, was the old cant term for a man.

COFFEE-SHOP, a water-closet, or house of office.

COG, to cheat at dice.—*Shakespere.* Also, to agree with, as one cog-wheel does with another.

COLD BLOOD, a house licensed for the sale of beer "NOT to be drunk on the premises."

COLD COOK, an undertaker.

COLD MEAT, a corpse.

COLD SHOULDER, "to show or give any one the COLD SHOULDER," to assume a distant manner towards them, to evince a desire to cease acquaintanceship. Sometimes it is termed "cold shoulder of *mutton.*"

COLLAR, "out of COLLAR," *i.e.*, out of place, no work.

COLLAR, to seize, to lay hold of.

COLLY-WOBBLES, a stomach ache, a person's bowels,—supposed by many of the lower orders to be the seat of feeling and nutrition; an idea either borrowed from, or transmitted by, the ancients.—*Devonshire.*

COLT'S TOOTH, elderly persons of juvenile tastes are said to have a colt's tooth.

COMB-CUT, mortified, disgraced, "down on one's luck."—*See* CUT.

COME, a slang verb used in many phrases; "A'nt he COMING IT?" *i.e.*, is he not proceeding at a great rate? "Don't COME TRICKS here," "don't COME THE OLD SOLDIER over me," *i.e.*, we are aware of your practices, and "twig" your manœuvre. COMING IT STRONG, exaggerating, going a-head, the opposite of "*drawing it mild*." COMING IT also means informing or disclosing.

COME DOWN, to pay down.

COMMISSION, a shirt.—*Ancient cant. Italian*, CAMICIA.

COMMISTER, a chaplain or clergyman.

COMMON SEWER, a DRAIN, or drink.

COMMONS, rations, because eaten *in common*.—*University*. SHORT COMMONS (derived from the University slang term), a scanty meal, a scarcity.

CONK, a nose; CONKY, having a projecting or remarkable nose. The Duke of Wellington was frequently termed "Old CONKY" in satirical papers and caricatures.

CONSTABLE, "to overrun the CONSTABLE," to exceed one's income, get deep in debt.

CONVEY, to steal; "CONVEY, the wise it call."

CONVEYANCER, a pick-pocket. *Shakespere* uses the cant expression, CONVEYER, a thief. The same term is also *French slang*.

COOK, a term well known in the Bankruptcy Courts, referring to accounts that have been meddled with, or COOKED, by the bankrupt; also the forming a balance sheet from general trade inferences; stated by a correspondent to have been first used in reference to the celebrated alteration of the accounts of the Eastern Counties Railway, by George Hudson, the Railway King.

COOK ONE'S GOOSE, to kill or ruin any person.—*North*.

COOLIE, a soldier, in allusion to the *Hindoo* COOLIES, or day labourers.

COON, abbreviation of Racoon.—*American*. A GONE COON—*ditto*, one in an awful fix, past praying for. This expression is said to have originated in the American war with a spy, who dressed himself in a racoon skin, and ensconced himself in a tree. An English rifleman taking him for a veritable coon levelled his piece at him, upon which he exclaimed, "Don't shoot, I'll come down of myself, I know I'm a GONE COON." The Yankees say the Britisher was so flummuxed, that he flung down his rifle and "made tracks" for home. The phrase is pretty usual in England.

COOPER, stout half-and-half, *i.e.*, half stout and half porter.

COOPER, to destroy, spoil, settle, or finish. COOPER'D, spoilt, "done up," synonymous with the Americanism, CAVED IN, fallen in and ruined. The vagabonds' hieroglyphic ▽, chalked by them on gate posts and houses, signifies that the place has been spoilt by too many tramps calling there.

COOPER, to forge, or imitate in writing; "COOPER a moneker," to forge a signature.

COP, to seize or lay hold of anything unpleasant; used in a similar sense to *catch* in the phrase "to COP (or catch) a beating," "to get COPT."

COPER, properly HORSE-COUPER, a Scotch horse-dealer,—used to denote a dishonest one.

COPPER, a policeman, *i.e.*, one who COPS, which see.

COPPER, a penny. COPPERS, mixed pence.

COPUS, a Cambridge drink, consisting of ale combined with spices, and varied by spirits, wines, &c. Corruption of HIPPOCRAS.

CORINTHIANISM, a term derived from the classics, much in vogue some years ago, implying pugilism, high life, "sprees," roistering, &c.—*Shakespere*. The immorality of *Corinth* was proverbial in Greece. *Κοριυθίαζ εσθαι*, to *Corinthianise*, indulge in the company of courtesans, was a *Greek* slang expression. Hence the proverb—

Οὐ παντὸς ἀνδρὸς εἰς Κόρινθον ἔσθ' ὁ πλοῦς,

and *Horace*, Epist. lib. 1, xvii. 36—

Non cuivis homini contingit adire Corinthum,

in allusion to the spoliation practised by the "betæræ" on those who visited them.

CORK, "to draw a CORK," to give a bloody nose.—*Pugilistic.*

CORKS, money; "how are you off for corks?" a soldier's term of a very expressive kind, denoting the means of "keeping afloat."

CORNED, drunk or intoxicated. Possibly from soaking or pickling oneself like CORNED beef.

CORNERED, hemmed in a corner, placed in a position from which there is no escape. —*American.*

CORPORATION, the protuberant front of an obese person.

CORPSE, to confuse or put out the actors by making a mistake. —*Theatrical.*

COSSACK, a policeman.

COSTERMONGERS, street sellers of fish, fruit, vegetables, poultry, &c. The London costermongers number more than 30,000. They form a distinct class, occupying whole neighbourhoods, and are cut off from the rest of metropolitan society by their low habits, general improvidence, pugnacity, love of gambling, total want of education, disregard for lawful marriage ceremonies, *and their use of a cant* (or so-called *back slang*) *language.*

COSTER, the short and slang term for a costermonger, or costard-monger, who was originally an apple seller. COSTERING, *i.e.*, costermongering.

COTTON, to like, adhere to, or agree with any person; "to COTTON on to a man," to attach yourself to him, or fancy him, literally, to stick to him as cotton would. *Vide Bartlett*, who claims it as an Americanism; and *Halliwell*, who terms it an Archaism; also *Bacchus and Venus*, 1737.

COUNCIL OF TEN, the toes of a man who turns his feet inward.

COUNTER JUMPER, a shopman, a draper's assistant.

COUNTY-CROP (*i.e.*, COUNTY-PRISON CROP), hair cut close and round, as if guided by a basin—an indication of having been in prison.

COUTER, a sovereign. HALF-A-COUTER, half-a-sovereign.

COVE, or COVEY, a boy or man of any age or station. A term generally preceded by an expressive adjective, thus a "flash COVE," a "rum COVE," a "downy COVE," &c. The feminine, COVESS, was once popular, but it has fallen into disuse. *Ancient cant*, originally (temp. Henry VIII.) COFE, or CUFFIN, altered in *Decker's* time to COVE. Probably connected with CUIF, which, in the North of England, signifies a lout or awkward fellow. Amongst *Negroes*, CUFFEE.

COVENTRY, "to send a man to COVENTRY," not to speak to or notice him. Coventry was one of those towns in which the privilege of practising most trades was anciently confined to certain privileged persons, as the freemen, &c. Hence a stranger stood little chance of custom, or countenance, and "to send a man to COVENTRY," came to be equivalent to putting him out of the pale of society.

COVER-DOWN, a tossing coin with a false cover, enabling either head or tail to be shown, according as the cover is left on or taken off.

COWAN, a sneak, an inquisitive or prying person.—*Masonic term. Greek*, κύων, a dog.

COW'S GREASE, butter.

COW-LICK, the term given to the lock of hair which costermongers and thieves usually twist forward from the ear; a large greasy curl upon the cheek, seemingly licked into shape. The opposite of NEWGATE-KNOCKER, which see.

COXY-LOXY, good-tempered, drunk.—*Norfolk.*

CRAB, or GRAB, a disagreeable old person. *Name of a wild and sour fruit.* "To catch a CRAB," to fall backwards by missing a stroke in rowing.

CRAB, to offend, or insult; to expose or defeat a robbery, to inform against.

CRABSHELLS, or TROTTING CASES, shoes.—*See* CARTS.

CRACK, first rate, excellent; "a CRACK HAND," an adept; a "CRACK article," a good one.—*Old.*

CRACK, dry firewood.—*Modern Gipsey.*

CRACK, "in a CRACK (of the finger and thumb)," in a moment.

CRACK A BOTTLE, to drink. *Shakespere* uses CRUSH in the same slang sense.

CRACK A KIRK, to break into a church or chapel.

CRACK-FENCER, a man who sells nuts.

CRACK-UP, to boast or praise.—*Ancient English.*

CRACKED-UP, penniless, or ruined.

CRACKSMAN, a burglar.

CRAM, to lie or deceive, implying to fill up or CRAM a person with false stories; to acquire learning quickly, to "*grind*," or prepare for an examination.

CRAMMER, a lie; or a person who commits a falsehood.

CRANKY, foolish, idiotic, ricketty, capricious, not confined to persons. *Ancient cant,* CRANKE, simulated sickness. *German,* KRANK, sickly.

CRAP, to ease oneself, to evacuate. *Old word* for refuse; also *old cant,* CROP.

CRAPPING CASE, or KEN, a privy, or water-closet.

CRAPPED, hanged.

CREAM OF THE VALLEY, gin.

CRIB, house, public or otherwise; lodgings, apartments.

CRIB, a situation.

CRIB, to steal or purloin.

CRIB, a literal translation of a classic author.—*University.*

CRIB BITER, an inveterate grumbler; properly said of a horse which has this habit, a sign of its bad digestion.

CRIBBAGE FACED, marked with the small pox, full of holes like a cribbage board.

CRIKEY, profane exclamation of astonishment; "Oh, CRIKEY, you don't say so!" corruption of "*Oh, Christ.*"

CRIMPS, men who trepan others into the clutches of the recruiting sergeant. They generally pretend to give employment in the colonies, and in that manner cheat those mechanics who are half famished. *Nearly obsolete.*

CRIPPLE, a bent sixpence.

CROAK, to die—from the gurgling sound a person makes when the breath of life is departing.—*Oxon.*

CROAKER, one who takes a desponding view of everything; an alarmist. *From the croaking of a raven.—Ben Jonson.*

CROAKER, a beggar.

CROAKER, a corpse, or dying person beyond hope.

CROAKS, last dying speeches, and murderers' confessions.

CROCODILES' TEARS, the tears of a hypocrite. An ancient phrase, introduced into this country by Mandeville, or other early English traveller.—*Othello*, iv., 1.

CROCUS, or CROAKUS, a quack or travelling doctor; CROCUS-CHOVEY, a chemist's shop.

CRONY, a termagant or malicious old woman; an intimate friend. *Johnson* calls it cant.

CROOKY, to hang on to, to lead, walk arm-in-arm; to court or pay addresses to a girl.

CROPPIE, a person who has had his hair cut, or CROPPED, in prison.

CROPPED, hanged.

CROSS, a general term amongst thieves expressive of their plundering profession, the opposite of SQUARE. "To get anything on the CROSS" is to obtain it surreptitiously. "CROSS-FANNING in a crowd," robbing persons of their scarf pins.

CROSS COVE and MOLLISHER, a man and woman who live by thieving.

CROSS-CRIB, a house frequented by thieves.

CROW, one who watches whilst another commits a theft, a confederate in a robbery. The CROW looks to see that the way is clear, whilst the SNEAK, his partner, commits the depredation.

CROW, "a regular CROW," a success, a stroke of luck,—equivalent to a FLUKE.

CROW, "I have a CROW to pick with you," *i.e.*, an explanation to demand, a disagreeable matter to settle; "to COCK-CROW over a person," to exalt over his abasement or misfortune.

CRUG, food.—*Household Words*, No. 183.

CRUMBS, "to pick up one's CRUMBS," to begin to have an appetite after an illness; to improve in health, circumstances, &c., after a loss thereof.

CRUMMY, fat, plump.—*North.*

CRUMMY-DOSS, a lousy or filthy bed.

CRUNCH, to crush. *Corruption;* or, perhaps from the sound of teeth grinding against each other.

CRUSHER, a policeman.

CRUSHING, excellent, first rate.

CRUSTY, ill tempered, petulant, morose.—*Old.*

CULL, a man or boy.—*Old cant.*

CULLING, or CULING, stealing from the carriages on race-courses.

CUPBOARD HEADED, an expressive designation of one whose head is both wooden and hollow.—*Norfolk.*

CURE, an odd person; a contemptuous term, abridged from CURIOSITY—which was formerly the favourite expression.—Compare STIPE.

CURSE OF SCOTLAND, the Nine of Diamonds. Various hypotheses have been set up as to this appellation—that it was the card on which the "Butcher Duke" wrote a cruel order with respect to the rebels after the battle of Culloden; that the diamonds are the nine lozenges in the arms of Dalrymple, Earl of Stair, detested for his share in the Massacre of Glencoe; that it is a corruption of *Cross of Scotland*, the nine diamonds being arranged somewhat after the fashion of a St. Andrew's Cross; but the most probable explanation is, that in the game of Pope Joan the nine of diamonds is the POPE, of whom the Scotch have an especial horror.

CURTAIL, to cut off. *Originally a cant word, vide Hudibras, and Bacchus and Venus,* 1737.

CUSHION THUMPER, polite rendering of TUB THUMPER, a clergyman, a preacher.

CUSTOMER, synonymous with CHAP, a fellow; "a rum CUSTOMER," *i. e.*, an odd fish, or curious person.—*Shakespere.*

CUSTOMHOUSE OFFICER, an aperient pill.

CUT, to run away, move off quickly; to cease doing anything; CUT AND RUN, to quit work, or occupation, and start off at once; to CUT DIDOES, synonymous with to CUT CAPERS; CUT A DASH, make a show; CUT A CAPER, to dance or show off in a strange manner; CUT A FIGURE, to make either a good or bad appearance; CUT OUT, to excel, thus in affairs of gallantry one Adonis is said to "*cut the other out*" in the affections of the wished for lady; CUT THAT! be quiet, or stop; CUT OUT OF, done out of; CUT OF ONE'S GIB, the expression or cast of his countenance [*see* GIB]; TO CUT ONE'S COMB, to take down a conceited person, from the practice of cutting the combs of capons [*see* COMB-CUT]; CUT AND COME AGAIN, plenty, if one cut does not suffice, plenty remains to "come again;" CUT UP, mortified, to criticise severely, or expose; CUT UP SHINES, to play tricks; CUT ONE'S STICK, to be off quickly, *i. e.*, be in readiness for a journey, further elaborated into AMPUTATE YOUR MAHOGANY [*see* STICK]; CUT IT FAT, to exaggerate or show off in an extensive manner; to CUT UP FAT, to die, leaving a large property; CUT UNDER, to undersell; CUT YOUR LUCKY, to run off; CUT ONE'S CART, to expose their tricks; CUT AN ACQUAINTANCE, to cease friendly intercourse with them—*Cambridge. Old;* CUTTE, to say.

CUT, in theatrical language, means to strike out portions of a dramatic piece, so as to render it shorter for representation. A late treasurer of one of the so called *Patent Theatres*, when asked his opinion of a new play, always gave utterance to the brief, but safe piece of criticism, "*wants* CUTTING."

CUT, tipsey.—*Household Words*, No. 183.

CUT, to compete in business.

CUT-THROAT, a butcher, a cattle slaughterer; a ruffian.

CUTE, sharp, cunning. Abbreviation of ACUTE.

CUTTER, a ruffian, a cut purse. Of *Robin Hood* it was said—

> "So being outlawed (as 'tis told),
> He with a crew went forth
> Of lusty CUTTERS, bold and strong,
> And robbed in the north."

This ancient cant word now survives in the phrase, "to swear like a CUTTER."

CUTTY PIPE, a short clay pipe. *Scotch,* CUTTY, short. *Cutty-sark,* a scantily draped lady is so called by *Burns.*

DAB, or DABSTER, an expert person. Johnson says, "in low language, an artist."

DAB, a bed.

DAB, street term for a flat fish of any kind.—*Old.*

DACHA-SALTEE, tenpence. Probably from the *Lingua Franca. Modern Greek,* δεκα; *Italian,* DIECI SOLDI, tenpence; Gipsey, DIK, ten. So also DACHA-ONE, *i.e., dieci uno,* elevenpence.—*See* SALTEE.

DADDLES, hands; "tip us your DADDLES, *i. e.,* shake hands.

DADDY, the stage manager.—*Theatrical.* Also the person who gives away the bride at weddings.

DAGS, feat or performance; "I'll do your DAGS," *i.e*, I will do something that you cannot do.

DAISY CUTTER, a horse which trots or gallops without lifting its feet much from the ground.

DAISY KICKERS, the name hostlers at large inns used to give each other, now nearly obsolete. DAISY-KICKER, or GROGHAM, was likewise the cant term for a horse.

The DAISY-KICKERS were sad rogues in the old posting-days; frequently the landlords rented the stables to them, as the only plan to make them return a profit.

DAMPER, a shop till; to DRAW A DAMPER, *i.e.,* rob a till.

DANCE UPON NOTHING, to be hanged.

DANCERS, stairs.—*Old cant.*

DANDER, passion, or temper; "to get one's DANDER up," to rouse his passion.—*Old.*

DANDY, a fop, or fashionable nondescript. This word, in the sense of a fop, is of modern origin. *Egan* says it was first used in 1820, and *Bee* in 1816. Johnson does not mention it, although it is to be found in all late dictionaries. DANDIES wore stays, studied feminity, and tried to undo their manhood. Lord Petersham headed them. At the present day dandies of this stamp are fast disappearing. The feminine of DANDY was DANDIZETTE, but the term only lived for a short season.

DANDYPRAT, a funny little fellow, a mannikin; originally a half-farthing.

DANNA, excrement; DANNA DRAG, a nightman's or dustman's cart.

DARBIES, handcuffs.—*Old cant.*

DARBLE, the devil.—*French,* DIABLE.

DARK, "keep it DARK," *i.e.*, secret. DARK HORSE, in racing phraseology a horse whose chance of success is unknown, and whose capabilities have not been made the subject of comment.

DARKEY, twilight. DARKMANS, the night.

DARN, vulgar corruption of d——n.—*American.*

DASHING, showy, fast.

DAVID'S SOW, "as drunk as DAVID'S SOW," *i.e.*, beastly drunk. —See origin of the phrase in *Grose's Dictionary.*

DAVY, "on my DAVY," on my affidavit, of which it is a vulgar corruption. Latterly DAVY has become synonymous in street language with the name of the Deity; "so help me DAVY," slang rendering of the conclusion of the oath usually exacted of witnesses.

DAVY'S LOCKER, or DAVY JONES' LOCKER, the sea, the common receptacle for all things thrown overboard;—a nautical phrase for death, the other world.

DAWDLE, to loiter, or fritter away time.

DAYLIGHTS, eyes; "to darken his DAYLIGHTS," to give a person black eyes.

DEAD ALIVE, stupid, dull.

DEAD HORSE, "to draw the DEAD HORSE," DEAD-HORSE work, —working for wages already paid; also any thankless or unassisted service.

DEAD-LURK, entering a dwelling-house during divine service.

DEAD MEN, the term for wine bottles after they are emptied of their contents.—*Old.*—*See* MARINES.

DEAD-SET, a pointed attack on a person.

DEANER, a shilling. *Provincial Gipsey,* DEANEE, a pound.

DEATH, "to dress to DEATH," *i.e.*, to the very extreme of fashion, perhaps so as to be KILLING.

DEATH-HUNTERS, running patterers, who vend last dying speeches and confessions.

DECK, a pack of cards.—*Old.* Used by Bulwer as a cant term. General in the *United States.*

DEE, a pocket book, term used by tramps.—*Gipsey.*

DEMIREP (or RIP), a courtesan. Contraction of DEMI-REPUTATION—*Grose.*

DESPATCHES, false "dice with two sides, double four, double five, and double six."—*Times*, 27th November, 1856.

DEUCE, the devil.—*Old.* Stated by *Junius* and others to be from DEUS.

DEUCE, twopence; DEUCE at cards or dice, one with two pips or holes.

DEVIL, a printer's youngest apprentice, an errand boy.

DEVIL-DODGERS, clergymen; also people who go sometimes to church and sometimes to meeting.

DEVIL'S-TEETH, dice.

DEVOTIONAL HABITS, horses weak in the knees and apt to stumble and fall are said to have these.—*Stable.*

DEWSKITCH, a good thrashing.

DIBBS, money; so called from the huckle bones of sheep, which have been used from the earliest times for gambling purposes, being thrown up five at a time and caught on the back of the hand like halfpence.

DICKEY, bad, sorry, or foolish; food or lodging is pronounced DICKEY when of a poor description; "it's all DICKEY with him," *i.e.*, all over with him.

DICKEY, formerly the cant for a worn out shirt, but means now-a-days a front or half-shirt. DICKEY was originally TOMMY (from the Greek, τομη, a section), a name which I understand was formerly used in Trinity College, Dublin. The students are said to have invented the term, and the GYPS changed it to DICKEY, in which dress it is supposed to have been imported into England.

DICKEY, a donkey.

DICKENS, synonymous with devil; "what the DICKENS are you after?" what the d—l are you doing? Used by *Shakespere* in the *Merry Wives of Windsor.*

DIDDLE, to cheat, or defraud.—*Old.*

DIDDLE, old cant word for geneva, or gin.

DIDDLER, or JEREMY DIDDLER, an artful swindler

DIDOES, pranks or capers; "to cut up DIDOES," to make pranks.

DIES, last dying speeches, and criminal trials.

DIGS, hard blows.

DIGGERS, spurs; also the spades on cards.

DIGGINGS, lodgings, apartments, residence; an expression probably imported from California, or Australia, with reference to *the gold diggings.*

DILLY DALLY, to trifle.

DIMBER, neat or pretty.—*Worcestershire*, but old cant.

DIMBER DAMBER, very pretty; a clever rogue who excels his fellows; chief of a gang. *Old cant* in the latter sense.—*English Rogue.*

DIMMOCK, money; "how are you off for DIMMOCK?" diminutive of DIME, a small foreign silver coin.

DINARLY, money; "NANTEE DINARLY," I have no money, corrupted from the *Lingua Franca*, "NIENTE DINARO," not a penny. *Turkish*, DINARI; *Spanish*, DINERO; *Latin*, DENARIUS.

DING, to strike; to throw away, or get rid of anything; to pass to a confederate.

DIPPED, mortgaged.—*Household Words*, No. 183.

DISGUISED, intoxicated.—*Household Words*, No. 183.

DISH, to stop, to do away with, to suppress; DISHED, done for, floored, beaten, or silenced. A correspondent suggests that meat is usually DONE BROWN before being DISHED, and conceives that the latter term may have arisen as the natural sequence of the former.

DISHABBILLY, the ridiculous corruption of the *French*, DESHABILLE, amongst fashionably affected, but ignorant "stuck-up" people.

DITHERS, nervous or cold shiverings. "It gave me the DITHERS."

DIVE, to pick pockets.

DIVERS, pickpockets.

DO, this useful and industrious verb has for many years done service as a slang term. To DO a person is to cheat him. Sometimes another tense is employed, such as "I DONE him," meaning I cheated or "paid him out;" DONE BROWN, cheated thoroughly, befooled; DONE OVER, upset, cheated, knocked down, ruined; DONE UP, used up, finished, or quieted. DONE also means convicted, or sentenced; so does DONE-FOR. To DO a person in pugilism is to excel him in fisticuffs. Humphreys, who fought Mendoza, a Jew, wrote this laconic note to his supporter—"Sir,—I have DONE the Jew, and am in good health. Rich. Humphreys." Tourists use the expression "I have DONE France and Italy," meaning I have completely explored those countries.

DOCTOR, to adulterate or drug liquor; also to falsify accounts. —*See* COOK.

DODGE, a cunning trick. "DODGE, that homely but expressive phrase."—*Sir Hugh Cairns on the Reform Bill*, 2nd March, 1859. *Anglo Saxon*, DEOGIAN, to colour, to conceal. The TIDY DODGE, as it is called by street-folk, consists in dressing up a family clean and *tidy*, and parading the streets to excite compassion and obtain alms. A correspondent suggests that the verb DODGE may have been formed (like *wench* from *wink*) from DOG, *i.e.*, to double quickly and unexpectedly, as in coursing.

DODGER, a tricky person, or one who, to use the popular phrase, "knows too much."—*See* DEVIL-DODGER.

DODGER, a dram. In *Kent*, a DODGER signifies a nightcap; which name is often given to the last dram at night.

DOG, to follow in one's footsteps on the sly, to track.

DOG-CHEAP, or DOG-FOOLISH, very, or singularly cheap, or foolish. Latham, in his *English Language*, says:—"This has nothing to do with dogs. The first syllable is god = *good* transposed, and the second, the ch—p, is chapman, *merchant*: compare EASTCHEAP."—*Old term.*

DOG-LATIN, barbarous Latin, such as was formerly used by lawyers in their pleadings.

DOG-ON-IT, a form of mild swearing used by boys. It is just worthy of mention that DOGONE, in *Anglo-Norman*, is equivalent to a term of contempt. *Friesic*, DOGENIET.

DOGSNOSE, gin and beer, so called from the mixture being *cold*, like a dog's nose.

DOLDRUMS, difficulties, low spirits, dumps.—*Sea.*

DOLLOP, a lump or portion.—*Norfolk. Ang. Sax.* DAEL, *dole.*

DOLLOP, to *dole up*, give up a share.—*Ib.*

DOLLYMOP, a tawdrily-dressed maid servant, a street walker.

DOLLY SHOP, an illegal pawnshop,—where goods, or stolen property, not good enough for the pawnbroker, are received, and charged at so much per day. If not redeemed the third day the goods are forfeited. *Anglo Saxon*, DAEL, a part,—to dole?—*See* NIX. A correspondent thinks it may have been derived from the *black doll*, the usual sign of a rag shop.

DOMINE, a parson.

DOMINOS, the teeth.

DON, a clever fellow, the opposite of a muff; a person of distinction in his line or walk. At the Universities, the Masters and Fellows are THE DONS. DON is also used as an adjective, "a DON hand at a knife and fork," *i.e.*, a first-rate feeder at a dinner table.—*Spanish.*

K 2

DONE FOR A RAMP, convicted for thieving.

DONKEY, "three more and up goes the DONKEY," a vulgar street phrase for extracting as much money as possible before performing any task. The phrase had its origin with a travelling showman, the *finale* of whose performance was the hoisting of a DONKEY on a pole or ladder; but this consummation was never arrived at unless the required number of "browns" was first paid up, and "three more" was generally the unfortunate deficit.

DONNA AND FEELES, a woman and children. *Italian* or *Lingua Franca*, DONNE E FIGLIE.

DOOKIN, fortune telling. *Gipsey*, DUKKERIN.

DOSE, three months' imprisonment as a known thief.—*See* BRAGGADOCIO.

DOSS, a bed.—*North*. Probably from DOZE. Mayhew thinks it is from the Norman, DOSSEL, a hanging, or bed canopy.

DOSS, to sleep, formerly spelt DORSE. Perhaps from the phrase to lie on one's *dorsum*, back.

DOSS-KEN, a lodging house.

DOUBLE, "to tip (or give) the DOUBLE," to run away from any person; to double back, turn short round upon one's pursuers and so escape, as a hare does.—*Sporting*.

DOUBLE-UP, to pair off, or "chum," with another man; to beat severely.

DOUBLE-SHUFFLE, a low, shuffling, noisy dance, common amongst costermongers.—*See* FLIP-FLAPS.

DOUSE, to put out; "DOUSE that glim," put out that candle.—*Sea*.

DOWD, a woman's nightcap.—*Devonshire;* also an *American* term; possibly from DOWDY, a slatternly woman.

DOWN, to be aware of, or awake to, any move—in this meaning, synonymous with UP; "DOWN upon one's luck," unfortunate; "DOWN in the mouth," disconsolate; "to be DOWN on one," to treat him harshly or suspiciously, to pounce upon him, or detect his tricks.

DOWN THE DOLLY, a favourite gambling contrivance, often seen in the tap rooms of public houses, at race-courses, and fairs, consisting of a round board and the figure of an old man or "doll," down which is a spiral hole. A marble is dropped "down the dolly," and stops in one of the small holes or pits (numbered) on the board. The bet is decided according as the marble stops on a high or low figure.

DOWN THE ROAD, stylish, showy, after the fashion.

DOWNER, a sixpence; apparently the *Gipsey* word, TAWNO, "little one," in course of metamorphosis into the more usual "*tanner*."

DOWNS, Tothill Fields' prison.

DOWNY, knowing or cunning; "a DOWNY COVE," a knowing or experienced sharper.

DOWRY, a lot, a great deal; "DOWRY of parny," lot of rain or water.—*See* PARNY. Probably from the *Gipsey*.

DOXY, the female companion of a thief or beggar. In the West of England, the women frequently call their little girls DOXIES, in a familiar or endearing sense. A learned divine once described *orthodoxy* as being a man's own DOXY, and *heterodoxy* another man's DOXY.—*Ancient cant.*

DRAB, a vulgar or low woman.—*Shakespere.*

DRAG, a cart of any kind, a coach; gentlemen drive to the races in DRAGS.

DRAG, a street, or road; BACK-DRAG, back-street.

DRAG, or THREE MOON, three months in prison.

DRAGGING, robbing carts, &c.

DRAGSMEN, fellows who cut trunks from the backs of carriages. They sometimes have a light cart, and "drop behind" the plundered vehicle, and then drive off in an opposite direction with the booty.

DRAIN, a drink; "to do a DRAIN," to take a friendly drink—"do a wet;" sometimes called a COMMON SEWER.

DRAW, "come, DRAW it mild!" *i.e.*, don't exaggerate; opposite of "come it strong." From the phraseology of the bar (of a PUBLIC), where customers desire the beer to be DRAWN mild.

DRAWERS, formerly the ancient cant name for very long stockings, now a hosier's term.

DRAWING TEETH, wrenching off knockers.

DRIVE-AT, to aim at; "what is he DRIVING AT?" what does he intend to imply?" a phrase often used when a circuitous line of argument is adopted by a barrister, or a strange set of questions asked, the purpose of which is not very evident.

DRIVE, a term used by tradesmen in speaking of business; "he's DRIVING a *roaring* trade," *i.e.*, a very good one; hence, to succeed in a bargain, "I DROVE a good bargain," *i.e.*, got the best end of it.

DRIZ, lace. In a low lodging house this singular autograph inscription appeared over the mantelpiece, "Scotch Mary, with DRIZ (lace), bound to Dover and back, please God."

DRIZ FENCER, a person who sells lace.

DROP, to quit, go off, or turn aside; "DROP the main Toby," go off the main road.

DROP, "to DROP INTO a person," to give him a thrashing.—*See* SLIP and WALK. "To DROP ON to a man," to accuse or rebuke him suddenly.

DRUM, a house, a lodging, a street; HAZARD-DRUM, a gambling house; FLASH-DRUM, a house of ill-fame.

DRUMMER, a robber who first makes his victims insensible by drugs or violence, and then plunders them.

DUB, to pay or give; "DUB UP," pay up.

DUBBER, the mouth; "mum your DUBBER," hold your tongue.

DUBLIN PACKET, to turn a corner; to "take the DUBLIN PACKET," viz., run round the corner.

DUBS, a bunch of keys.—*Nearly obsolete.*

DUBSMAN, or SCREW, a turnkey.

DUCKS AND DRAKES, "to make DUCKS AND DRAKES of one's money," to throw it away childishly,—derived from children "shying" flat stones on the surface of a pool, which they call DUCKS AND DRAKES, according to the number of skips they make.

DUDDERS, or DUDSMEN, persons who formerly travelled the country as pedlars, selling gown-pieces, silk waistcoats, &c., to countrymen. In selling a waistcoat-piece for thirty shillings or two pounds, which cost them perhaps five shillings, they would show great fear of the revenue officer, and beg of the purchasing clodhopper *to kneel down in a puddle of water, crook his arm, and swear that it might never become straight if he told an exciseman, or even his own wife.* The term and practice are nearly obsolete. In Liverpool, however, and at the east end of London, men dressed up as sailors, with pretended silk handkerchiefs and cigars "only just smuggled from the Indies," are still to be plentifully found.

DUDDS, clothes, or personal property. *Gaelic*, DUD; *Ancient cant;* also *Dutch.*

DUFF, pudding; vulgar pronunciation of DOUGH.—*Sea.*

DUFFER, a hawker of "Brummagem" or sham jewellery; a sham of any kind; a fool, or worthless person. DUFFER was formerly synonymous with DUDDER, and was a general term given to pedlars. It is mentioned in the *Frauds of London* (1760), as a word in frequent use in the last century to express cheats of all kinds. From the *German*, DURFEN, to want?

DUFFING, false, counterfeit, worthless.

DUKE, gin.—*Household Words*, No. 183.

DUMB-FOUND, to perplex, to beat soundly till not able to speak. Originally a cant word. *Johnson* cites the *Spectator* for the earliest use. *Scotch*, DUMFOUNDER.

DUMMACKER, a knowing or acute person.

DUMMIES, empty bottles and drawers in an apothecary's shop, labelled so as to give an idea of an extensive stock.

DUMMY, in three-handed whist the person who holds two hands plays DUMMY.

DUMMY, a pocket book.

DUMP FENCER, a man who sells buttons.

DUMPY, short and stout.

DUMPISH, sullen, or glumpy.

DUN, to solicit payment.—*Old cant*, from the French DONNEZ, give; or from JOE DUN, the famous bailiff of Lincoln; or simply a corruption of DIN, from the *Anglo Saxon* DUNAN, to clamour?

DUNAKER, a stealer of cows or calves *Nearly obsolete.*

DUNDERHEAD, a blockhead.

DUNG, an operative who works for an employer who does not give full or "society" wages.

DUNNAGE, baggage, clothes. Also, a *Sea* term for wood or loose faggots laid at the bottom of ships, upon which is placed the cargo.

DUNNY-KEN, a water-closet.—*See* KEN.

DURRYNACKING, offering lace or any other article as an introduction to fortune-telling; generally pursued by women.

DUST, money; "down with the DUST," put down the money. —*Ancient.* Dean Swift once took for his text, "He who giveth to the poor lendeth to the Lord." His sermon was short. "Now, my brethren," said he, "if you are satisfied with the security, down with the DUST."

DUST, a disturbance, or noise, "to raise a DUST," to make a row.

DUTCH CONSOLATION, "thank God it is no worse."

DUTCH CONCERT, where each performer plays a different tune.

DUTCH COURAGE, false courage, generally excited by drink,—*pot-valour*.

DUTCH FEAST, where the host gets drunk before his guest.

DUTCH UNCLE, a personage often introduced in conversation, but exceedingly difficult to describe; "I'll talk to him like a DUTCH UNCLE!" conveys the notion of anything but a desirable relation.—*Americanism.*

DOUBLE DUTCH, gibberish, or any foreign tongue.

EARL OF CORK, the ace of diamonds.—*Hibernicism.*

> "What do you mean by the Earl of Cork?" asked Mr. Squander. "The ace of diamonds, your honour. It's the worst ace, and the poorest card in the pack, and is called the Earl of Cork, because he's the poorest nobleman in Ireland."—*Carleton's Traits and Stories of the Irish Peasantry.*

EARWIG, a clergyman, also one who prompts another maliciously.

EARWIGGING, a rebuke in private; a WIGGING is more public.

EASE, to rob; "EASING a bloak," robbing a man.

EGG, or EGG on, to excite, stimulate, or provoke one person to quarrel with another, &c. *Cor. of edge, or edge on.—Ancient.*

ELBOW, "to shake one's ELBOW," to play at cards.

ELBOW GREASE, labour, or industry.

ELEPHANT, "to have SEEN THE ELEPHANT," to be "*up* to the latest move," or "*down* to the last new trick;" to be knowing, and not "green," &c. Possibly a metaphor taken from the travelling menageries, where the ELEPHANT is the *finale* of the exhibition.—Originally an *Americanism. Bartlett* gives conflicting examples. *General* now, however.

EVAPORATE, to go, or run away.

EVERLASTING STAIRCASE, the treadmill. Sometimes called "Colonel Chesterton's everlasting staircase," from the gallant inventor or improver.

EXTENSIVE, frequently applied in a slang sense to a person's appearance or talk; "rather EXTENSIVE that!" intimating that the person alluded to is showing off, or "cutting it fat."

EYE WATER, gin.

FAD, a hobby, a favourite pursuit.

FADGE, a farthing.

FADGE, to suit or fit; "it won't FADGE," it will not do. Used by *Shakespere,* but now heard only in the streets.

FAG, to beat, also one boy working for another at school.

FAG, a schoolboy who performs a servant's offices to a superior school-mate. *Grose* thinks FAGGED OUT is derived from this.

FAGOT, a term of opprobrium used by low people to children; "you little FAGOT, you!" FAGOT was originally a term of contempt for a dry, shrivelled old woman, whose bones were like a bundle of sticks, only fit to burn.—Compare the French expression for a heretic, *sentir le fagot.*

FAKE, to cheat, or swindle; to do anything; to go on, or continue; to make or construct; to steal, or rob,—a verb variously used. FAKED, done, or done for; "FAKE away, there's no down," go on, there is nobody looking. *Mayhew* says it is from the *Latin,* FACIMENTUM.

FAKEMENT, a false begging petition, any act of robbery, swindling, or deception.

FAKEMENT CHARLEY, the owner's private mark.

FAKER, one who makes or FAKES anything.

FAKING A CLY, picking a pocket.

FAMBLES, or FAMMS, the hands.—*Ancient cant. German,* FAUGEN.

FAMILY MEN, or PEOPLE, thieves, or burglars.

FAN, a waistcoat.

FANCY, the favourite sports, pets, or pastime of a person, *the tan of low life.* Pugilists are sometimes termed THE FANCY. *Shakespere* uses the word in the sense of a favourite, or pet; and the paramour of a prostitute is still called her FANCY-MAN.

FANCY-BLOAK, a fancy or sporting man.

FAN-TAIL, a dustman's hat.

FAST, gay, spreeish, unsteady, thoughtless,—an Americanism that has of late ascended from the streets to the drawing-room. The word has certainly now a distinct meaning, which it had not thirty years ago. QUICK is the synonyme for FAST, but a QUICK MAN would not convey the meaning of a FAST MAN,—a person who by late hours, gaiety, and continual rounds of pleasure, lives too fast and wears himself out. In polite society a FAST young lady is one who affects mannish habits, or makes herself conspicuous by some unfeminine accomplishment,—talks slang, drives about in London, smokes cigarettes, is knowing in dogs, horses, &c. An amusing anecdote is told of a FAST young lady, the daughter of a right reverend prelate, who was an adept in *horseflesh.* Being desirous of ascertaining the opinion of a candidate for ordination, who had the look of a bird of the same feather, as to the merits of some cattle just brought to her father's palace for her to select from, she was assured by him they were utterly unfit for a lady's use. With a knowing look at the horses' points, she gave her decision in these choice words, "Well, I agree with you; they *are* a rum lot, as the Devil said of the ten commandments."

FAST, embarrassed, wanting money. Synonymous with HARD UP.—*Yorkshire.*

FAT, a printer's term signifying the void spaces on a page, for which he is paid at the same rate as full or unbroken pages. This work afforded much FAT for the printers.

FAT, rich, abundant, &c.; "a FAT lot;" "to cut it FAT," to exaggerate, to show off in an extensive or grand manner, to assume undue importance; cut up FAT," see under CUT. As a *Theatrical* term, a part with plenty of FAT in it, is one which affords the actor an opportunity of effective display.

FATHER, or FENCE, a buyer of stolen property.

FAWNEY, a finger ring.

FAWNEY BOUNCING, selling rings for a wager. This practice is founded upon the old tale of a gentleman laying a wager that if he was to offer "real gold sovereigns" at a penny a piece at the foot of London Bridge, the English public would be too incredulous to buy. The story states that the gentleman stationed himself with sovereigns in a tea tray, and sold only two within the hour,—winning the bet. This tale the FAWNEY BOUNCERS tell the public, only offering brass, double gilt rings, instead of sovereigns.

FAWNEY, or FAWNEY RIG, ring dropping. A few years ago, this practice, or RIG, was very common. A fellow purposely dropped a ring, or a pocket book with some little articles of jewellery, &c., in it, and when he saw any person pick it up, ran to claim half. The ring found, the question of how the booty was to be divided had then to be decided. The *Fawney* says, "if you will give me eight or nine shillings for my share the things are yours." This the FLAT thinks very fair. The ring of course is valueless, and the swallower of the bait discovers the trick too late.

FEATHERS, money, wealth; "in full FEATHER," rich.

FEEDER, a spoon.—*Old cant.*

FEELE, a daughter, or child.—*Corrupted French.*

FELT, a hat.—*Old term, in use in the sixteenth century.*

FENCE, or FENCER, a purchaser or receiver of stolen goods; FENCE, the shop or warehouse of a FENCER.—*Old cant.*

FENCE, to sell or pawn stolen property to a FENCER.

FERRICADOUZER, a knock down below, a good thrashing. Probably derived through the *Lingua Franca* from the *Italian*, FAR' CADER' MORTO, to knock down dead.

FIB, to beat, or strike.—*Old cant.*

FIDDLE, a whip.

FIDDLE FADDLE, twaddle, or trifling discourse.—*Old cant.*

FIDDLE STICKS! nonsense.

FIDDLER, or FADGE, a farthing.

FIDDLER, a sixpence.—*Household Words*, No. 183.

FIDDLER, a sharper, a cheat; also one who dawdles over little matters, and neglects great ones.

FIDDLERS' MONEY, a lot of sixpences;—6d. was the remuneration to fiddlers from each of the company in old times.

FIDDLING, doing any odd jobs in the streets, holding horses, carrying parcels, &c., for a living. Among the middle classes, FIDDLING means idling away time, or trifling; and amongst sharpers, it means gambling.

FID FAD, a game similar to chequers, or drafts, played in the West of England.

FIDLUM BEN, thieves who take anything they can lay their hands upon.

FIELD-LANE-DUCK, a baked sheep's head. *Field-lane* is a low London thoroughfare, leading from the foot of Holborn-hill to the purlieus of Clerkenwell. It was formerly the market for stolen pocket handkerchiefs.

FIG, "to FIG a horse," to play improper tricks with one in order to make him lively.

FIG, "in full FIG," *i.e.*, full dress costume, "extensively got up."

FIGURE, "to cut a good or bad FIGURE," to make a good or indifferent appearance; "what's the FIGURE?" how much is to pay? FIGURE-HEAD, a person's face.—*Sea term.*

FILCH, to steal, or purloin. Originally a cant word, derived from the FILCHES, or hooks, thieves used to carry, to hook clothes, or any portable articles from open windows. —*Vide Decker.* It was considered a cant or Gipsey term up to the beginning of the last century. *Harman* has "FYLCHE, to robbe."

FILE, a deep, or artful man, a jocose name for a cunning person.

Originally a term for a pickpocket, when TO FILE was to cheat or rob. FILE, an artful man, was used in the thirteenth and fourteenth centuries.

FILLIBRUSH, to flatter, praise ironically.

FIMBLE-FAMBLE, a lame prevaricating excuse.—*Scand.*

FIN, a hand; "come, tip us your FIN," viz., let us shake hands. —*Sea.*

FINDER, one who FINDS bacon and meat at the market before they are lost, *i.e.*, steals them.

FINUF, a five-pound note. DOUBLE FINUF, a ten-pound note. —*German*, FUNF, five.

FISHY, doubtful, unsound, rotten—a term used to denote a suspicion of a "screw being loose," or "something rotten in the state of Denmark," in alluding to an unsafe speculation.

FISH, a person; "a queer FISH," "a loose FISH," &c.

FIX, a predicament, dilemma; "an awful FIX," a terrible position; "to FIX one's flint for him," *i.e.*, to "settle his *hash*," "put a spoke in his wheel."

FIZZING, first-rate, very good, excellent; synonymous with STUNNING.

FLABERGAST, or FLABBERGHAST, to astonish, or strike with wonder.—*Old.*

FLAG, a groat, or 4d.—*Ancient cant.*

FLAG, an apron.

FLAG OF DISTRESS, poverty—when the end of a person's shirt protrudes through his trousers.

FLAM, nonsense, blarney, a lie.—*Kentish; Anglo Saxon.*

FLAME, a sweetheart.

FLANNEL, or HOT FLANNEL, the old term for gin and beer, drank hot, with nutmeg, sugar, &c. Also called FLIP. There is an anecdote told of Goldsmith helping to drink a quart of FLANNEL in a night house, in company with George Parker, Ned Shuter, and a demure grave looking gentleman, who continually introduced the words CRAP, STRETCH, SCRAG, and SWING. Upon the Doctor's asking who this strange person might be, and being told his profession, he rushed from the place in a frenzy, exclaiming, "Good God! and have I been sitting all this while with a hangman?"

FLARE UP, a jovial social gathering, a "break down," a "row."

FLASH, showy, smart, knowing; a word with various meanings.

A person is said to be dressed FLASH when his garb is showy, and after a fashion, but without taste. A person is said to be FLASH when he apes the appearance or manners of his betters, or when he is trying to be superior to his friends and relations. FLASH also means "fast," roguish, and sometimes infers counterfeit or deceptive,—and this, perhaps, is its general signification. "FLASH, my young friend, or slang, as others call it, is the classical language of the Holy Land; in other words, St. Giles' Greek."—*Tom and Jerry, by Moncreiff.* Vulgar language was first termed FLASH in the year 1718, by Hitchin, author of "*The Regulator of Thieves, &c., with account of* FLASH *words.*"

FLASH IT, show it—said when any bargain is offered.

FLAT, a fool, a silly or "soft" person, the opposite of SHARP. The term appears to be shortenings for "sharp-witted" and "flat-witted." "Oh! Messrs. Tyler, Donelson, and the rest, what FLATS you are."—*Times*, 5th September, 1847.

FLATTIES, rustic, or uninitiated people.

FLATTY-KEN, a public house, the landlord of which is ignorant of the practices of the thieves and tramps who frequent it.

FLESH AND BLOOD, brandy and port in equal quantities.

FLESH-BAG, a shirt.

FLICK, or OLD FLICK, an old chap or fellow.

FLICK, or FLIG, to whip by striking, and drawing the lash back at the same time, which causes a stinging blow.

FLIM FLAMS, idle stories.—*Beaumont and Fletcher.*

FLIMP, to hustle, or rob.

FLIMSIES, bank notes.

FLIMSY, the thin prepared copying paper used by newspaper reporters and "penny-a-liners" for making several copies at once, thus enabling them to supply different papers with the same article without loss of time.—*Printers' term.*

FLINT, an operative who works for a "society" master, *i.e.*, for full wages.

FLIP, corruption of FILLIP, a light blow.

FLIP-FLAPS, a peculiar rollicking dance indulged in by costermongers when merry or excited—better described, perhaps, as the DOUBLE SHUFFLE, danced with an air of extreme *abandon.*

FLIPPER, the hand; "give us your FLIPPER," give me your hand.—*Sea.* Metaphor taken from the flipper or paddle of a turtle.

FLOG, to whip. Cited both by *Grose* and the author of *Bacchus and Venus* as a cant word. It would be curious to ascertain the earliest use; *Richardson* cites Lord Chesterfield.—*Latin.*

FLOGGER, a whip.—*Obsolete.*

FLOOR, to knock down.—*Pugilistic.*

FLOORER, a blow sufficiently strong to knock a man down.

FLOWERY, lodging, or house entertainment; "square the omee for the FLOWERY," pay the master for the lodging.

FLUE FAKERS, chimney sweeps; also low sporting characters, who are so termed from their chiefly betting on the *Great Sweeps.*

FLUFF IT, a term of disapprobation, implying "take it away, I don't want it."

FLUKE, at billiards, playing for one thing and getting another. Hence, generally what one gets accidentally, an unexpected advantage, "more by luck than wit."

FLUMMERY, flattery, gammon, genteel nonsense.

FLUMMUX, to perplex, hinder; FLUMMUXED, stopped, used up

FLUMMUXED, done up, sure of a month in QUOD, or prison. In mendicant freemasonry, the sign chalked by rogues and tramps upon a gate-post or house corner, to express to succeeding vagabonds that it is unsafe for them to call there, is known as ⨀, or FLUMMUXED, which signifies that the only thing they would be likely to get upon applying for relief would be "a month in QUOD."—*See* QUOD.

FLUNKEY, a footman, servant.—*Scotch.*

FLUSH, the opposite of HARD UP, in possession of money, not poverty stricken.—*Shakespere.*

FLY, to lift, toss, or raise; "FLY the *mags,*" *i e.,* toss up the halfpence; "to FLY a window," *i.e.,* to lift one for the purpose of stealing.

FLY, knowing, wide awake, fully understanding another's meaning.

FLY THE KITE, or RAISE THE WIND, to obtain money on bills, whether good or bad, alluding to tossing paper about like children do a kite.

FLY THE KITE, to evacuate from a window,—term used in padding kens, or low lodging houses.

FLYING-MESS, "to be in FLYING MESS" is a soldier's phrase for being hungry and having to mess where he can.—*Military.*

FLYING STATIONERS, paper workers, hawkers of penny

ballads; "Printed for the Flying Stationers" is the *imprimatur* on hundreds of penny histories and sheet songs of the last and present centuries.

FLYMY, knowing, cunning, roguish.

FOALED, "thrown from a horse."—*Hunting term.*—*See* PURLED, and SPILT.

FOGEY, or OLD FOGEY, a dullard, an old-fashioned or singular person. *Grose* says it is a nickname for an invalid soldier, from the *French*, FOURGEAUX, fierce or fiery, but it has lost this signification now. FOGGER, *old word* for a huckster or servant.

FOGGY, tipsy.

FOGLE, a silk handkerchief—not a CLOUT, which is of *cotton.* It has been hinted that this may have come from the *German*, VOGEL, a bird, from the *bird's eye* spots on some handkerchiefs [*see* BIRD'S-EYE-WIPE, under BILLY], but a more probable derivation is the Italian slang (*Fourbesque*) FOGLIA, a pocket, or purse; or from the *French argot*, FOUILLE, also a pocket.

FOGUS, tobacco.—*Old cant.* FOGO, *old word for stench.*

FOONT, a sovereign, or 20s.

FOOTING, "to pay FOOTING."—*See* SHOE.

FORAKERS, a water-closet, or house of office.—Term used by the boys at *Winchester school.*

FORK OUT, to bring out one's money, to pay the bill, to STAND FOR or treat a friend; to hand over what does not belong to you.—Old cant term for picking pockets, and very curious it is to trace its origin. In the early part of the last century, a little book on purloining was published, and of course it had to give the latest modes. FORKING was the newest method, and it consisted in thrusting the fingers stiff and open into the pocket, and then quickly closing them and extracting any article.

FORKS, or GRAPPLING IRONS, fingers.

FORTY GUTS, vulgar term for a fat man.

FOUR AND NINE, or FOUR AND NINEPENNY GOSS, a cheap hat, so called from 4s. 9d., the price at which a noted advertising hat maker sold his hats—

> "Whene'er to slumber you incline,
> Take a *short* NAP at 4 and 9."—1844.

FOU, slightly intoxicated.—*Scotch.*

FOURTH, or FOURTH COURT, the court appropriated to the

water-closets at Cambridge; from its really being No. 4 at Trinity College. A man leaving his room to go to this FOURTH COURT, writes on his door "*gone to the* FOURTH," or, in algebraic notation, "GONE 4"—the Cambridge slang phrase.

FOX, to cheat or rob.—*Eton College.*

FOXING, watching in the streets for any occurrence which may be turned to a profitable account.—*See* MOOCHING.

FOXING, to pretend to be asleep like a fox, which is said to take its rest with one eye open.

FOXY, rank, tainted.—*Lincolnshire.*

FREE, to steal—generally applied to horses.

FREE AND EASY, a club held at most public houses, the members of which meet in the taproom or parlour for the purpose of drinking, smoking, and hearing each other sing and "talk politics." The name indicates the character of the proceedings.

FREEMAN'S QUAY, "drinking at FREEMAN'S QUAY," *i.e.*, at another's cost. This quay was formerly a celebrated wharf near London Bridge, and the saying arose from the beer which was given gratis to porters and carmen who went there on business.

FRENCH CREAM, brandy.

FRENCH LEAVE, to leave or depart slyly, without saying anything.

FRESH, said of a person slightly intoxicated.

FRISK, to search; FRISKED, searched by a constable or other officer.

FRISK A CLY, to empty a pocket.

FRIZZLE, champagne.

FROG, a policeman.

FRONTISPIECE, the face.

FROW, a girl, or wife. *German*, FRAU; *Dutch*, VROUW.

FRUMMAGEMMED, annihilated, strangled, garotted, or spoilt. —*Old cant.*

FRUMP, a slatternly woman, a gossip.—*Ancient.*

FRUMP, to mock, or insult.—*Beaumont and Fletcher.*

FUDGE, nonsense, stupidity. *Todd and Richardson* only trace the word to *Goldsmith*. *Disraeli*, however, gives the origin to a Captain Fudge, a great fibber, who told monstrous stories, which made his crew say in answer to any improbability, "you FUDGE it!"—*See Remarks on the Navy*, 1700.

FULLAMS, false dice, which always turn up high.—*Shakes.*

FULLY, "to be FULLIED," to be committed for trial. From the slang of the penny-a-liner, "the prisoner was *fully* committed for trial."

FUNK, to smoke out.—*North.*

FUNK, trepidation, nervousness, cowardice. To FUNK, to afraid, or nervous.

FUNNY-BONE, the extremity of the elbow—or rather, the muscle which passes round it between the two bones, a blow on which causes painful tingling in the fingers. Facetiously derived, from its being the extremity of the *humerus* (humorous).

FYE-BUCK, a sixpence. *Nearly obsolete.*

GAB, GABBER, or GABBLE, talk; "gift of the GAB," loquacity, or natural talent for speech-making.—*Anglo Norman.*

GAD, a trapesing, slatternly woman.—*Gipsey. Anglo Saxon,* GADELYNG.

GADDING THE HOOF, going without shoes. GADDING, roaming about, although used in an old translation of the Bible, is now only heard amongst the lower orders.

GAFF, a fair, or penny-playhouse.—*See* PENNY GAFF.

GAFFING, tossing halfpence, or counters.—*North,* where it means tossing up three pennies.

GALENY, old cant term for a fowl of any kind; now a respectable word in the West of England, signifying a Guinea fowl.—*Vide Grose. Latin,* GALLINA.

GALLAVANT, to wait upon the ladies.—*Old.*

GALORE, abundance. *Irish,* GO LEOR, in plenty.

GALLOWS, very, or exceedingly - a disgusting exclamation; "GALLOWS poor," very poor.

GAME, a term variously applied; "are you GAME?" have you courage enough? "what's your little GAME?" what are you going to do? "come, none of your GAMES," be quiet, don't annoy me; "on the GAME," out thieving.

GAMMON, to hoax, to deceive merrily, to laugh at a person, to tell an untrue but plausible story, to make game of, or in the provincial dialect, to make GAME ON; "who's thou makin' thy GAM' ON?" *i. e.,* who are you making a fool of? —*Yorkshire.*

GAMMON, deceit, humbug, a false and ridiculous story. *Anglo Saxon*, GAMEN, game, sport.

GAMMY, bad, unfavourable, poor tempered. Those householders who are known enemies to the street folk and tramps, are pronounced by them to be GAMMY. GAMMY sometimes means forged, as "GAMMY-MONEKER," a forged signature; GAMMY STUFF, spurious medicine; GAMMY LOWR, counterfeit coin. *Hants*, GAMY, dirty. The hieroglyphic used by beggars and cadgers to intimate to those of the tribe coming after that things are not very favourable, is known as ☐, or GAMMY.

GAMMY-VIAL (Ville), a town where the police will not let persons hawk.

GANDER MONTH, the period when the monthly nurse is in the ascendant, and the husband has to shift for himself.

GAR, euphuistic corruption of the title of the Deity; "be GAR, you don't say so!"—*Franco-English.*

GARRET, the head.

GARRET, the fob pocket.

GARGLE, medical student Slang for physic.

GAS, "to give a person GAS," to scold him or give him a good beating. Synonymous with "to give him JESSIE."

GASSY, liable to "flare up" at any offence.

GATTER, beer; "shant of GATTER," a pot of beer. A curious street melody, brimful and running over with slang, known in Seven Dials as *Bet, the Coaley's Daughter*, thus mentions the word in a favourite verse:—

> "But when I strove my flame to tell
> Says she, '*Come, stow that patter*,'
> If you're a *cove* wot likes a gal
> Vy don't you *stand* some GATTER?
> *In course* I instantly complied—
> Two brimming quarts of porter,
> With four *goes* of gin beside,
> Drained Bet the Coaley's daughter."

GAWFS, cheap red-skinned apples, a favourite fruit with costermongers, who rub them well with a piece of cloth, and find ready purchasers.

GAWKY, a lanky, or awkward person; a fool. *Saxon*, GEAC; *Scotch*, GOWK.

GAY, loose, dissipated; "GAY woman," a kept mistress, or prostitute.

GEE, to agree with, or be congenial to a person.

GEN, a shilling. Also, GENT, silver. Abbreviation of the *French*, ARGENT.

GENT, a contraction of "gentleman,"—in more senses than one. A dressy, showy, foppish man, with a little mind, who vulgarises the prevailing fashion.

GENT, silver. From the *French*, ARGENT.

GET-UP, a person's appearance, or general arrangements. Probably derived from the decorations of a play.

> "There's so much GETTING UP to please the town,
> It takes a precious deal of coming down."
> *Planché's Mr. Buckstone's Ascent of Parnassus.*

GHOST, "the GHOST does'nt walk," *i e.*, the manager is too poor to pay salaries as yet.—*Theat.*; *Ho. Words, No.* 183.

GIB-FACE, properly the lower lip of a horse; "TO HANG ONE'S GIB," to pout the lower lip, be angry or sullen.

GIBBERISH, unmeaning jargon; the language of the Gipseys, synonymous with SLANG, another *Gipsey* word. Somner says, "*French*, GABBER; *Dutch*, GABBEREN; and our own GAB, GABBER; hence also, I take it, our GIBBERISH, a kind of canting language used by a sort of rogues we vulgarly call Gipseys, a *gibble gabble* understood only among themselves." —*Gipsey*. *See Introduction.*

GIFFLE GAFFLE, nonsense.—*See* CHAFF. *Icelandic*, GAFLA.

GIFT, any article which has been stolen and afterwards sold at a low price.

GIG, a farthing. Formerly, GRIG.

GIG, fun, frolic, a spree.

> "In search of *lark*, or some delicious GIG,
> The mind delights on, when 'tis in *prime twig*."
> *Randall's Diary*, 1820.

GIGLAMPS, spectacles. In my first edition I stated this to be a *University* term. Mr. CUTHBERT BEDE, however, in a communication to *Notes and Queries*, of which I have availed myself in the present edition, says—"If the compiler has taken this epithet from *Verdant Green*, I can only say that I consider the word not to be a 'University' word in general, but as only due to the inventive genius of Mr. Bouncer in particular." The term, however, has been adopted, and is now in general use.

GILL, a homely woman; "Jack and GILL," &c.—*Ben Jonson.*

GILLS, the lower part of the face.—*Bacon.* "To grease one's GILLS," "to have a good feed," or make a hearty meal.

GILLS, shirt collars.

GILT, money. *German*, GELD; *Dutch*, GELT.

GIMCRACK, a bijou, a slim piece of mechanism. *Old slang* for "a spruce wench."—*N. Bailey*.

GIN AND GOSPEL GAZETTE, the *Morning Advertiser*, so called from its being the organ of the dissenting party, and of the Licensed Victuallers' Association. Sometimes termed the TAP TUB, or the 'TIZER.

GINGER, a showy, fast horse—as if he had been FIGGED with GINGER under his tail.

GINGERLY, to do anything with great care.—*Cotgrave*.

GINGER HACKLED, having flaxen light yellow hair.—*See* HACKLE.

GINGUMBOB, a bauble.

GIVE, to strike or scold; "I'll GIVE it to you," I will thrash you. Formerly, *to rob*.

GLASGOW MAGISTRATES, salt herrings.—*Scotch*.

GLAZE, glass—generally applied to windows.

GLIM, a light, a lamp; "dowse the GLIM," put the candle out. —*Sea, and old cant*.

GLIM LURK, a begging paper, giving a certified account of a dreadful fire—which never happened.

GLOAK, a man.—*Scotch*.

GLUMP, to sulk.

GLUMPISH, of a stubborn, sulky temper.

GNOSTICS, knowing ones, or sharpers. *Nearly obsolete in this vulgar sense*.

GO, a GO of gin a quartern of that liquor; GO is also synonymous with circumstance or occurrence; "a rummy GO," and "a great GO," signify curious and remarkable occurrences; "no GO," no good; "here's a pretty GO!" here's a trouble! "to GO the jump," to enter a house by the window; "all the GO," in fashion.—*See* LITTLE GO.

> "Gemmen (says he), you all well know
> The joy there is whene'er we meet;
> It's what I call the prinest GO,
> And rightly named, 'tis—'quite a treat.'"
>
> *Jack Randall's Diary*, 1820

GO-ALONG, a thief.—*Household Words*, No. 183.

GOB, the mouth; mucus, or saliva.—*North*. Sometimes used for GAB, talk—

> "There was a man called *Job*,
> Dwelt in the land of Uz;
> He had a good gift of the GOB;
> The same case happen us."
>
> ZACH. BOYD.

GOB, a portion.

GODS, the people in the upper gallery of a theatre; "up amongst the GODS," a seat amongst the low persons in the gallery—so named from the high position of the gallery, and the blue sky generally painted on the ceiling of the theatre; termed by the *French*, PARADIS.

GODS, the quadrats used by printers in throwing on the imposing stone, similar to the movement in casting dice.—*Printers' term*.

GO IT, a term of encouragement, implying "keep it up!" Sometimes amplified to GO IT, YE CRIPPLES; said to have been a facetious rendering of the last line of *Virgil's Eclogues*—

"Ite domum Saturæ, Venit Hesperus, *ite capellæ*;"

or, "GO IT, YE CRIPPLES, CRUTCHES ARE CHEAP."

GOLDFINCH, a sovereign.

GOLGOTHA, a hat, "place of a skull."

GOLOPSHUS, splendid, delicious, luscious.—*Norwich*.

GOOSE, to ruin, or spoil. Also, to hiss a play.—*Theatrical*.

GOOSE, a tailor's pressing iron.—Originally a slang term, but now in most dictionaries.

GOOSEBERRY, to "play up old GOOSEBERRY" with any one, to defeat or silence a person in a quick or summary manner.

GOOSECAP, a booby, or noodle.—*Devonshire*.

GOOSER, a settler, or finishing blow.

GORMED, a Norfolk corruption of a profane oath. So used by Mr. Peggotty, one of Dickens' characters.

GORGER, a swell, a well dressed, or *gorgeous* man—probably derived from that word.

GOSPEL GRINDER, a city missionary, or tract distributor.

GOSS, a hat—from the gossamer silk with which modern hats are made.

GONNOF, or GUN, a fool, a bungler, an amateur pickpocket. A correspondent thinks this may be a corruption of *gone off*, on the analogy of GO-ALONG; but the term is really as old as *Chaucer's* time. During Kett's rebellion in Norfolk, in the reign of Edward VI., a song was sung by the insurgents in which the term occurs—

"The country GNOFFES, Hob, Dick, and Hick,
With clubbes and clouted shoon,
Shall fill up Dussyn dale
With slaughtered bodies soone."

GOUROCK HAM, salt herrings. Gourock, on the Clyde, about

twenty-five miles from Glasgow, was formerly a great fishing village.—*Scotch.*

GOVERNMENT SIGNPOST, the gallows.

GOVERNOR, a father, a master or superior person, an elder; "which way, GUV'NER, to Cheapside?"

GRABB, to clutch, or seize.

GRABBED, caught, apprehended.

GRABBERS, the hands.

GRACE-CARD, the ace of hearts.

GRAFT, to work; "where are you GRAFTING?" *i.e.*, where do you live, or work?

GRANNY, to know, or recognise; "de ye GRANNY the bloke?" do you know the man?

GRANNY, importance, knowledge, pride; "take the GRANNY off them as has white hands," viz., remove their self-conceit. —*Mayhew*, vol. i., p. 364.

GRAPPLING IRONS, fingers.—*Sea.*

GRASS, "gone to GRASS," dead,—a coarse allusion to *burial;* absconded, or disappeared suddenly; "oh, go to GRASS," a common answer to a troublesome or inquisitive person,—possibly a corruption of "go to GRACE," meaning, of course, a directly opposite fate.

GRASS-WIDOW, an unmarried mother; a deserted mistress. In the United States, during the gold fever in California, it was common for an adventurer to put both his GRASS-WIDOW and his children to *school* during his absence.

GRAVEL, to confound, to bother; "I'm GRAVELLED," *i.e.*, perplexed or confused.—*Old.*

GRAVEL-RASH, a scratched face,—telling its tale of a drunken fall.

GRAY-COAT-PARSON, a lay impropriator, or lessee of great tithes.

GRAYS, or SCOTCH GRAYS, lice.—*Scotch.*

GRAYS, halfpennies, with either two "heads" or two "tails,"—both sides alike. *Low gamblers* use GRAYS, and they cost from 2d. to 6d. each.

GREASE-SPOT, a minute remnant, the only distinguishable remains of an antagonist after a terrific contest.

GREASING a man is bribing; SOAPING is flattering him.

GREEKS, the low Irish. ST. GILES' GREEK, slang or cant language. *Cotgrave* gives MERIE GREEK as a definition for a roystering fellow, a drunkard.—*Shakespere.*—*See* MEDICAL GREEK.

GREEN, ignorant, not wide awake, inexperienced.—*Shakespere.* "Do you see any GREEN in my eye?" ironical question in a dispute.

GREEN-HORN, a fresh, simple, or uninitiated person.

GRIDDLER, a person who sings in the streets without a printed copy of the words.

GRIEF, "to come to GRIEF," to meet with an accident, be ruined.

GRIFFIN, in India, a newly arrived cadet; general for an inexperienced youngster. "Fast" young men in London frequently term an umbrella a GRIFFIN.

GRIND, "to take a GRIND," *i.e.*, a walk, or constitutional.—*University.*

GRIND, to work up for an examination, to cram with a GRINDER, or private tutor.—*Medical.*

GRINDERS, teeth.

GROGGY, tipsy; when a prize-fighter becomes "weak on his pins," and nearly beaten, he is said to be GROGGY.—*Pugilistic.* The same term is applied to horses in a similar condition. *Old English,* AGGROGGYD, weighed down, oppressed.—*Prompt. Parvulorum.*

GRUB, meat, or food, of any kind,—GRUB signifying food, and BUB, drink.

GRUBBING-KEN, or SPINIKIN, a workhouse; a cook-shop.

GRUBBY, musty, or old-fashioned.—*Devonshire.*

GULFED, a University term, denoting that a man is unable to enter for the classical examination, from having failed in the mathematical. Candidates for classical honours were compelled to go in for both examinations. From the alteration of the arrangements the term is now obsolete.—*Camb.*

GULPIN, a weak, credulous fellow.

GUMMY, thick, fat—generally applied to a woman's ancles, or to a man whose flabby person betokens him a drunkard.

GUMPTION, or RUMGUMPTION, comprehension, capacity. From GAUM, to comprehend; "I canna GAUGE it, and I canna GAUM it," as a Yorkshire exciseman said of a hedgehog.

GURRELL, a fob.

GUTTER BLOOD, a low or vulgar man—*Scotch.*

GUTTER LANE, the throat.

GUY, a fright, a dowdy, an ill-dressed person. Derived from the effigy of Guy Fawkes carried about by boys on Nov. 5.

GYP, an undergraduate's valet at *Cambridge.* Corruption of GYPSEY JOE (*Saturday Review*); popularly derived by Cantabs from the *Greek,* GYPS (γύψ), a vulture, from their dishonest rapacity. At *Oxford* they are called SCOUTS.

HACKLE, "to show HACKLE," to be willing to fight. HACKLES are the long feathers on the back of a cock's neck, which he erects when angry,—hence the metaphor.

HADDOCK, a purse.—*See* BEANS.

HALF A BEAN, half a sovereign.

HALF A BULL, two shillings and sixpence.

HALF A COUTER, half a sovereign.

HALF A HOG, sixpence; sometimes termed HALF A GRUNTER.

HALF A STRETCH, six months in prison.

HALF A TUSHEROON, half a crown.

HALF AND HALF, a mixture of ale and porter, much affected by medical students; occasionally *Latinized* into DIMIDIUM DIMIDIUMQUE.—*See* COOPER.

HALF BAKED, soft, doughy, half-witted, silly.

HALF FOOLISH, ridiculous; means often *wholly* foolish.

HALF JACK.—*See* JACKS.

HALF ROCKED, silly, half-witted.—Compare HALF BAKED.

HALF SEAS OVER, reeling drunk.—*Sea.* Used by *Swift.*

HAND, a workman, or helper, a person. "A cool HAND," explained by Sir Thomas Overbury to be "one who accounts bashfulness the wickedest thing in the world, and therefore studies impudence."

HANDER, a second, or assistant, in a prize fight.

HANDLE, a nose; the title appended to a person's name; also a term in boxing, "HANDLING one's fists."

HAND-SAW, or CHIVE FENCER, a man who sells razors and knives in the streets.

HANDSELLER, or CHEAP JACK, a street or open air seller, a man who carries goods to his customers, instead of waiting for his customers to visit him,

HANG OUT, to reside,—in allusion to the ancient custom of *hanging out* signs.

HANGMAN'S WAGES, thirteenpence halfpenny.

HANSEL, or HANDSALE, the *lucky money*, or first money taken in the morning by a pedlar.—*Cocker's Dictionary*, 1724. "Legs of mutton (street term for sheep's trotters, or feet) two for a penny; who'll give me a HANSEL? who'll give me a HANSEL?"—*Cry at Cloth Fair at the present day.* Hence, earnest money, first fruits, &c. In Norfolk, HANSELLING a thing, is using it for the first time, as wearing a new coat, taking seizin of it, as it were.—*Anglo Saxon. N. Bailey.*

HA'PURTH OF LIVELINESS, the music at a low concert, or theatre.

HARD LINES, hardship, difficulty.—*Soldiers' term* for hard duty on the *lines* in front of the enemy.

HARD UP, in distress, poverty stricken.—*Sea.*

HARD-UPS, cigar-end finders, who collect the refuse pieces of smoked cigars from the gutter, and having dried them, sell them as tobacco to the very poor.

HARRY, or OLD HARRY (*i.e. Old Hairy?*) the Devil; "to play OLD HARRY with one," *i.e.*, ruin or annoy him.

HARRY-SOPH (ἐρίσοφος, very wise indeed), an undergraduate in his last year of residence.—*Cambridge.*

HASH, a mess, confusion; "a pretty HASH he made of it;" to HASH UP, to jumble together without order or regularity.

HATCHET, "to throw the HATCHET," to tell lies.

HAWSE-HOLES, the apertures in a ship's bows through which the cables pass; "he has crept in through the HAWSE-HOLES," said of an officer who has risen from the grade of an ordinary seaman.—*Navy.*

HAY BAG, a woman.

HAZY, intoxicated.—*Household Words*, No. 183.

HEAD OR TAIL, "I can't make HEAD OR TAIL of it," *i.e.*, cannot make it out.

HEAP, "a HEAP of people," a crowd; "struck all of a HEAP," suddenly astonished.

HEAVY WET, porter or beer,—because the more a man drinks of it, the heavier he becomes.

HEDGE, to secure a doubtful bet by making others.—*Turf.*

HEEL-TAPS, small quantities of wine or other beverage left in the bottom of glasses, considered as a sign that the liquor is not liked, and therefore unfriendly and unsocial to the host and the company.

HEIGH HO! a cant term for stolen yarn, from the expression used to apprize the dishonest manufacturer that the speaker has stolen yarn to sell.—*Norwich cant.*

HELL, a fashionable gambling house. In printing offices, the term is generally applied to the old tin box in which is thrown the broken or spoilt type, purchased by the founders for re-casting. *Nearly obsolete.*

HEN AND CHICKENS, large and small pewter pots.

HEN-PECKED, said of one whose wife "wears the breeches."

HERRING POND, the sea; "to be sent across the HERRING POND," to be transported.

HIDING, a thrashing. *Webster* gives this word, but not its root, HIDE, to beat, flay by whipping.

HIGGLEDY-PIGGLEDY, all together,—as hogs and pigs lie.

HIGH AND DRY, an epithet applied to the *soi disant* "orthodox" clergy of the last century, for whom, while ill-paid curates did the work, the *comforts* of the establishment were its greatest charms.

> "Wherein are various ranks, and due degrees,
> The Bench for honour, and the Stall for ease."

Though often confounded with, they are utterly dissimilar to, the modern High Church or Anglo-Catholic party. Their equally uninteresting opponents deserved the corresponding appellation of LOW AND SLOW; while the so-called "Broad Church" is defined with equal felicity as the BROAD AND SHALLOW.

HIGH FLY, "ON THE HIGH FLY," on the begging or cadging system.

HIGH JINKS, "ON THE HIGH JINKS," taking up an arrogant position, assuming an undue superiority.

HIGH-FLYER, a genteel beggar, or swindler.

HIGH FLYERS, large swings, in frames, at fairs and races.

HIGH-LOWS, laced boots reaching a trifle higher than ancle-jacks.

HIGHFALUTEN, showy, affected, tinselled, affecting certain pompous or fashionable airs, stuck up; "come, none of yer HIGHFALUTEN games," *i.e.*, you must not show off or imitate the swell here.—*American* slang from the *Dutch*, VERLOOTEN.

HIP INSIDE, inside coat pocket.

HIP OUTSIDE, outside coat pocket.

HIVITE, a student of St. Begh's College, Cumberland; pronounced ST. BEE'S.—*University*

HOAX, to deceive, or ridicule,—*Grose* says was originally a *University* cant word. Corruption of HOCUS, to cheat.

HOCKS, the feet; CURBY HOCKS, round or clumsy feet.

HOCUS, to drug a person, and then rob him. The HOCUS generally consists of snuff and beer.

HOCUS POCUS, Gipsey words of magic, similar to the modern "presto fly." The Gipseys pronounce "*Habeas Corpus*," HAWCUS PACCUS (*see Crabb's Gipsey's Advocate*, p. 18); can this have anything to do with the origin of HOCUS POCUS? *Turner* gives OCHUS BOCHUS, an old demon. Pegge, however, states that it is a burlesque rendering of the words of the unreformed church service at the delivery of the host, HOC EST CORPUS, which the early Protestants considered as a species of conjuring, and ridiculed accordingly.

HODGE, a countryman or provincial clown. I don't know that it has been elsewhere remarked, but most country districts in England have one or more families of the name of HODGE; indeed, GILES and HODGE appear to be the favourite hobnail nomenclature. Not in any way writing disrespectfully, was the slang word taken from Hog—with the *g* soft, which gives the *dg* pronunciation? In old canting dictionaries HODGE stands for a country clown; so, indeed, does ROGER, another favourite provincial name. — *Vide Bacchus and Venus.*

HOG, "to go the whole HOG," to do anything with a person's entire strength, not "by halves;" realised by the phrase "in for a penny in for a pound." *Bartlett* claims this to be a pure *American* phrase; whilst *Ker*, of course, gives it a *Dutch* origin.—*Old.*

HOG, a shilling.—*Old cant.*

HOISTING, shoplifting.

HOLLOW, "to beat HOLLOW," to excel.

HOLY LAND, Seven Dials,—where the St. Giles' Greek is spoken.

HOOK, to steal or rob.—*See the following.*

HOOK OR BY CROOK, by fair means or foul—in allusion to the hook which footpads used to carry to steal from open windows, &c., and from which HOOK, to take or steal, has been derived. Mentioned in *Hudibras* as a cant term.

HOOK IT, "get out of the way," or "be off about your business;" "TO HOOK IT," to run away, to decamp; "on one's own HOOK," dependant upon one's own exertions.—*See the preceding for derivation.*

HOOKS, "dropped off the HOOKS," said of a deceased person—derived from the ancient practice of suspending on hooks the quarters of a traitor or felon sentenced by the old law to be hung, drawn, and quartered, and which dropped off the hooks as they decayed.

HOOKEY WALKER! ejaculation of incredulity, usually shortened to WALKER!—which see. A correspondent thinks HOOKEY WALKER may have been a certain *Hugh K. Walker.*

HOOK-UM SNIVEY (formerly "hook *and* snivey"), a low expression meaning to cheat by feigning sickness or other means. Also a piece of thick iron wire crooked at one end, and fastened into a wooden handle, for the purpose of undoing from the outside the wooden bolt of a door.

HOP, a dance.—*Fashionable slang.*

HOP THE TWIG, to run away, or BOLT, which see.—*Old.*

HOP-MERCHANT, a dancing-master.

HOPPING GILES, a cripple. St. Ægidius or Giles, himself similarly afflicted, was their patron saint. The ancient lazar houses were dedicated to him.

HORRID HORN, term of reproach amongst the street Irish, meaning a fool, or half-witted fellow. From the *Erse* OMADHAUN, a brainless fellow. A correspondent suggests HERRIDAN, a miserable old woman.

HORRORS, the low spirits, or "blue devils," which follow intoxication.

HORSE, contraction of Horsemonger-lane Gaol.

HORSE CHAUNTER, a dealer who takes worthless horses to country fairs and disposes of them by artifice. He is flexible in his ethics, and will put in a glass-eye, or perform other tricks.—*See* COPER.

HORSE NAILS, money.—*Compare* BRADS.

HORSE'S NIGHTCAP, a halter; "to die in a HORSE'S NIGHTCAP," to be hung.

HORSE MARINE, an awkward person. In ancient times the "JOLLIES" or Royal Marines, were the butts of the sailors, from their ignorance of seamanship. "Tell that to the MARINES, the blue jackets won't believe it!" was a common rejoinder to a "stiff yarn." Now-a-days they are deservedly appreciated as the finest regiment in the service. A HORSE MARINE (an impossibility) was used to denote one more awkward still.

HOT COPPERS, the feverish sensations experienced next morning by those who have been drunk over night.

HOT TIGER, an Oxford mixture of hot-spiced ale and sherry.

HOUSE OF COMMONS, a water-closet.

HOXTER, an inside pocket.—*Old English*, OXTER.

HUEY, a town or village.

HUFF, to vex, or offend; a poor temper.

HUFF, a dodge or trick; "don't try that HUFF on me," or "that HUFF won't do."—*Norwich*.

HULK, to hang about in hopes of an invitation.—*See* MOOCH.

HULKY, extra sized.—*Shropshire*.

HUM AND HAW, to hesitate, raise objections.—*Old English*.

HUMBLE PIE, to "eat HUMBLE PIE," to knock under, be submissive. The UMBLES, or entrails of a deer, were anciently made into a dish for servants, while their masters feasted off the haunch.

HUMBUG, an imposition, or a person who imposes upon others. A very expressive but slang word, synonymous at one time with HUM AND HAW. Lexicographers have fought shy at adopting this word. Richardson uses it frequently to express the meaning of other words, but omits it in the alphabetical arrangement as unworthy of recognition! In the first edition of this work, 1785 was given as the earliest date at which the word could be found in a printed book. Since then I have traced HUMBUG half a century farther back, on the title-page of a singular old jest-book—"*The Universal Jester;* or a pocket companion for the Wits: being a choice collection of merry conceits, facetious drolleries, &c., clenchers, closers, closures, bon-mots, and HUMBUGS," by *Ferdinando Killigrew*. London, about 1735-40.

I have also ascertained that the famous Orator Henley was known to the mob as ORATOR HUMBUG. The fact may be learnt from an illustration in that exceedingly curious little collection of *Caricatures*, published in 1757, many of which were sketched by Lord Bolingbroke—Horace Walpole filling in the names and explanations. *Halliwell* describes HUMBUG as "a person who hums," and cites Dean Milles' MS., which was written about 1760. It has been stated that the word is a corruption of Hamburgh, from which town so many false bulletins and reports came during the war in the last century. "Oh, that is *Hamburgh* [or HUMBUG]," was the answer to any fresh piece of news which smacked of improbability. *Grose* mentions it in his Dictionary, 1785; and in a little printed squib, published in 1808, entitled *Bath Characters*, by *T. Goosequill*, HUMBUG is thus mentioned in a comical couplet on the title page:—

> "Wee Thre Bath Deities bee,
> HUMBUG, Follie, and Varietee."

Gradually from this time the word began to assume a place in periodical literature, and in novels not written by squeamish or over-precise authors. In the preface to a flat, and, I fear, unprofitable poem, entitled, *The Reign of* HUMBUG, *a Satire*, 8vo., 1836, the author thus apologises for the use of the word—"I have used the term HUMBUG to designate this principle [wretched sophistry of life generally], considering that it is now adopted into our language as much as the words *dunce, jockey, cheat, swindler*, &c., which were formerly only colloquial terms." A correspondent, who in a late number of *Adersaria* ingeniously traced *bombast* to the inflated Doctor Paracelsus Bombast, considers that HUMBUG may, in like manner, be derived from *Homberg*, the distinguished chemist of the court of the Duke of Orleans, who, according to the following passage from Bishop Berkeley's "Siris," was an ardent and successful seeker after the philosopher's stone!

> "§ 194.—Of this there cannot be a better proof than the experiment of Monsieur Homberg, WHO MADE GOLD OF MERCURY BY INTRODUCING LIGHT INTO ITS PORES, but at such trouble and expense, that, I suppose, nobody will try the experiment for profit. By this injunction of light and mercury, both bodies became fixed, and produced a third different to either, to wit, real gold. For the truth of which FACT I refer to the memoirs of the French Academy of Sciences."—*Berkeley's Works*, vol. ii., p. 366, (Wright's edition).

The universal use of this term is remarkable; in California there is a town called *Humbug Flat*—a name which gives a significant hint of the acuteness of the first settler.

HUM-DRUM, tedious, tiresome, boring; "a society of gentlemen who used to meet near the Charter House, or at the King's Head, St. John's-street. They were characterised by less mystery and more pleasantry than the Freemasons."—*Bacchus and Venus*, 1737. In the *West* a low cart.

HUMP, to botch, or spoil.

HUMP UP, "to have one's HUMP UP," to be cross or ill-tempered—like a cat with its back set up.—*See* MONKEY.

HUMPTY DUMPTY, short and thick.

HUNCH, to shove, or jostle.

HUNTER PITCHING, cockshies, or three throws a penny.—*See* COCKSHY.

HUNTING THE SQUIRREL, when hackney and stage coachmen try to upset each other's vehicles on the public roads. *Nearly obsolete.*

HURDY-GURDY, a droning musical instrument shaped like a large fiddle, and turned by a crank, used by Savoyards and itinerant foreign musicians in England, now nearly superseded by the hand-organ. A correspondent suggests that the name is derived from being *girded* on the HARDIES, loins or buttocks.—*Scotch ; Tam o'Shanter.* In *Italy* the instrument is called VIOLA.

HUSH-MONEY, a sum given to quash a prosecution or evidence.

HUSH-SHOP, or CRIB, a shop where beer or spirits is sold "on the quiet"—no licence being paid.

HYPS, or HYPO, the blue devils. *From Hypochondriasis.*—SWIFT.

IN, "to be IN with a person," to be even with, or UP to him.

IN FOR IT, in trouble or difficulty of any kind.

IN FOR PATTER, waiting for trial.

INEXPRESSIBLES, UNUTTERABLES, UNWHISPERABLES, or SIT-UPONS, trousers, the nether garments.

INNINGS, earnings, money coming in; "he's had long INNINGS," *i.e.*, a good run of luck, plenty of cash flowing in.

INSIDE LINING, dinner, &c.

INTERESTING, "to be in an INTERESTING situation," applied to females when *enceinte.*

INTO, "hold my hat, Jim, I'll be INTO him," *i.e.*, I will fight him. In this sense equivalent to PITCH INTO or SLIP INTO.

INVITE, an invitation—a corruption used by stuck-up people of mushroom origin.

IPSAL DIXAL, Cockney corruption of *ipse dixit*—said of one's simple uncorroborated assertion.

IT'S GOOD ON THE STAR, it's easy to open.

IVORIES, teeth; "a box" or "cage of IVORIES," a set of teeth, the mouth; "wash your IVORIES," *i.e.*, "drink." The word is also used to denote DICE.

JABBER, to talk, or chatter. A cant word in *Swift's* time.

JACK, a low prostitute.

JACK KETCH, the public hangman.—*See* KETCH.

JACK SPRAT, a diminutive boy or man.

JACK TAR, a sailor.

JACK-AT-A PINCH, one whose assistance is only sought on an emergency; JACK-IN-THE-WATER, an attendant at the watermen's stairs on the river and sea-port towns, who does not mind wetting his feet for a customer's convenience, in consideration of a douceur.

JACKS, HALF JACKS, card counters, resembling in size and appearance sovereigns and half-sovereigns, for which they are occasionally passed to simple persons. In large gambling establishments the "heaps of gold" are frequently composed mainly of JACKS.

JACKETING, a thrashing.

JACKEY, gin.

JACOB, a ladder. *Grose* says from Jacob's dream.—*Old cant.*

JAGGER, a gentleman.—*German*, JAGER, a sportsman.

JAIL-BIRD, a prisoner, one who has been in jail.

JAMES, a sovereign, or twenty shillings.

JANNOCK, sociable, fair dealing.—*Norfolk.*

JAPAN, to ordain.—*University.*

JARK, a seal, or watch ornament.—*Ancient cant.*

JARVEY, the driver of a hackney coach; JARVEY'S UPPER BENJAMIN, a coachman's over-coat.

JAW, speech, or talk; "hold your JAW," don't speak any more; "what are you JAWING about?" *i.e.*, what are you making a noise about?

JAW-BREAKERS, hard or many-syllabled words.

JAZEY, a wig. A corruption of JERSEY, the name for flax prepared in a peculiar manner, and of which common wigs were formerly made.

JEAMES, (a generic for "flunkies.") the *Morning Post* newspaper—the organ of Belgravia and the "Haristocracy."

JEHU, old slang term for a coachman, or one fond of driving.

JEMMY, a crowbar.

JEMMY, a sheep's head.—*See* SANGUINARY JAMES.

JEMMY JESSAMY, a dandy.

JERRY, a beer house.

JERRY, a chamber utensil, abbreviation of JEROBOAM.—*Swift.* JERRY-COME-TUMBLE, a water-closet.

JERRY, a fog.

JERUSALEM-PONY, a donkey.

JESSIE, "to give a person JESSIE," to beat him soundly.—*See* GAS.

JEW'S EYE, a popular simile for anything valuable. Probably a corruption of the *Italian,* GIOJE; *French,* JOUAILLE, a jewel. In ancient times, when a king was short of cash, he generally issued orders for so many *Jew's eyes,* or equivalent sums of money. The Jews preferred paying the ransom, although often very heavy. We thus realise the popularly believed origin of JEW'S EYE. Used by *Shakespere.*

JEW-FENCER, a Jew street salesman.

JIB, the face, or a person's expression; "the cut of his JIB," *i.e.* his peculiar appearance. The sail of a ship, which in position and shape corresponds to the nose on a person's face.—*See* GIB.—*Sea.*

JIB, or JIBBER, a horse that starts or shrinks. *Shakespere* uses it in the sense of a worn out horse.

JIBB, the tongue.—*Gipsey and Hindoo.*

JIFFY, "in a JIFFY," in a moment.

JIGGER, a secret still, illicit spirits.—*Scotch.*

JIGGER, "I'm JIGGERED if you will," a common form of mild swearing.—*See* SNIGGER.

JIGGER, a door; "dub the JIGGER," shut the door. *Ancient cant,* GYGER. In billiards the *bridge* on the table is often termed the JIGGER.

JIGGER-DUBBERS, term applied to jailors or turnkeys.

JILT, a crowbar or housebreaking implement.

JINGO, "by JINGO," a common form of oath, said to be a corruption of St. *Gingoulph.*—*Vide Halliwell.*

JOB, a short piece of work, a prospect of employment. *Johnson* describes JOB as a low word, without etymology. It is, and was, however, a cant word, and a JOB, two centuries ago, was an arranged robbery. Even at the present day it is mainly confined to the streets, in the sense of employment for a short time. Amongst undertakers a JOB signifies a funeral; "to do a JOB," conduct any one's funeral; "by the JOB," *i.e., piece*-work, as opposed to *time*-work. A JOB in political phraseology is a Government office or contract, obtained by secret influence or favouritism.

To JOE BLAKE THE BARTLEMY, to visit a low woman.

JOEY, a fourpenny piece. The term is derived (like BOBBY from

Sir Robert Peel) from Joseph Hume, the late respected M.P. The explanation is thus given in *Hawkins' History of the Silver Coinage of England.*

> "These pieces are said to have owed their existence to the pressing instance of Mr. Hume, from whence they, for some time, bore the nickname of JOEYS. As they were very convenient to pay short cab fares, the Hon. M.P. was extremely unpopular with the drivers, who frequently received only *a groat* where otherwise they would have received a sixpence without any demand for change." The term originated with the London cabmen, who have invented many others.

JOG-TROT, a slow but regular trot, or pace.

JOGUL, to play up, at cards or other game. *Spanish*, JUGAR.

JOHN THOMAS, a generic for "flunkies,"—footmen popularly represented with large calves and bushy whiskers.

JOLLY, a word of praise, or favourable notice; "chuck Harry a JOLLY, Bill!" *i.e.*, go and praise up his goods, or buy of him, and speak well of the article, that the crowd standing around his stall may think it a good opportunity to lay out their money. "Chuck a JOLLY," literally translated, is to throw a shout or a good word.

JOLLY, a Royal Marine.—*See* HORSE MARINE.

JOMER, a sweetheart, or favourite girl.—*See* BLOWER.

JORDAN, a chamber utensil.—*Saxon.*

JOSKIN, a countryman.

JUG, a prison, or jail.

JUMP, to seize, or rob; "to JUMP a man," to pounce upon him, and either rob or maltreat him; "to JUMP a house," to rob it.—*See* GO.

JUNIPER, gin.—*Household Words*, No. 183.

JUNK, salt beef.—*See* OLD HORSE.

KEEL-HAULING, a good thrashing or mauling, rough treatment,—from the old nautical custom of punishing offenders by throwing them overboard with a rope attached and hauling them up from under the ship's keel.

KEEP IT UP, to prolong a debauch, or the occasion of a rejoicing—a metaphor drawn from the game of shuttlecock.—*Grose.*

KEN, a house.—*Ancient cant.* KHAN, *Gipsey* and *Oriental.*

*** All slang and cant words which end in KEN, such as SPIELKEN, SPINIKEN, BAWDYKEN, or BOOZINGKEN, refer to *houses*, and are partly of *Gipsey* origin.

KEN-CRACKERS, housebreakers.

KENNEDY, to strike or kill with a poker. A St. Giles' term, so given from a man of that name being killed by a poker. Frequently shortened to NEDDY.

KENT RAG, or CLOUT, a cotton handkerchief.

KERTEVER-CARTZO, the venereal disease. From the *Lingua Franca*, CATTIVO, bad, and CAZZO, the male generative organ.

KETCH, or JACK KETCH, the popular name for a public hangman—derived from a person of that name who officiated in the reign of Charles II.—*See Macaulay's History of England*, p. 626.

KIBOSH, nonsense, stuff, humbug; "it's all KIBOSH," *i. e.*, palaver or nonsense; "to put on the KIBOSH," to run down, slander, degrade, &c.—*See* BOSH.

KICK, a moment; "I'll be there in a KICK," *i. e.*, in a minute.

KICK, a sixpence; "two and a KICK," two shillings and sixpence.

KICK, a pocket.

KICK THE BUCKET, to die.—*Norfolk*. According to Forby, a metaphor taken from the descent of a well or mine, which is of course absurd. The Rev. E. S. Taylor supplies me with the following note from his MS. additions to the work of the East-Anglian lexicographer:—

> "The allusion is to the way in which a slaughtered pig is hung up, viz., by passing the ends of a bent piece of wood behind the tendons of the hind legs, and so suspending it to a hook in a beam above. This piece of wood is locally termed *a bucket*, and so by a coarse metaphor the phrase came to signify to die. Compare the Norfolk phrase "as wrong as a bucket."

The natives of the West Indies have converted the expression into KICKERABOO.

KICK-UP, a noise or disturbance.

KICK UP, "to KICK UP a *row*," to create a tumult.

KICKSHAWS, trifles; made, or French dishes—not English, or substantial. Corruption of the *French*, QUELQUES CHOSES.

KICKSIES, trousers.

KICKSY, troublesome, disagreeable.

KID, an infant, or child.

KID, to joke, to quiz, to hoax anybody.

KID-ON, to entice, or incite a person on to the perpetration of an act.

KID-RIG, cheating children in the streets sent on errands, or entrusted with packages. *Nearly obsolete.*

KIDDEN, a low lodging house for boys.

KIDDIER, a pork-butcher.

KIDDILY, fashionably, or showily; "KIDDILY togg'd," showily dressed.

KIDDLEYWINK, a small shop where they retail the commodities of a village store. Also, a loose woman.

KIDDY, a man or boy. Formerly a low thief.

KIDDYISH, frolicsome, jovial.

> "Think on the KIDDYISH spree we had on such a day."
> *Randall's Diary*, 1820.

KIDMENT, a pocket-handkerchief fastened to the pocket, and partially hung out to entrap thieves.

KIDNAPPER, one who steals children or adults. From KID, a child, and NAB (corrupted to NAP), to steal, or seize.

KIDNEY, "of that KIDNEY," of such a stamp: "strange KIDNEY," odd humour; "two of a KIDNEY," two persons of a sort, or as like as two peas, *i.e.*, resembling each other like two kidneys in a bunch.—*Old.* "Attempt to put their hair out of KIDNEY."—*Terræ Filius*, 1763.

KIDSMAN, one who trains boys to thieve and pick pockets successfully.

KILKENNY CAT, a popular simile for a voracious or desperate animal or person, from the story of the two cats in that county, who are said to have fought and bitten each other until a small portion of the tail of one of them alone remained.

KILLING, bewitching, fascinating. The term is akin to the phrase "dressing to DEATH."

KIMBO, or A KIMBO, holding the arms in a bent position from the body, and resting the hands upon the hips, in a bullying attitude. Said to be from A SCHEMBO, *Italian;* but more probably from KIMBAW, the old cant for beating, or bullying.—*See Grose.*

KINCHIN, a child.—*Old cant.* From the *German* diminutive, KINDCHEN, a baby.

KINCHIN COVE, a man who robs children; a little man.—*Ancient cant.*

KINGSMAN, the favourite coloured neckerchief of the costermongers. The women wear them thrown over their shoulders. With both sexes they are more valued than any other article of clothing. A coster's *caste*, or position, is at stake, he imagines, if his KINGSMAN is not of the most approved pattern. When he fights, his KINGSMAN is tied either around his waist as a belt, or as a garter around his leg. This very singular partiality for a peculiar coloured neckcloth was doubtless derived from the Gipseys, and probably refers to an Oriental taste or custom long forgotten by these vagabonds. A singular similarity of taste for certain colours exists amongst the Hindoos, Gipseys, and London costermongers. Red and yellow (or orange) are the great favourites, and in these hues the Hindoo selects his turban and his robe; the Gipsey his breeches, and his wife her shawl or gown; and the costermonger his plush waistcoat and favourite KINGSMAN. Amongst either class, when a fight takes place, the greatest regard is paid to the favourite coloured article of dress. The Hindoo lays aside his turban, the Gipsey folds up his scarlet breeches or coat, whilst the pugilistic costermonger of Covent Garden or Billingsgate, as we have just seen, removes his favourite neckerchief to a part of his body, by the rules of the "ring," comparatively out of danger. Amongst the various patterns of kerchiefs worn by the wandering tribes of London, red and yellow are the oldest and most in fashion. Blue, intermixed with spots, is a late importation, probably from the Navy, through sporting characters.

KING'S PICTURES (now, of course, QUEEN'S PICTURES), money.

KISKY, drunk, fuddled.

KISS CURL, a small curl twisted on the temple.—*See* BOW-CATCHER.

KISS-ME-QUICK, the name given to the very small bonnets worn by females since 1850.

KITE, *see* FLY THE KITE.

KNACKER, an old horse; a horse slaughterer.—*Gloucestershire.*

KNAP, to receive, to take, to steal.

KNAPPING-JIGGER, a turnpike-gate; "to dub at the KNAPPING-JIGGER," to pay money at the turnpike.

KNARK, a hard-hearted or savage person.

KNIFE, "to KNIFE a person," to stab, an un-English but now-a-days a very common expression.

KNIFE IT, "cut it," cease, stop, don't proceed.

KNIFE-BOARD, the seat running along the roof of an omnibus.

KNIGHT, a common and ironical prefix to a man's calling,—thus, "KNIGHT of the whip," a coachman; "KNIGHT of the thimble," a tailor.

KNOCK ABOUT THE BUB, to hand or pass about the drink.

KNOCK DOWN, or KNOCK ME DOWN, strong ale.

KNOCK OFF, to give over, or abandon. A saying used by workmen about dinner, or other meal times, for upwards of two centuries.

KNOCKED UP, tired, jaded, used up, done for. In the United States, amongst females, the phrase is equivalent to being *enceinte*, so that Englishmen often unconsciously commit themselves when amongst our Yankee cousins.

KNOCK-IN, the game of *loo*.

KNOCK-OUTS, or KNOCK-INS, disreputable persons who visit auction rooms and unite to buy the articles at their own prices. One of their number is instructed to buy for the rest, and after a few small bids as blinds to the auctioneer and bystanders, the lot is knocked down to the KNOCK-OUT bidders, at a nominal price—the competition to result from an auction being thus frustrated and set aside. At the conclusion of the sale the goods are paid for, and carried to some neighbouring public house, where they are re-sold or KNOCKED-OUT, and the difference between the first purchase and the second—or tap-room KNOCK-OUT—is divided amongst the gang. As generally happens with ill-gotten gains, the money soon finds its way to the landlord's pocket, and the KNOCK-OUT is rewarded with a red nose or a bloated face. Cunning tradesmen join the KNOCK-OUTS when an opportunity for money making presents itself. The lowest description of KNOCK-OUTS, fellows with more tongue than capital, are termed BABES,—which see.

KNOCKING-SHOP, a brothel, or disreputable house frequented by prostitutes.

KNOWING, a slang term for sharpness; "KNOWING codger," or "a KNOWING blade," one who can take you in, or cheat you, in any transaction you may have with him. It implies also deep cunning and foresight, and generally signifies dishonesty.

> "Who, on a spree with black eyed Sal, his blowen,
> So swell, so prime, so nutty and so KNOWING."
>
> *Don Juan.*

KNOWLEDGE-BOX, the head.—*Pugilistic.*

KNUCKLE, to pick pockets after the most approved method.

KNUCKLE TO, or KNUCKLE UNDER, to yield or submit.

KNUCKLER, a pickpocket.

KNULLER, old term for a chimney-sweep, who solicited jobs by ringing a bell. From the *Saxon*, CNYLLAN, to knell, or sound a bell.—*See* QUERIER.

KOTOOING, misapplied flattery.—*Illustrated London News*, 7th January, 1860.

KYPSEY, a basket.

LA! a euphuistic rendering of LORD, common amongst females and very precise persons; imagined by many to be a corruption of LOOK! but this is a mistake. Sometimes pronounced LAW, or LAWKS.

LACING, a beating. From the phrase "I'll LACE your jacket." —*L'Estrange*. Perhaps to give a beating with a *lace* or *lash*.

LADDER, "can't see a hole in a LADDER," said of any one who is intoxicated.

LADDLE, a lady. Term with chimney-sweeps on the 1st of May. A correspondent suggests that the term may come from the brass *ladles* for collecting money, always carried by the sweeps' ladies.

LAG, a returned transport, or ticket-of-leave convict.

LAG, to void urine.—*Ancient cant.*

LAGGED, transported for a crime.

LAGGER, a sailor.

LAME DUCK, a stock jobber who speculates beyond his capital and cannot pay his losses. Upon retiring from the Exchange he is said to "waddle out of the Alley."

LAMMING, a beating.—*Old English*, LAM; used by *Beaumont and Fletcher*.

LAND LUBBER, sea term for a landsman."—*See* LOAFER.

LAND-SHARK, a sailor's definition of a lawyer.

LAP THE GUTTER, to get drunk.

LARK, fun, a joke; "let's have a jolly good LARK," let us have a piece of fun. *Mayhew* calls it "a convenient word covering much mischief."—*Anglo Saxon*, LAC, sport; but more probably from the nautical term SKYLARKING, *i.e.*, mounting to the highest yards and sliding down the ropes for amusement, which is allowed on certain occasions.

LARRUP, to beat, or thrash.

LARRUPING, a good beating or "hiding."—*Irish.*

LATCHPAN, the lower lip—properly a dripping pan; "to hang one's LATCHPAN," to pout, be sulky.—*Norfolk.*

LAVENDER, "to be laid up in LAVENDER," in pawn; or, when a person is out of the way for an especial purpose.—*Old.*

LAY, to watch; "on the LAY," on the look out —*Shakespere.*

LED CAPTAIN, a fashionable spunger, a swell who, by artifice ingratiates himself into the good graces of the master of the house, and lives at his table.

LEARY, to look, or be watchful; shy.—*Old cant.*

LEARY, flash, or knowing.

LEARY BLOAK, a person who dresses showily.

LEATHER, to beat or thrash. From the leather belt worn by soldiers and policemen, often used as a weapon in street rows.

LEAVING SHOP, an unlicensed house where goods are taken in to pawn at exorbitant rates of interest.—*Daily Telegraph*, 1st August, 1859.

LEEF, "I'd as LEEF do it as not," *i.e.*, I have no objection to do it.—*Corruption* of LIEF, or LEAVE. *Old English*, LIEF, inclined to.

LEG IT, to run; LEG BAIL, to run off; "to give a LEG," to assist, as when one mounts a horse; "making a LEG," a countryman's bow,—projecting the leg from behind as a balance to the head bent forward.—*Shakespere.*

LEGGED, in irons.

LEGS, or BLACKLEGS, disreputable sporting characters, and race-course *habitués.*

LEGS OF MUTTON, inflated street term for sheeps' trotters, or feet.

LENGTH, forty-two lines of a dramatic composition.—*Theat.*

LENGTH, six months' imprisonment.—*See* STRETCH.

LET DRIVE, to strike, or attack with vigour.

LET IN, to cheat or victimise.

LET ON, to give an intimation of having some knowledge of a subject. *Ramsay* employs the phrase in the *Gentle Shepherd.* Common in Scotland.

LETTY, a bed. *Italian,* LETTO.

LEVANTER, a card sharper, or defaulting gambler. A correspondent states that it was formerly the custom to give out to the creditors, when a person was in pecuniary difficulties, and it was convenient for him to keep away, that he was gone to the *East*, or the LEVANT; hence, when one loses a bet, and decamps without settling, he is said to LEVANT.

LICK, a blow; LICKING, a beating; "to put in big LICKS," a curious and common phrase meaning that great exertions are being made.—*Dryden; North.*

LICK, to excel, or overcome; "if you aint sharp he'll LICK

you," *i.e.*, be finished first. Signifies, also, to whip, chastise, or conquer. *Ancient cant*, LYCKE.

LIFER, a convict who is sentenced to transportation *for life*.

LIFT, to steal, pick pockets; "there's a clock been LIFTED," said when a watch has been stolen. The word is as old as the Border forays, and is used by *Shakespere*. SHOPLIFTER is a recognised term.

LIGHT, "to be able to get a LIGHT at a house" is to get credit.

LIGHT-FEEDERS, silver spoons.

LIGHTS, a "cake," a fool, a soft or "doughy" person.

LIGHTS, the eyes.

LIGHTNING, gin; "FLASH O' LIGHTNING," a glass of gin.

LIMB OF THE LAW, a lawyer, or clerk articled to that profession.

LINE, calling, trade, profession; "what LINE are you in?" "the building LINE."

LINGO, talk, or language. Slang is termed LINGO amongst the lower orders. *Italian*, LINGUA.

LIP, bounce, impudence; "come, none o' yer LIP!"

LIQUOR, or LIQUOR UP, to drink drams.—*Americanism*. IN LIQUOR, tipsy, or drunk.

LITTLE GO, the "Previous Examination," at Cambridge the first University examination for undergraduates in their second year of matriculation. At Oxford, the corresponding term is THE SMALLS.

LITTLE SNAKES-MAN, a little thief, who is generally passed through a small aperture to open any door to let in the rest of the gang.

LIVE-STOCK, vermin of the *insect* kind.

LOAFER, a lazy vagabond. Generally considered an *Americanism*. LOPER, or LOAFER, however, was in general use as a cant term in the early part of the last century. LAND-LOPER, was a vagabond who begged in the attire of a sailor; and the sea phrase, LAND-LUBBER, was doubtless synonymous.—*See the Times*, 3rd November, 1859, for a reference to LOAFER.

LOAVER, money.—*See* LOUR.

LOB, a till, or money drawer.

LOBB, the head.—*Pugilistic*.

LOBLOLLY, gruel.—*Old*: used by *Markham* as a sea term for grit gruel, or hasty pudding.

LOBLOLLY BOY, a derisive term for a surgeon's mate in the navy.

LOBS, words.—*Gipsey.*

LOBSTER, a soldier. A *policeman* from the colour of his coat is styled an *unboiled*, or *raw* LOBSTER.

LOBSTER-BOX, a barrack, or military station.

LOLLY, the head.—*See* LOBB.—*Pugilistic.*

LONG-BOW, "to draw," or "shoot with the LONG BOW," to exaggerate.

LONG-TAILED-ONES, bank notes, or FLIMSIES, for a large amount.

LOOF FAKER, a chimney-sweep.—*See* FLUE FAKER.

LOOSE.—*See* ON THE LOOSE.

LOOT, swag, or plunder.—*Hindoo.*

LOP-SIDED, uneven, one side larger than the other.—*Old.*

LOPE, this old form of *leap* is often heard in the streets.

LORD, "drunk as a LORD," a common saying, probably referring to the facilities a man of fortune has for such a gratification; perhaps a sly sarcasm at the supposed habits of the "haristocracy."

LORD, a hump-backed man.—*See* MY LORD.

LORD OF THE MANOR, a sixpence.

LOUD, flashy, showy, as applied to dress or manner.—*See* BAGS.

LOUR, or LOWR, money; "gammy LOWR," bad money.—*Ancient cant*, and *Gipsey*.

LOUSE-TRAP, a small tooth comb.—*Old cant.*—*See* CATCH 'EM ALIVE.

LOVE, at billiards "five to none" would be "five LOVE,"—a LOVE being the same as when one player does not score at all.

LOVEAGE, tap droppings, a mixture of spirits, sweetened and sold to habitual dram-drinkers, principally females. Called also ALLS.

LUBBER, a clown, or fool.—*Ancient cant*, LUBBARE.

LUBBER'S HOLE, an aperture in the maintop of a ship, by which a timid climber may avoid the difficulties of the "futtock shrouds"—hence, a sea term for any cowardly way of evading duty.

LUCK, "down on one's LUCK," wanting money, or in difficulty.

LUCKY, "to cut one's LUCKY," to go away quickly.—*See* STRIKE.

LUG, "my togs are in LUG," *i.e.*, in pawn.

LUG, the ear.—*Scotch.*

LUG, to pull, or slake thirst.—*Old.*

LUG CHOVEY, a pawnbroker's shop.

LULLY PRIGGERS, rogues who steal wet clothes hung on lines to dry.

LUMBER, to pawn or pledge.—*Household Words,* No. 183.

LUMMY, jolly, first-rate.

LUMPER, a contractor. On the river, more especially a person who contracts to deliver a ship laden with timber.

LUMP THE LIGHTER, to be transported.

LUMP WORK, work contracted for, or taken by the *lump.*

LUMPERS, low thieves who haunt wharves and docks, and rob vessels; persons who sell old goods for new.

LUMPY, intoxicated.

LUNAN, a girl.—*Gipsey.*

LURK, a sham, swindle, or representation of feigned distress.

LURKER, an impostor who travels the country with false certificates of fires, shipwrecks, &c.

LUSH, intoxicating drinks of all kinds, but generally used for beer. The *Globe,* 8th September, 1859, says "LUSH and its derivatives claim *Lushington,* the brewer, as sponsor."

LUSH, to drink, or get drunk.

LUSH-CRIB, a public house.

LUSHINGTON, a drunkard, or one who continually soaks himself with drams, and pints of beer. Some years since there was a "Lushington Club" in Bow-street, Covent Garden.

LUSHY, intoxicated. Johnson says "opposite to pale," so red with drink.

MAB, a cab, or hackney coach.

MACE, a dressy swindler who victimizes tradesmen.

MACE, to spunge, swindle, or beg, in a polite way; "give it him (a shopkeeper) on the MACE," *i.e.,* obtain goods on credit and never pay for them; also termed "striking the MACE."

MADZA, half. *Italian,* MEZZA. This word enters into combination with various cant phrases, mainly taken from the *Lingua Franca,* as MADZA CAROON, half-a-crown, two-and-sixpence; MADZA SALTEE, a halfpenny [*see* SALTEE]; MADZA POONA, half-a-sovereign; MADZA ROUND THE BULL, half-a pound of steak, &c.

MAG, a halfpenny.—*Ancient cant*, MAKE. MEGGS were formerly guineas.—*B. M. Carew*.

MAG, to talk. A corruption of NAG.—*Old;* hence MAGPIE.

MAGGOTTY, fanciful, fidgetty. Whims and fancies were formerly termed MAGGOTS, from the popular belief that a maggot in the brain was the cause of any odd notion or caprice a person might exhibit.

MAGSMAN, a street swindler, who watches for countrymen and "gullable" persons.

MAHOGANY, "to have one's feet under another man's MAHOGANY," to sit at his table, be supported on other than one's own resources; "amputate your MAHOGANY," *i.e.*, go away, or "cut your stick."

MAIN-TOBY, the highway, or the main road.

MAKE, a successful theft, or swindle.

MAKE, to steal.

MAKE UP, personal appearance.—*Theatrical*.

MANG, to talk.—*Scotch*.

MARE'S NEST, a Cockney discovery of marvels, which turn out no marvels at all. An old preacher in Cornwall, up to very lately employed a different version, viz.: "a cow calving up in a tree."

MARINATED, transported;—from the salt-pickling fish undergo in Cornwall.—*Old cant*.

MARINE, or MARINE RECRUIT, an empty bottle. This expression having once been used in the presence of an officer of marines, he was at first inclined to take it as an insult, until some one adroitly appeased his wrath by remarking that no offence could be meant, as all that it could possibly imply was, "one who had done his duty, and was ready to do it again."—*See* HORSE MARINE.—*Naval*.

MARRIAGE LINES, a marriage certificate.—*Provincial*.

MARROWSKYING.—*See* MEDICAL GREEK.

MARYGOLD, one million sterling.—*See* PLUM.

MASSACRE OF THE INNOCENTS, when the leader of the House of Commons goes through the doleful operation of devoting to extinction a number of useful measures at the end of the session, for want of time to pass them.—*Vide Times*, 20th July, 1859: Mr. C. Foster, on altering the time of the legislative sessions.—*Parliamentary slang*.

MATE, the term a coster or low person applies to a friend, partner, or companion; "me and my MATE did so and so," is a common phrase with a low Londoner.—Originally a *Sea term.*

MAULEY, a signature, from MAULEY, a fist; "put your FIST to it," is sometimes said by a low tradesman when desiring a fellow trader to put his signature to a bill or note.

MAULEY, a fist, that with which one strikes as with a MALL.—*Pugilistic.*

MAUND, to beg; "MAUNDERING on the fly," begging of people in the streets.—*Old cant.* MAUNG, to beg, is a term in use amongst the *Gipseys,* and may also be found in the *Hindoo* Vocabulary. MAUND, however, is pure *Anglo Saxon,* from MAND, a basket. Compare "beg," which is derived from BAG, a curious parallel.

MAW, the mouth; "hold your MAW," cease talking.

MAX, gin; MAX-UPON TICK, gin obtained upon credit.

M. B. COAT, *i.e., Mark of the Beast,* a name given to the long surtout worn by the clergy,—a modern Puritan form of abuse, said to have been accidentally disclosed to a Tractarian customer by a tailor's orders to his foreman.

MEALY-MOUTHED, plausible, deceitful.

MEDICAL GREEK, the slang used by medical students at the hospitals. At the London University they have a way of disguising English, described by Albert Smith as the *Gower-street Dialect,* which consists in transposing the initials of words, *e.g.*, "*poke a smipe,*"—smoke a pipe, "*flutter-by*"—butterfly, &c. This disagreeable nonsense is often termed MARROWSKYING. — *See* GREEK, St. Giles' Greek, or the "*Ægidiac*" dialect, Language of ZIPH, &c.

MENAGERY, the orchestra of a theatre.—*Theatrical.*

MIDDY, abbreviation of MIDSHIPMAN.—*Naval.*

MIDGE NET, a lady's veil.

MIKE, to loiter; or, as a costermonger defined it, to "lazy about." The term probably originated at St. Giles', which used to be thronged with Irish labourers (Mike being so common a term with them as to become a generic appellation for Irishmen with the vulgar) who used to loiter about the Pound, and lean against the public-houses in the "Dials" waiting for hire.

MILKY ONES, white linen rags.

MILL, a fight, or SET TO. *Ancient cant,* MYLL, to rob.

MILL, to fight or beat.

MILL, the tread*mill,* prison.

MILL-TOG, a shirt—most likely the prison garment.

MISH, a shirt, or chemise. From COMMISSION, the *Ancient cant* for a shirt, afterwards shortened to K'MISH or SMISH, and then to MISH. *French*, CHEMISE; *Italian*, CAMICIA.

> "With his snowy CAMESE and his shaggy capote."—*Byron*.

MITTENS, fists.—*Pugilistic*.

MIZZLE, to run away, or decamp; to disappear as in a mist. From MIZZLE, a drizzling rain; a Scotch mist.

> "And then one *mizzling* Michaelmas night
> The Count he MIZZLED too."—*Hood*.

MOB. Swift informs us, in his *Art of Polite Conversation*, that MOB was, in his time, the slang abbreviation of *Mobility*, just as NOB is of *Nobility* at the present day.—*See* SCHOOL.

MOBILITY, the populace; or, according to *Burke*, the "great unwashed." *Johnson* calls it a cant term, although *Swift* notices it as a proper expression.

MOBS, companions; MOBSMEN, dressy swindlers.

MOKE, a donkey.—*Gipsey*.

MOKO, a name given by sportsmen to pheasants killed by mistake in partridge shooting during September, before the pheasant shooting comes in. They pull out their tails, and roundly assert they are no pheasants at all, but MOKOS.

MOLL, a girl; nickname for Mary.—*Old cant*.

MOLL'D, followed, or accompanied by a woman.

MOLLISHER, a low girl or woman; generally a female cohabiting with a man, and jointly getting their living by thieving.

MOLLSACK, a reticule, or market basket.

MOLL-TOOLER, a female pickpocket.

MOLLYCODDLE, an effeminate man; one who caudles amongst the women, or does their work.

MOLLYGRUBS, or MULLIGRUBS, stomach-ache, or sorrow—which to the costermonger is much the same, as he believes, like the ancients, that the viscera is the seat of all feeling.

MOLROWING, "out on the *spree*," in company with so-called gay women." In allusion to the amatory serenadings of the London cats.

MONEKEER, a person's name or signature.

MONKEY, spirit, or ill temper; "to get one's MONKEY up," to rouse his passion. A man is said to have his MONKEY up, or the MONKEY on his back, when he is "*riled*," or out of temper; also to have his BACK or HUMP up.

MONKEY, a padlock.

MONKEY, the instrument which drives a rocket.—*Army*.

MONKEY, £500.

MONKEY WITH A LONG TAIL, a mortgage.—*Legal*.

MONKEY'S ALLOWANCE, to get blows instead of alms, more kicks than half-pence.

MONKERY, the country, or rural districts. *Old* word for a quiet, or monastic life.—*Hall*.

MOOCH, to sponge; to obtrude yourself upon friends just when they are about to sit down to dinner, or other lucky time—of course quite accidentally.—Compare HULK. To slink away, and allow your friend to pay for the entertainment. *In Wiltshire*, ON THE MOUTCH is to shuffle.

MOOCHING, or ON THE MOOCH, on the look out for any articles or circumstances which may be turned to a profitable account; watching in the streets for odd jobs, scraps, horses to hold, &c.

MOOE, the mouth; the female generative organ.—*Gipsey* and *Hindoo*. *Shakespere* has MOE, to make mouths.

MOON, a month—generally used to express the length of time a person has been sentenced by the magistrate; thus "ONE MOON" is one month.—*See* DRAG. It is a curious fact that the Indians of America and the roaming vagabonds of England should both calculate time by the MOON.

MOONEY, intoxicated.—*Household Words*, No. 183.

MOONLIGHT, or MOONSHINE, smuggled gin.

MOONSHINE, palaver, deception, humbug.

MOP, a hiring place (or fair) for servants. Steps are being taken to put down these assemblages, which have been proved to be greatly detrimental to the morality of the poor.

MOP UP, to drink, or empty a glass.—*Old*.

MOPS AND BROOMS, intoxicated.—*Ho. Words*, No. 183.

MOPUSSES, money; "MOPUSSES ran taper," money ran short.

MORRIS, to decamp, be off. Probably from the ancient MORESCO, or MORRIS DANCE.

MORTAR-BOARD, the term given by the vulgar to the square college caps.

MOTT, a girl of indifferent character. Formerly *Mort*. *Dutch*, MOTT-KAST, a harlotry.

MOUNTAIN-DEW, whisky, advertised as from the Highlands.

MOUNTAIN PECKER, a sheep's head.—*See* JEMMY.

MOUNTER, a false swearer. Derived from the borrowed clothes men used to MOUNT, or dress in, when going to swear for a consideration.

MOUTHPIECE, a lawyer, or counsel.

MOVE, a "dodge," or cunning trick; "up to a move or two," acquainted with tricks.

MRS. JONES, the house of office, a water-closet.

MRS. HARRIS and MRS. GAMP, nicknames of the *Morning Herald* and *Standard* newspapers, while united under the proprietorship of Mr. Baldwin. MRS. GAMP, a monthly nurse, was a character in Mr. Charles Dickens' popular novel of *Martin Chuzzlewit*, who continually quoted an imaginary *Mrs. Harris* in attestation of the superiority of her qualifications, and the infallibility of her opinions; and thus afforded a parallel to the two newspapers, who appealed to each other as independent authorities, being all the while the production of the same editorial staff.

MUCK, to beat, or excel; "it's no use, luck's set in him; he'd MUCK a thousand."—*Mayhew*, vol. i, p. 18. To RUN A MUCK, or GO A MUCKER, to rush headlong into certain ruin. From a certain religious phrenzy, which is common among the Malays, causing one of them, kreese in hand, to dash into a crowd and devote every one to death he meets with, until he is himself killed, or falls from exhaustion—*Malay*, AMOK, slaughter.

MUCK OUT, to clean out,—often applied to one utterly ruining an adversary in gambling. From the *Provincial* MUCK, dirt.

MUCK-SNIPE, one who has been "MUCKED OUT," or beggared, at gambling.

MUCKENDER, or MUCKENGER, a pocket handkerchief.—*Old.*

MUDFOG, "The British Association for the Promotion of Science."—*University.*

MUD-LARKS, men and women who, with their clothes tucked above knee, grovel through the mud on the banks of the Thames, when the tide is low, for silver spoons, old bottles, pieces of iron, coal, or any articles of the least value, deposited by the retiring tide, either from passing ships or the sewers. Occasionally those men who cleanse the sewers, with great boots and sou' wester hats.

MUFF, a silly, or weak-minded person; MUFF has been defined to be "a soft thing that holds a lady's hand without squeezing it."

MUFFIN-WORRY, an old ladies' tea party.

MUFTI, the civilian dress of a naval or military officer when off duty.—*Anglo Indian.*

MUG, to fight, or chastise.

MUG, "to MUG oneself," to get tipsy.

MUG, the mouth, or face.—*Old.*

MUGGING, a thrashing,—synonymous with SLOGGING, both terms of the "ring," and frequently used by fighting men.

MUGGY, drunk.

MUG-UP, to paint one's face.—*Theatrical.* To "cram" for an examination.—*Army.*

MULL, "to make a MULL of it," to spoil anything, or make a fool of oneself.—*Gipsey.*

MULLIGRUBS.—*Vide* MOLLYGRUBS.

MULTEE KERTEVER, very bad.—*Italian,* MOLTO CATTIVO.

MUMMER, a performer at a travelling theatre.—*Ancient.* Rustic performers at Christmas in the West of England.

MUMPER, a beggar.—*Gipsey.* Possibly a corruption of MUMMER.

MUNDUNGUS, trashy tobacco. *Spanish,* MONDONGO, black pudding.

MUNGARLY, bread, food. MUNG is an *old word* for mixed food, but MUNGARLY is doubtless derived from the *Lingua Franca,* MANGIAR, to eat.—See the following.

MUNGARLY CASA, a baker's shop; evidently a corruption of some *Lingua Franca* phrase for an eating house. The well known "Nix mangiare" stairs at Malta derive their name from the endless beggars who lie there and shout NIX MANGIARE, *i.e.,* "nothing to eat," to excite the compassion of the English who land there,—an expression which exhibits remarkably the mongrel composition of the *Lingua Franca,* MANGIARE being *Italian,* and *Nix* an evident importation from Trieste, or other Austrian seaport.

MUNGING, or "MOUNGING," whining, begging, muttering.—*North.*

MUNS, the mouth. *German,* MUND.—*Old cant.*

MURERK, the mistress of the house.—*See* BURERK.

MURKARKER, a monkey,—vulgar cockney pronunciation of MACAUCO, a species of monkey. *Jackey Macauco* was the name of a famous fighting monkey, which used about thirty years ago to display his prowess at the Westminster pit, where, after having killed many dogs, he was at last "chawed up" by a bull terrier.

MURPHY, a potato. Probably from the Irish national liking for potatoes, MURPHY being a common surname amongst the Irish.—*See* MIKE. MURPHIES (*edible*) are sometimes called DUNNAMANS.

MURPHY, "in the arms of MURPHY," *i.e.*, fast asleep. Corruption of MORPHEUS.

MUSH, an umbrella. Contraction of *mushroom*.

MUSH, (or MUSHROOM) FAKER, an itinerant mender of umbrellas.

MUSLIN, a woman or girl; "he picked up a bit of MUSLIN.

MUTTON, a lewd woman.—*Shakespere.*

MUTTON-WALK, the saloon at Drury Lane Theatre.

MUZZLE, to fight or thrash.

MUZZLE, the mouth.

MUZZY, intoxicated.—*Household Words*, No. 183.

MY AUNT, a water-closet, or house of office.

MY LORD, a nickname given to a hunchback.

MY TULIP, a term of endearment used by the lower orders to persons and animals; "kim up, MY TULIP," as the coster said to his donkey when thrashing him with an ash stick.

MY UNCLE, the pawnbroker,—generally used when any person questions the whereabouts of a domestic article, "Oh! only at MY UNCLE'S" is the reply. UP THE SPOUT has the same meaning.

NAB, to catch, to seize; "NAB the rust," to take offence.—*Ancient*, fourteenth century.

NABOB, an Eastern prince, a retired Indian official,—hence a slang term for a capitalist.

NAIL, to steal, or capture; "paid on the NAIL," *i.e.*, ready money; NAILED, taken up, or caught—probably in allusion to the practice of NAILING bad money to the counter. We say "as dead as a DOOR-NAIL;"—why? *Shakespere* has the expression in Henry IV.—

> "*Falstaff*. What! is the old king dead?
> *Pistol*. As nail in door."

A correspondent thinks the expression is only alliterative humour, and compares as "*Flat as a Flounder*," "straight as a soldier," &c.

NAM, a policeman. Evidently *back slang*.

NAMBY PAMBY, particular, over nice, effeminate. This, I think, was of Pope's invention, and first applied by him to the affected short-lined verses addressed by Ambrose Phillips to Lord Carteret's infant children.—*See Johnson's Life of Pope.*

NAMUS, or NAMOUS, some one, *i.e.*, "be off, somebody is coming."—*Back slang*, but general.—*See* VAMOS.

NANNY-SHOP, a disreputable house.

NANTEE, not any, or "I have none." *Italian*, NIENTE, nothing. —*See* DINARLY.

NANTEE PALAVER, no conversation, *i.e.*, hold your tongue. —*Lingua Franca.*—*See* PALAVER.

NAP, or NAB, to take, steal, or receive; "you'll NAP it," *i.e.*, you will catch a beating!—*North;* also *old cant.*—*Bulwer's Paul Clifford.*

NAP, or NAPPER, a hat. From NAB, a hat, cap, or head.—*Old cant.*

NAP ONE'S BIB, to cry, shed tears, or carry one's point.

NAP THE REGULARS, to divide the booty.

NAP THE TEAZE, to be privately whipped in prison.

NARK, a person in the pay of the police; a common informer; one who gets his living by laying traps for publicans, &c.

NARK, to watch, or look after, "NARK the titter;" watch the girl.

NARP, a shirt.—*Scotch.*

NARY ONE, provincial for NE'ER A ONE, neither.

NASTY, ill-tempered, cross-grained.

NATION, very, or exceedingly. Corruption of DAMNATION.

NATTY, pretty, neat, tidy.—*Old.*

NATURAL, an idiot, a simpleton.

NECK, to swallow. NECK-OIL, drink of any kind.

NECK OR NOTHING, desperate.—*Racing phrase.*

NEDDY, a life preserver.—Contraction of KENNEDY, the name of the first man, it is said in St. Giles', who had his head broken by a poker.—*Vide Mornings at Bow Street.*

NEDDY, a donkey.

NEDS, guineas. HALF-NEDS, half-guineas.

NED STOKES, the four of spades.—*North Hants.*—*See Gentleman's Magazine* for 1791, p. 141.

NEEDFUL, money, cash.

NEEDY, a nightly lodger, or tramp.

NEEDY MIZZLER, a shabby person; a tramp who runs away without paying for his lodging.

NESTS, varieties.—*Old*

NEVER-TRUST-ME, an ordinary phrase with low Londoners, and common in Shakespere's time, *vide Twelfth Night*. It is generally used instead of an oath, calling vengeance on the asseverator, if such and such does not come to pass.

NEWGATE FRINGE, or FRILL, the collar of beard worn under the chin; so called from its occupying the position of the rope when Jack Ketch operates. Another name for it is a TYBURN COLLAR.

NEWGATE KNOCKER, the term given to the lock of hair which costermongers and thieves usually twist back towards the ear. The shape is supposed to resemble the knocker on the prisoners' door at Newgate—a resemblance that would appear to carry a rather unpleasant suggestion to the wearer. Sometimes termed a COBBLER'S KNOT, or COW-LICK, which see.

NEWMARKET, in tossing halfpence, when it is agreed that the first toss shall be decisive, the play is said to be NEWMARKET.

NIBBLE, to take, or steal. NIBBLER, a petty thief.

NIBS, the master, or chief person; a man with no means but high pretensions,—a "shabby genteel."

NICK, or OLD NICK, the evil spirit.—*Scandinavian.*

NICK, to hit the mark; "he's NICKED it," *i.e.*, won his point.

NICK-KNACK, a trifle.—Originally *cant.*

NIGGLING, trifling, or idling; taking short steps in walking.—*North.*

NIL, half; half profits, &c.

NILLY-WILLY, *i.e.*, *Nill ye, will ye*, whether you will or no, a familiar version of the *Latin*, NOLENS VOLENS.

NIMMING, stealing. Immediately from the *German*, NEHMEN. Motherwell, the Scotch poet, thought the old word NIM (to snatch or pick up) was derived from *nam*, *nam*, the tiny words or cries of an infant, when eating anything which pleases its little palate. A negro proverb has the word:—

"Buckra man *nam* crab,
Crab *nam* buckra man."

Or, in the buckra man's language—

"White man eat [or steal] the crab,
And the crab eats the white man."

NINCOMPOOP, a fool, a hen pecked husband, a "Jerry Sneak."—Corruption of *non compos mentis.*

NINE CORNS, a pipeful of tobacco.

NINES, "dressed up to the NINES," in a showy or *recherché* manner.

NINEPENCE, "right as NINEPENCE," all right, right to a nicety.

NIP, to steal, take up quickly.

NIPPER, a small boy. *Old cant* for a *boy* cut-purse.

NIX, nothing, "NIX my doll," synonymous with NIX. *German*, NICHTS, nothing.—*See* MUNGARLY.

NIX! the signal word of school boys to each other that the master, or other person in authority, is approaching.

NIZZIE, a fool, a coxcomb.—*Old cant, vide Triumph of Wit.*

NOAH'S ARK, a long closely buttoned overcoat, recently in fashion. So named by *Punch* from the similarity which it exhibits to the figure of Noah and his sons in children's toy arks.

NOB, the head—*Pugilistic;* "BOB A NOB," a shilling a head. *Ancient cant*, NEB. NOB is an early English word, and is used in the Romance of Kynge Alisaunder (thirteenth century) for a head; originally, no doubt, the same as *knob.*

NOB, a person of high position, a "swell," a *nob*leman,—of which word it may be an abbreviation.—*See* SNOB.

NOBBA, nine. *Italian*, NOVE; *Spanish*, NOVA,—the *b* and *v* being interchangeable, as Se*b*astópol and Se*v*astópol.

NOBBA SALTEE, ninepence. *Lingua Franca*, NOVE SOLDI.

NOBBING, collecting money; "what NOBBINGS?" *i.e.*, how much have you got?

NOBBLE, to cheat, to overreach; to discover.

NOBBLERS, confederates of thimble-rigs, who play earnestly as if strangers to the "RIG," and thus draw unsuspecting persons into a game.

NOBBY, or NOBBISH, fine or showy; NOBBILY, showily.—*See* SNOB for derivation.

NOMMUS, be off.—*See* NAMUS.

NO ODDS, no matter, of no consequence.—*Latimer's sermon before Edward VI.*

NOSE, a thief who turns informer, or Queen's evidence; a spy or watch; "on the NOSE," on the look out.

NOSE, "to pay through the NOSE," to pay an extravagant price.

NOSE-BAGS, visitors at watering places, and houses of refreshment, who carry their own victuals.—*Term applied by waiters.*

NOSE EM, or FOGUS, tobacco.

NOSER, a bloody or contused nose.—*Pugilistic.*

NOUSE, comprehension, perception.—*Old,* apparently from the *Greek,* νοῦς.

NUB, a husband.

NUDDIKIN, the head.

For Cant Numerals, see under SALTEE.

NURSE, a curious term lately applied to competition in omnibuses. Two omnibuses are placed on the road to NURSE, or oppose, each opposition "buss," one before, the other behind. Of course the central or NURSED buss has very little chance, unless it happens to be a favourite with the public. NURSE, to cheat, or swindle; trustees are said to NURSE property, *i.e.*, gradually eat it up themselves.

NUT, to be "off one's NUT," to be in liquor, or "ALL MOPS AND BROOMS."

NUTS, to be NUTS upon anything or person is to be pleased with or fond of it; a self-satisfied man is said to be NUTS upon himself. NUTTED, taken in by a man who professed to be NUTS upon you.

NUTTY, amorous.

NYMPH OF THE PAVE (*French,* PAVÈ), a street-walker, a girl of the town.

OAK, the outer door of college rooms; to "sport one's OAK," to be "not at home" to visitors.—*See* SPORT.—*University.*

OBFUSCATED, intoxicated.

OBSTROPOLOUS, Cockney corruption of *obstreperous.*

OCHRE, money, generally applied to *gold,* for a very obvious reason.

O'CLOCK, or A'CLOCK, "like ONE O'CLOCK," a favourite comparison with the lower orders, implying briskness; "to know what O'CLOCK it is," to be wide awake, sharp, and experienced.

ODD MAN, a street or public-house game at tossing. The number of players is three. Each tosses up a coin, and if two come down head, and one tail, or *vice versâ,* the last is ODD MAN, and loses or wins as may have been agreed upon. Frequently used to victimise a "flat." If all three be alike, then the toss goes for nothing, and the coppers are again "*skied.*"

OD DRAT IT, OD RABBIT (*Colman's Broad Grins*), OD'S BLOOD, and all other exclamations commencing with OD, are nothing but softened or suppressed oaths. OD is a corruption of GOD, and DRAT of ROT.—*Shakespere.*

OFF AND ON, vacillating; "an OFF AND ON kind of a chap," one who is always undecided.

OFF ONE'S FEED, real or pretended want of appetite.—*Stable slang.*

OFFISH, distant, not familiar.

OFFICE, "to give the OFFICE," to give a hint dishonestly to a confederate, thereby enabling him to win a game or bet, the profits being shared.

OGLE, to look, or reconnoitre.

OGLES, eyes.—*Old cant. French,* ŒIL.

OIL OF PALMS, or PALM OIL, money.

OINTMENT, medical student slang for butter.

OLD GOOSEBERRY (*see* GOOSEBERRY), OLD HARRY (query, *Old Hairy?*), OLD SCRATCH, all synonymes for the devil.

OLD GOWN, smuggled tea.

OLD HORSE, salt junk, or beef.—*Sea.*

OLD TOM, gin.

OLIVER, the moon; "OLIVER don't widdle," *i.e.*, the moon does not shine. *Nearly obsolete.—Bulwer's Paul Clifford.*

OMEE, a master or landlord; "the OMEE of the cassey's a nark on the pitch," the master of the house will not let us perform. *Italian,* UOMO, a man; "UOMO DELLA CASA," the master of the house.

ON, "to be ON," in public-house or vulgar parlance, is synonymous with getting "tight," or tipsy; "it's *Saint Monday* with him, I see he's ON again," *i.e.*, drunk as usual, or ON *the road* to it.

ON THE FLY, getting one's living by thieving or other illegitimate means; the phrase is applied to men the same as ON THE LOOSE is to women.

ON THE LOOSE, obtaining a living by prostitution, in reality, on the streets. The term is applied to females only, excepting in the case of SPREES, when men carousing are sometimes said to be ON THE LOOSE.

ON THE NOSE, on the watch or look out.—*See* NOSE.

ON THE SHELF, to be transported. With old maids it has another and very different meaning.

ON THE TILES, out all night "on the spree," or carousing,—in allusion to the London cats on their amatory excursions.

ONE IN TEN, a parson.

ONE-ER, that which stands for ONE, a blow that requires no more. In *Dickens'* amusing work, the "Marchioness" tells Dick Swiveller that "her missus is a ONE-ER at cards."

ORACLE, "to work the ORACLE," to plan, manœuvre, to succeed by a wily stratagem.

OTTER, eightpence.—*Italian*, OTTO, eight.

OTTOMY, a thin man, a skeleton, a dwarf. Vulgar pronunciation of *Anatomy*. *Shakespere* has 'ATOMY.

OUT, a dram glass. The *habitué* of a gin-shop, desirous of treating a brace of friends, calls for a quartern of gin and three OUTS, by which he means three glasses which will exactly contain the quartern.

OUT AND OUT, prime, excellent, of the first quality. OUT AND OUTER, "one who is of an OUT AND OUT description," UP to anything.

An ancient MS. has this couplet, which shows the antiquity of the phrase—

> "The Kyng was good alle aboute,
> And she was wycked *oute and oute.*"

OUT OF COLLAR, out of place,—in allusion to servants. When in place, the term is COLLARED UP.—*Theatrical* and *general*.

OUT ON THE LOOSE, "on the spree," in search of adventures.

OUT ON THE PICKAROON. PICARONE is *Spanish* for a thief, but this phrase does not necessarily mean anything dishonest, but ready for anything in the way of excitement to turn up; also to be in search of anything profitable.

OUT-SIDER, a person who does not habitually bet, or is not admitted to the "Ring." Also, a horse whose name does not appear among the "favourites."

OVER! or OVER THE LEFT, *i.e.*, the left shoulder—a common exclamation of disbelief in what is being narrated,—implying that the results of a proposed plan will be "over the left," *i.e.*, in the wrong direction, loss instead of gain.

OWNED, a canting expression used by the ultra-Evangelicals when a popular preacher makes many converts. The converts themselves are called his "SEALS."

P's AND Q's, particular points, precise behaviour; "mind your P'S AND Q'S," be very careful. Originating, according to some, from the similarity of p's and q's in the hornbook alphabet, and therefore the warning of an old dame to her pupils; or, according to others, of a French dancing master to his pupils, to mind their *pieds* (feet) and *queues* (wigs) when making a bow.

PACK, to go away; "now, then, PACK off there," *i.e.*, be off, don't stop here any longer. *Old*, "*Make speede to flee, be* PACKING *and awaie.*"—*Baret's Alvearie*, 1580.

PAD, "to stand PAD," to beg with a small piece of paper pinned on the breast, inscribed "I'm starving."

PAD, the highway; a tramp.—*Lincolnshire.*

PAD THE HOOF, to walk, not ride; "PADDING THE HOOF on the high toby," tramping or walking on the high road.

> "Trudge, plod away o' the hoof."
> *Merry Wives*, i., 3.

PADDING KENS, or CRIBS, tramps' and boys' lodging houses.

PADDLE, to go or run away.—*Household Words*, No. 183.

PADDY, PAT, or PADDY WHACK, an Irishman.

> "I'm PADDY WHACK, from Bally hack,
> Not long ago turned soldier;
> In storm and sack, in front attack,
> None other can be boulder."
> *Irish Song.*

PADRE, a clergyman.—*Anglo Indian.*

PAL, a partner, acquaintance, friend, an accomplice. *Gipsey*, a brother.

PALAVER, to ask, or talk,—not deceitfully, as the term usually signifies; "PALAVER to the nibs for a shant of bivvy," ask the master for a quart of beer. In this sense used by *tramps.*—Derived from *French*, PARLER.

PALL, to detect.

PALM OIL, or PALM SOAP, money.

PALMING, robbing shops by pairs,—one thief bargaining with apparent intent to purchase, whilst the other watches his opportunity to steal. An amusing example of PALMING came off some time since. A man entered a "ready made" boot and shoe shop and desired to be shown a pair of boots,—his companion staying outside and amusing himself by looking in at the window. The one who required to be fresh shod was apparently of a humble and deferential turn, for he placed his hat on the floor directly he stepped in the shop. Boot after boot was tried on until at last a fit was obtained,—when lo, forth came a man, snatched up the customer's hat left near the door, and down the street he ran as fast as his legs could carry him. Away went the customer after his hat, and Crispin, standing at the door, clapped his hands and shouted "go it, you'll catch him,"—little thinking that it was a concerted trick, and that neither his boots nor the customer would ever return. PALMING sometimes refers to secreting money or rings in the hand.

PAM, the knave of clubs; or, in street phraseology, Lord Palmerston.

PANNAM, food, bread.—*Lingua Franca,* PANNEN; *Latin,* PANIS; *Ancient cant,* YANNAM.

PANNAM-BOUND, stopping the prison food or rations to a prisoner. PANNAM-STRUCK, very hungry.

PANNIKIN, a small pan.

PANNY, a house—public or otherwise; "flash PANNY," a public-house used by thieves; PANNY MEN, housebreakers.

PANTILE, a hat. The term PANTILE is properly applied to the mould into which the sugar is poured which is afterwards known as "loaf sugar." Thus, PANTILE, from whence comes the phrase "a sugar-loaf hat," originally signified a tall, conical hat, in shape similar to that usually represented as the head gear of a bandit. From PANTILE, the more modern slang term TILE has been derived. *Halliwell* gives PANTILE SHOP, a meeting-house.

PANTILER, a dissenting preacher. Probably from the practice of the Quakers, and many dissenters, of not removing the hat in a place of worship.

PAPER MAKERS, rag gatherers and gutter rakers—similar to the chiffonniers of Paris. Also, those men who tramp through the country, and collect rags on the pretence that they are agents to a paper mill.

PAPER WORKERS, the wandering vendors of street literature; street folk who sell ballads, dying speeches and confessions, sometimes termed RUNNING STATIONERS.

PARADIS, *French* slang for the gallery of a theatre, "up amongst the GODS," which see.

PARISH LANTERN, the moon.

PARNEY, rain; "dowry of PARNEY," a quantity of rain. *Anglo-Indian* slang from the *Hindoo,* PĀNI, water; *Gipsey,* PANÉ. Old Indian officers always call brandy and water BRANDY PAWNEE.

PASH, to strike; now corrupted to BASH, which see.—*Shakes.*

PASTE-HORN, the nose. Shoemakers nickname any shopmate

with a large nose "old PASTEHORN," from the horn in which they keep their paste.

PATENT COAT, a coat with the pockets inside the skirts,—termed PATENT from the difficulty of picking them.

PATTER, a speech or discourse, a pompous street oration, a judge's summing up, a trial. *Ancient* word for muttering. Probably from the *Latin*, PATER NOSTER, or Lord's Prayer. This was said, before the Reformation, in a *low voice* by the priest, until he came to, "and lead us not into temptation," to which the choir responded, "but deliver us from evil." In our reformed Prayer Book this was altered, and the Lord's Prayer directed to be said "with a *loud voice*."—*Dr. Pusey* takes this view of the derivation in his *Letter to the Bishop of London*, p. 78, 1851. *Scott* uses the word twice in *Ivanhoe* and the *Bride of Lammermoor*.

PATTER, to talk. PATTER FLASH, to speak the language of thieves, talk cant.

PATTERERS, men who cry last dying speeches, &c., in the streets, and those who help off their wares by *long harangues* in the public thoroughfares. These men, to use their own term "are the haristocracy of the street sellers," and despise the costermongers for their ignorance, boasting that they live by their intellect. The public, they say, do not expect to receive from them an equivalent for their money—they pay to hear them talk.—*Mayhew*. PATTERERS were formerly termed "mountebanks."

PAWS, hands.

PAY, to beat a person, or "serve them out." Originally a nautical term, meaning to stop the seams of a vessel with pitch (*French*, POIX); "here's the d——l to PAY, and no pitch hot," said when any catastrophe occurs which there is no means of averting; "to PAY over face and eyes, as the cat did the monkey;" "to PAY through the nose," to give a ridiculous price,—whence the origin? *Shakespere* uses PAY in the sense of to beat, or thrash.

PEACH, to inform against or betray. *Webster* states that *impeach* is now the modification mostly used, and that PEACH is confined principally to the conversation of thieves and the lower orders.

PEACOCK HORSE, amongst undertakers, is one with a showy tail and mane, and holds its head up well,—*che va favorreggiando, &c., Italian*.

PEAKING, remnants of cloth.

PECK, food; "PECK and booze," meat and drink.—*Lincolnshire. Ancient cant*, PEK, meat.

PECKER, "keep your PECKER up," *i.e.*, don't get down-hearted,—literally, keep your beak or head well up, "never say die!"

PECKISH, hungry. *Old cant*, PECKIDGE, meat.

PEEL, to strip, or disrobe.—*Pugilistic.*

PEELER, a policeman; so called from Sir Robert Peel (*see* BOBBY); properly applied to the Irish constabulary rather than the City police, the former force having been established by Sir Robert Peel.

PEEPERS, eyes; "painted PEEPERS," eyes bruised or blackened from a blow.

PEERY, suspicious, or inquisitive.

PEG, brandy and soda water.

PEG, "to PEG away," to strike, run, or drive away; "PEG a hack," to drive a cab; "take down a PEG or two," to check an arrogant or conceited person.

PEG, a shilling.—*Scotch.*

PEG-TOPS, the loose trousers now in fashion, small at the ankle and swelling upwards, in imitation of the Zouave costume.

PENNY GAFFS, shops turned into temporary theatres (admission one penny), where dancing and singing take place every night. Rude pictures of the performers are arranged outside to give the front a gaudy and attractive look, and at night-time coloured lamps and transparencies are displayed to draw an audience.

PENNY A-LINER, a contributor of local news, accidents, fires, scandal, political and fashionable gossip, club jokes, and anecdotes, to a newspaper; not regularly "on the paper;" one who is popularly believed to be paid for each contribution at the rate of a *penny a line*, and whose interest is, therefore, that his article should be horribly stuffed with epithets.

PENISULAR, or MOLL TOOLER, a female pickpocket.

PENSIONER, a man of the lowest morals who lives off the miserable earnings of a prostitute.

PEPPER, to thrash, or strike.—*Pugilistic*, but used by *Shakespere.—East.*

PERCH, or ROOST, a resting place; "I'm off to PERCH," *i.e.*, I am going to bed.

PERSUADERS, spurs.

PESKY, an intensive expression, implying annoyance; a PESKY, troublesome fellow. Corruption of PESTILENT?

PETER, a partridge.—*Poacher's term.*

PETER, a bundle, or valise.—*Bulwer's Paul Clifford.*

PETER, to run short, or give out.

PETERER, or PETERMAN, one who follows hackney and stage coaches, and cuts off the portmanteaus and trunks from behind.—*Nearly obsolete. Ancient* term for a fisherman, still used at Gravesend.

PETTICOAT, a woman.

PEWTER, money, like TIN, used generally to signify silver; also, a pewter-pot.

PHYSOG, or PHIZ, the face. *Swift* uses the latter. Corruption of *physiognomy.*

PIC., the Piccadilly Saloon.

PICK, "to PICK oneself up," to recover after a beating or illness; "to PICK a man up," "to do," or cheat him.

PICKERS, the hands.—*Shakespere.*

PICKLE, a miserable or comical position; "he is in a sad PICKLE," said of any one who has fallen into the gutter, or got besmeared. "A PICKLE herring," a comical fellow, a merry Andrew.—*Old.*

PICKLES! gammon.

PIECE, a contemptuous term for a woman; a strumpet.—*Shakespere.*

PIG, or SOW'S BABY, a sixpence.

PIG, a mass of metal,—so called from its being poured in a fluid state from a sow, which see.—*Workmen's term.*

PIG AND TINDER-BOX, the vulgar rendering of the well-known tavern sign, "*Elephant and Castle.*"

PEPPER-BOXES, the buildings of the Royal Academy and National Gallery, in Trafalgar-square. The name was first given by a wag, in allusion to the cupolas erected by Wilkins, the architect, upon the roof, and which at a distance suggest to the stranger the fact of their being enlarged PEPPER-BOXES, from their form and awkward appearance. —*See* BOILERS.

PIGEON, a gullible or soft person. The *French* slang, or *argot,* has the word PIGEON, dupe—"PECHON, PESCHON DE RUBY, apprenti gueux, enfant (sans doute dérobé)." The vagabonds and brigands of Spain also use the word in their

Germania, or *Robbers' Language*, PALOMO (pigeon), ignorant, simple.

PIGEON, or BLUEY CRACKING, breaking into empty houses and stealing lead.

PIG-HEADED, obstinate.

PIG'S WHISPER, a low or inaudible whisper; also a short space of time, synonymous with COCKSTRIDE, *i.e.*, *cock's tread.*

PIKE, to run away.

PIKE, a turnpike; "to bilk a PIKE," to cheat the keeper of the toll-gate.

PILL, a doctor—*Military.* PILL-DRIVER, a peddling apothecary.

PIN, "to put in the PIN," to refrain from drinking. From the ancient peg tankard, which was furnished with a row of PINS, or pegs, to regulate the amount which each person was to drink. A MERRY PIN, a roisterer.

PINCH, to steal, or cheat; also, to catch, or apprehend.

PINDARIC HEIGHTS, studying the odes of Pindar.—*Oxford.*

PINK, to stab, or pierce.

PINK, the *acmé* of perfection.—*Shakespere.*

PINNERS-UP, sellers of old songs pinned against a wall, or framed canvas.

PINS, legs.

PIPE, to shed tears, or bewail; "PIPE one's eye.—*Sea term.*

> "He first began to eye his pipe,
> And then to PIPE HIS EYE."
> *Old Song.*

Metaphor from the boatswain's pipe, which calls to duty.

PIPE, "to put one's PIPE out," to traverse his plans, "take a rise" out of him.

PIPKIN, the stomach,—properly, an earthen round-bottomed pot.—*Norwich.*

PIT, a breast pocket.

PITCH, a fixed locality where a patterer can hold forth to a gaping multitude for at least some few minutes continuously; "to do a PITCH in the drag," to perform in the street.

PITCH INTO, to fight; "PITCH INTO him, Bill," *i.e.*, give him a thrashing.

PITCH THE FORK, to tell a pitiful tale.

PITCH THE NOB, PRICK THE GARTER, which see.

PLANT, a dodge, a preconcerted swindle; a position in the street to sell from. PLANT, a swindle, may be thus described: a coster will join a party of gambling costers that he never saw before, and commence tossing. When sufficient time has elapsed to remove all suspicions of companionship, his mate will come up and commence betting on each of his PAL's throws with those standing around. By a curious quickness of hand, a coster can make the toss tell favourably for his wagering friend, who meets him in the evening after the play is over and shares the spoil.

PLANT, to mark a person out for plunder or robbery, to conceal, or place.—*Old cant.*

PLEBS, a term used to stigmatise a tradesman's son at Westminster School. *Latin*, PLEBS, the vulgar.

PLOUGHED, drunk.—*Household Words*, No. 183. Also a *University* term equivalent to PLUCKED.

PLUCK, the heart, liver, and lungs of an animal,—all that is PLUCKED away in connection with the windpipe, from the chest of a sheep or hog; among low persons, courage, valour, and a stout heart.—*See* MOLLYGRUBS.

PLUCK'D-'UN, a stout or brave fellow; "he's a rare PLUCKED-'UN," *i.e.*, dares face anything.

During the Crimean war, PLUCKY, signifying courageous, seemed likely to become a favourite term in May-Fair, even among the ladies. An eminent critic, however, who had been bred a butcher, having informed the fashionable world that in his native town the *sheep's head* always went with the PLUCK, the term has been gradually falling into discredit at the West End.

It has been said that a brave soldier is PLUCKY in attack, and GAME when wounded. Women are more GAME than PLUCKY.

PLUCKED, turned back at an examination.—*University.*

PLUNDER, a common word in the horse trade to express profit. Also an *American* term for baggage, luggage.

PLUM, £100,000, usually applied to the dowry of a rich heiress, or a legacy.

PLUMMY, round, sleek, jolly, or fat; excellent, very good, first rate.

PLUMPER, a single vote at an election, not a "split ticket."

PODGY, drunk; dumpy, short and fat.

POGRAM, a dissenter, a fanatic, formalist, or humbug.

POKE, "come, none of your POKING fun at me," *i.e.*, you must not laugh at me.

POKE, a bag, or sack; "to buy a pig in a POKE," to purchase anything without seeing it.—*Saxon.*

POKER, "by the holy POKER and the tumbling Tom!" an Irish oath.

POKERS, the Cambridge slang term for the Esquire Bedels, who carry the silver maces (also called POKERS) before the Vice-Chancellor.

POKY, confined or cramped; "that corner is POKY and narrow." —*Times* article, 21st July, 1859.

POLE-AXE, vulgar corruption of policeman.

POLICEMAN, a fly.

POLISH OFF, to finish off anything quickly—a dinner for instance; also to finish off an adversary.—*Pugilistic.*

POLL, or POLLING, one thief robbing another of part of their booty.—*Hall's Union*, 1548.

POLL, the "ordinary degree" candidates for the B.A. Examination, who do not aspire to the "Honours" list. From the *Greek*, οἱ πόλλοι, "the many." Some years ago, at Cambridge, Mr. Hopkins being the most celebrated "honour coach," or private tutor for the wranglers, and Mr. Potts the principal "crammer" of the non-honour men, the latter was facetiously termed the "POLLY HOPKINS" by the undergraduates.

POLL, a prostitute; POLLED UP, living with a woman without being married to her.

POLONY, a *Bologna* sausage.

POONA, a sovereign.—Corruption of *pound;* or from the *Lingua Franca?*

PONY, twenty-five pounds.—*Sporting.*

POPS, pocket pistols.

POP, to pawn or pledge; "to POP up the spout," to pledge at the pawnbroker's,—an allusion to the spout up which the brokers send the ticketed articles until such times as they shall be redeemed. The spout runs from the ground floor to the wareroom at the top of the house.

POSH, a halfpenny, or trifling coin. Also a generic term for money.

POSTERIORS, a correspondent insists that the vulgar sense of this word is undoubtedly slang (Swift, I believe, first applied it as such), and remarks that it is curious the word *anterior* has not been so abused.

POST-HORN, the nose.—*See* PASTE-HORN.

POST-MORTEM, at Cambridge, the second examination which men who have been "plucked" have to undergo.—*University.*

POT, a sixpence, *i.e.*, the price of a pot or quart of half-and-half. A half crown, in medical student slang, is a FIVE-POT PIECE.

POT, "to GO TO POT," to die; from the classic custom of putting the ashes of the dead in an urn; also, to be ruined, or broken up,—often applied to tradesmen who fail in business. GO TO POT! *i.e.*, go and hang yourself, shut up and be quiet. *L'Estrange*, to PUT THE POT ON, to overcharge, or exaggerate.

POT, to finish; "don't POT me," term used at billiards. This word was much used by our soldiers in the Crimea, for firing at the enemy from a hole or ambush. These were called POT-SHOTS.

POT-HUNTER, a sportsman who shoots anything he comes across, having more regard to filling his bag than to the rules which regulate the sport.

POT-LUCK, just as it comes; to take POT-LUCK, *i.e.*, one's chance of a dinner,—a hearty term used to signify whatever the pot contains you are welcome to.

POT-WALLOPERS, electors in certain boroughs before the passing of the Reform Bill, whose qualification consisted in being housekeepers,—to establish which, it was only necessary to boil a pot within the limits of the borough, by the aid of any temporary erection. This implied that they were able to provide for themselves, and not necessitated to apply for parochial relief. WALLOP, a word of *Anglo Saxon* derivation, from the same root as *wall.*

POTTED, or POTTED OUT, cabined, confined; "the patriotic member of Parliament POTTED OUT in a dusty little lodging somewhere about Bury-street."—*Times* article, 21st July, 1859. Also applied to burial.

POTTY, indifferent, bad looking.

POTATO TRAP, the mouth. A humorous *Hibernicism.*

POWER, a large quantity.—Formerly *Irish,* but now general; "a POWER of money."

PRAD, a horse.

PRAD NAPPING, horse stealing.

PRANCER, a horse.—*Ancient cant.*

PRICK THE GARTER, or PITCH THE NOB, a gambling and cheating game common at fairs, and generally practised by thimble riggers. It consists of a "garter" or a piece of list doubled, and then folded up tight. The bet is made upon your asserting that you can, with a pin, "prick" the point at which the garter is doubled. The garter is then unfolded, and nine times out of ten you will find that you have been deceived, and that you pricked one of the false folds. The owner of the garter, I should state, holds the ends tightly with one hand. This was, doubtless, originally a Gipsey game, and we are informed by *Brand* that it was much practised by the Gipseys in the time of *Shakespere*. In those days, it was termed PRICKING AT THE BELT, or FAST AND LOOSE.

PRIG, a thief Used by *Addison* in the sense of a coxcomb. *Ancient cant*, probably from the *Saxon*, PRICC-AN, to filch, &c. —*Shakespere*. PRIG, to steal, or rob. PRIGGING, thieving. In *Scotland* the term PRIG is used in a different sense from what it is in England. In Glasgow, or at Aberdeen, "to PRIG a salmon," would be to cheapen it, or seek for an abatement in the price. A story is told of two Scotchmen, visitors to London, who got into sad trouble a few years ago by announcing their intention of "PRIGGING a hat" which they had espied in a fashionable manufacturer's window, and which one of them thought he would like to possess.

PRIME PLANT, a good subject for plunder.—*See* PLANT.

PRIMED, said of a person in that state of incipient intoxication that if he takes more drink it will become evident.

PRO, a professional.—*Theatrical.*

PROG, meat, food, &c. *Johnson* calls it "a low word."

PROP, a gold scarf pin.

PROP-NAILER, a man who steals, or rather snatches, pins from gentlemen's scarfs.

PROPS, crutches.

PROPER, very, exceedingly, sometimes ironically; "you are a PROPER nice fellow," meaning a great scamp.

PROS, a water-closet. Abbreviated form of πρὸς τινα τόπον.—*Oxford University.*

PROSS, breaking in, or instructing, a stage-infatuated youth.—*Theatrical.*

PSALM-SMITER, a "Ranter," one who sings at a conventicle. —*See* BRISKET BEATER.

PUB, or PUBLIC, a public-house

PUCKER, poor temper, difficulty, *déshabillé*.

PUCKER, or PUCKER UP, to get in a poor temper.

PUCKERING, talking privately.

PUDDING SNAMMER, one who robs a cook shop.

PUFF, to blow up, swell with praise, was declared by a writer in the *Weekly Register*, as far back as 1732, to be illegitimate.

> "PUFF has become a cant word, signifying the applause set forth by writers, &c., to increase the reputation and sale of a book, and is an excellent stratagem to excite the curiosity of gentle readers."

Lord Bacon, however, used the word in a similar sense a century before.

PULL, an advantage, or hold upon another; "I've the PULL over you," *i.e.*, you are in my power—perhaps an oblique allusion to the judicial sense.—*See the following*.

PULL, to have one apprehended; "to be PULLED up," to be taken before a magistrate.

PULL, to drink; "come, take a PULL at it," *i.e.*, drink up.

PULLEY, a confederate thief,—generally a woman.

PUMMEL, to thrash,—from POMMEL.

PUMP SHIP, to evacuate urine.—*Sea*.

PURE FINDERS, street collectors of dogs' dung.

PURL, hunting term for a fall, synonymous with FOALED, or SPILT; "he'll get PURLED at the rails."

PURL, a mixture of hot ale and sugar, with wormwood infused in it, a favourite morning drink to produce an appetite; sometimes with gin and spice added :—

> "Two penn'orth o' PURL—
> Good 'early PURL,'
> 'Gin all the world
> To put your hair into a curl,
> When you feel yourself queer of a mornin'."

PUSH, a crowd.—*Old cant*.

PUSSEY-CATS, corruption of *Puseyites*, a name constantly, but improperly, given to the "Tractarian" party in the Church, from the Oxford Regius Professor of Hebrew, who by no means approved of the Romanising tendencies of some of its leaders.

PUT, a game at cards.

PUT THE POT ON, to bet too much upon one horse.—*Sporting*.

PUT UP, to suggest, to incite, "he PUT me UP to it;" to have done with; PUT IT UP, is a vulgar answer often heard in the streets. PUT UP, to stop at an hotel or tavern for entertainment.

PUT UPON, cheated, deluded, oppressed.

PYGOSTOLE, the least irreverent of names for the peculiar "M.B." coats worn by Tractarian curates."—

> "It is true that the wicked make sport
> Of our PYGOSTOLES, as we go by;
> And one gownsman, in Trinity Court,
> Went so far as to call me a 'Guy,'"

QUARTEREEN, a farthing.—*Gibraltar term. Ital.*, QUATTRINO.

QUEAN (not QUEEN), a strumpet.

QUEER, an old cant word, once in continual use as a prefix, signifying base, roguish, or worthless,—the opposite of RUM, which signified good and genuine. QUEER, in all probability, is immediately derived from the cant language. It has been mooted that it came into use from a *quære* (?) being set before a man's name; but it is more than probable that it was brought into this country by the Gipseys from Germany, where QUER signifies "*cross*," or "*crooked*." At all events, it is believed to have been first used in England as a cant word.

QUEEN BESS, the Queen of Clubs,—perhaps because that queen, history says, was of a swarthy complexion.—*North Hants.—See Gentleman's Magazine for* 1791, p. 141.

QUEER, "to QUEER a flat," to puzzle or confound a "gull" or silly fellow.

> "Who in a *row* like Tom could lead the van,
> *Booze* in the *ken*, or at the *spellken* hustle?
> Who QUEER a flat," &c.
>
> *Don Juan*, canto xi., 19.

QUEER BAIL, worthless persons who for a consideration would stand bail for any one in court. Insolvent Jews generally performed this office, which gave rise to the term JEW-BAIL. —*See* MOUNTERS: both nearly obsolete.

QUEER BIT-MAKERS, coiners.

QUEER SCREENS, forged bank notes.

QUEER SOFT, bad money.

QUEER STREET, "in QUEER STREET," in difficulty or in want.

QUEER CUFFEN, a justice of the peace, or magistrate—a very ancient term, mentioned in the earliest slang dictionary.

QUERIER, a chimney-sweep who calls from house to house,—formerly termed KNULLER, which see.

QUI-HI, an English resident at Calcutta.—*Anglo Indian.*

QUICK STICKS, in a hurry, rapidly; "to cut QUICK STICKS," to be in a great hurry.

QUID, or THICK UN, a sovereign; "half a QUID," half a sovereign; QUIDS, money generally; "QUID for a QUOD," one good turn for another. The word is used by *Old French* writers:—

> "Des testamens qu'on dit le maistre
> De mon fait n'aura QUID ne QUOD."
> *Grand Testament de Villon.*

QUID, a small piece of tobacco—one mouthful. *Quid est hoc?* asked one, tapping the swelled cheek of another; *hoc est quid*, promptly replied the other, exhibiting at the same time "a chaw" of the weed. Probably a corruption of CUD.

QUIET, "on the QUIET," clandestinely, so as to avoid observation, "under the rose."

QUILL-DRIVER, a scrivener, a clerk—satirical phrase similar to STEEL-BAR-DRIVER, a tailor.

QUILT, to thrash, or beat.

QUISBY, bankrupt, poverty stricken.—*Ho. Words*, No. 183.

QUIZ, a prying person, an odd fellow. *Oxford slang;* lately admitted into dictionaries. Not noticed by *Johnson*.

QUIZ, to pry, or joke.

QUIZZICAL, jocose, humorous.

QUOCKERWODGER, a wooden toy figure, which, when pulled by a string, jerks its limbs about. The term is used in a slang sense to signify a pseudo-politician, one whose strings of action are pulled by somebody else.—*West.*

QUOD, a prison, or lock up; QUODDED, put in prison. A slang expression used by Mr. Hughes, in *Tom Brown's Schooldays* (Macmillan's Magazine, January, 1860), throws some light upon the origin of this now very common street term:—"Flogged or whipped in QUAD," says the delineator of student life, in allusion to chastisement inflicted within the *Quadrangle* of a college. Quadrangle is the term given to the prison inclosure within which culprits are allowed to walk, and where whippings were formerly inflicted. Quadrangle also represents a building of four sides; and to be "within FOUR WALLS," or prison, is the frequent slang lamentation of unlucky vagabonds.

RABBIT, when a person gets the worst of a bargain he is said "to have bought the RABBIT."

RACKET, a dodge, manœuvre, exhibition; a disturbance.

RACKETY, wild or noisy.

RACKS, the bones of a dead horse. Term used by horse slaughterers.

RACLAN, a married woman.—*Gipsey.*

RAFE, or RALPH, a pawnbroker's duplicate.—*Norwich.*

RAG, to divide or share; "let's RAG IT," or GO RAGS, *i.e.*, share it equally between us.—*Norwich.*

RAGAMUFFIN, a tattered vagabond, a tatterdemalion.

RAG SPLAWGER, a rich man.

RAGS, bank notes.

RAG-SHOP, a bank.

RAIN NAPPER, umbrella.

RAISE THE WIND, to obtain credit, or money—generally by pawning or selling off property.

RAMP, to thieve or rob with violence.

RAMPSMAN, a highway robber who uses violence when necessary.

RAMSHACKLE, to shatter as with a battering ram; RAMSHACKLED, knocked about, as standing corn is after a high wind. Corrupted from *ram-shatter*, or possibly from *ransack*.

RANDOM, three horses driven in line, a very appropriate term. —*See* TANDEM.

RANDY, rampant, violent, warm, amorous. *North*, RANDY-BEGGAR, a gipsey tinker.

RAN-TAN, "on the RAN-TAN," drunk.—*Ho. Words*, No. 183.

RANTIPOLE, a wild noisy fellow.

RAP, a halfpenny; frequently used generically for money, thus: "I hav'nt a RAP," *i.e.*, I have no money whatever; "I don't care a RAP," &c. Originally a species of counterfeit coin used for small change in *Ireland*, against the use of which a proclamation was issued, 5th May, 1737. Small copper or base metal coins are still called RAPPEN in the Swiss cantons. Irish robbers are called RAPPAREES.

RAP, to utter; "he RAPPED out a volley of oaths."

RAPPING, enormous; "a RAPPING big lie."

RAPSCALLION, a low tattered wretch.

RAT, a sneak, an informer, a turn-coat, one who changes his party for interest. The late Sir Robert Peel was called the RAT, or the TAMWORTH RATCATCHER, for altering his views on the Roman Catholic question. From rats deserting vessels about to sink.

RAT, term amongst printers to denote one who works under price. *Old cant* for a clergyman.

RATHER! a ridiculous street exclamation synonymous with yes; "do you like fried chickens?" "RATHER!" "are you going out of town?" "RATHER!"

RATHER OF THE RATHEREST, a phrase applied to anything slightly in excess or defect.

RATTLECAP, an unsteady, volatile person.

RATTLER, a cab, coach, or cart.—*Old cant.*

RATTLERS, a railway; "on the RATTLERS to the stretchers," *i.e.*, going to the races by railway.

RAW, uninitiated; a novice.—*Old.* Frequently a JOHNNY RAW.

RAW, a tender point, a foible; "to touch a man up on the RAW" is to irritate one by alluding to, or joking him on, anything on which he is peculiarly susceptible or "thin-skinned."

READER, a pocket-book; "give it him for his READER," *i.e.*, rob him of his pocket-book.—*Old cant.*

READY, or READY GILT (properly GELT), money. Used by *Arbuthnot*, "Lord Strut was not very *flush* in READY.

REAM, good or genuine. From the *Old cant*, RUM.

REAM-BLOAK, a good man.

RECENT INCISION, the busy thoroughfare on the Surrey side of the Thames, known by sober people as the NEW CUT.

REDGE, gold.

RED HERRING, a soldier.

RED LANE, the throat.

RED LINER, an officer of the Mendicity Society.

RED RAG, the tongue.

REGULARS, a thief's share of the plunder. "They were quarrelling about the REGULARS."—*Times*, 8th January, 1856.

RELIEVING OFFICER, a significant term for a father.—*Univ.*

RENCH, vulgar pronunciation of RINSE. "*Wrench* your mouth out," said a fashionable dentist one day.—*North.*

RE-RAW, "on the RE-RAW," tipsy or drunk.—*Household Words*, No. 183.

RHINO, ready money.

RHINOCERAL, rich, wealthy, abounding in RHINO.

RIB, a wife.—*North.*

RIBBONS, the reins.—*Middlesex.*

RIBROAST, to beat till the ribs are sore,—*Old;* but still in use:—

> "And he departs, not meanly boasting
> Of his magnificent RIBROASTING."—*Hudibras.*

RICH, spicy; also used in the sense of "too much of a good thing;" "a RICH idea," one too absurd or unreasonable to be adopted.

RIDE, "to RIDE THE HIGH HORSE," or RIDE ROUGH-SHOD over one, to be overbearing or oppressive; to RIDE THE BLACK DONKEY, to be in an ill humour.

RIDER, in a University examination, a problem or question appended to another, as directly arising from or dependent on it;—beginning to be generally used for any corollary or position which naturally arises from any previous statement or evidence.

RIG, a trick, "spree," or performance; "run a RIG," to play a trick—*Gipsey;* "RIG the market," in reality to play tricks with it,—a mercantile slang phrase often used in the newspapers.

RIGGED, "well RIGGED," well dressed.—*Old slang*, in use 1736. —*See Bailey's Dictionary*.—*Sea.*

RIGHT AS NINEPENCE, quite right, exactly right.

RIGHTS, "to have one to RIGHTS," to be even with him, to serve him out.

RIGMAROLE, a prolix story.

RILE, to offend, to render very cross, irritated, or vexed. Properly, to render liquor turbid.—*Norfolk.*

RING, a generic term given to horse-racing and pugilism,—the latter is sometimes termed the PRIZE-RING. From the practice of forming the crowd into a *ring* around the combatants, or outside the race-course.

RING, "to go through the RING," to take advantage of the Insolvency Act, or be *whitewashed.*

RING DROPPING, *see* FAWNEY.

RINGING CASTORS, changing hats.

RINGING THE CHANGES, changing bad money for good.

RIP, a rake; "an old RIP," an old libertine, or debauchee. Corruption of *Reprobate.* A person reading the letters R. I. P. (*Requiescat in Pace*) on the top of a tombstone as one word, said, soliloquising, "Rip! well, he *was* an old RIP, and no mistake.—*Cuthbert Bede.*

RIPPER, a first-rate man or article.—*Provincial.*

RIPPING, excellent, very good.

RISE, "to take a RISE out of a person," to mortify, outwit, or cheat him, by superior cunning.

RISE (or RAISE) A BARNEY, to collect a mob.

ROARER, a broken-winded horse.

ROARING TRADE, a very successful business.

ROAST, to expose a person to a running fire of jokes at his expense from a whole company, in his presence. QUIZZING is done by a single person only.

ROCK A LOW, an overcoat. Corruption of the *French* ROQUELAURE.

ROCKED, "he's only HALF-ROCKED," *i.e.*, half witted.

ROLL OF SNOW, a piece of Irish linen.

ROMANY, a Gipsey, or the Gipsey language; the speech of the Roma or Zincali.—*Spanish Gipsey.*

ROOK, a clergyman, not only from his black attire, but also, perhaps, from the old nursery favourite, the *History of Cock Robin.*

> "I, says the ROOK,
> With my little book,
> I'll be the parson."

ROOK, a cheat, or tricky gambler; the opposite of PIGEON.—*Old.*

ROOKERY, a low neighbourhood inhabited by dirty Irish and thieves—as ST. GILES' ROOKERY.—*Old.* In *Military slang* that part of the barracks occupied by subalterns, often by no means a pattern of good order.

ROOKY, rascally, rakish, scampish.

ROOST, synonymous with PERCH, which see.

ROOTER, anything good, or of a prime quality; "that *is* a ROOTER," *i.e.*, a first-rate one of the sort.

ROSE, an orange.

ROSE, "under the ROSE" (frequently used in its *Latin* form, *Sub rosâ*), *i.e.*, under the obligation of silence and secresy, of which the rose was anciently an emblem, perhaps, as Sir Thomas Browne remarks, from the closeness with which its petals are enfolded in the bud. The Rose of Venus was given, says the classic legend, to Harpocrates, the God of Silence, by Cupid, as a bribe not to "peach" about the Goddess' amours. It was commonly sculptured on the ceilings of banquetting rooms, as a sign that what was said in free conversation there was not afterwards to be divulged; and about 1526 was placed over the Roman confessionals as an emblem of secrecy. The White Rose was also an emblem of the Pretender, whose health, as king, his secret adherents used to drink "under the ROSE."

ROT, nonsense, anything bad, disagreeable, or useless.

ROT GUT, bad small beer,—in *America*, cheap whisky.

ROUGH, bad; "ROUGH fish," bad or stinking fish.

ROUGH IT, to put up with chance entertainment, to take pot luck, and what accommodation "turns up," without sighing for better. ROUGHING IT *in the Bush*" is the title of an interesting work on Backwoods life.

ROUGHS, coarse, or vulgar men.

ROULEAU, a packet of sovereigns.—*Gaming*.

ROUND, to tell tales, to "SPLIT," which see; "to ROUND on a man," to swear to him as being the person, &c. Synonymous with "BUFF," which see. *Shakespere* has ROUNDING, whispering.

ROUND, "ROUND dealing," honest trading; "ROUND sum," a large sum. Synonymous also in a *slang* sense with SQUARE, which see.

ROUNDS, shirt collars—apparently a mere shortening of "All Rounds," or "All Rounders," names of fashionable collars.

ROUNDS (in the language of the street), the BEATS or usual walks of the costermonger to sell his stock. A term used by street folk generally.

> "Watchmen, sometimes they made their sallies,
> And walk'd their ROUNDS through streets and allies."
> *Ned Ward's Vulgus Britannicus*, 1710.

ROUND ROBIN, a petition, or paper of remonstrance, with the signatures written in a circle,—to prevent the first signer, or ringleader, from being discovered.

ROUNDABOUTS, large swings of four compartments, each the size, and very much the shape, of the body of a cart, capable of seating six or eight boys and girls, erected in a high frame, and turned round by men at a windlass. Fairs and merry-makings generally abound with them. The frames take to pieces, and are carried in vans by miserable horses, from fair to fair, &c.

ROW, a noisy disturbance, tumult, or trouble. Originally *Cambridge*, now universal. Seventy years ago it was written ROUE, which would indicate a *French* origin from *roué*, a profligate, or disturber of the peace.—*Vide George Parker's Life's Painter*, 1789, p. 122.

ROWDY, money. In *America*, a ruffian, a brawler, "rough."

ROWDY-DOW, low, vulgar; "not the CHEESE," or thing.

RUB, a quarrel, or impediment; "there's the RUB," *i.e.*, that is the difficulty.—*Shakespere and L'Estrange*.

RUBBER, a term at whist, &c., two games out of three.—*Old*, 1677.

RUCK, the undistinguished crowd; "to come in with the RUCK," to arrive at the winning post among the non-winning horses. —*Racing term.*

RUGGY, fusty, frowsy.

RUM, like its opposite, QUEER, was formerly a much used prefix, signifying, fine, good, gallant, or valuable, perhaps in some way connected with ROME. Now-a-days it means indifferent, bad, or questionable, and we often hear even persons in polite society use such a phrase as "what a RUM fellow he is, to be sure," in speaking of a man of singular habits or appearance. The term, from its frequent use, long since claimed a place in our dictionaries; but, with the exception of *Johnson*, who says RUM, a cant word for a clergyman (?), no lexicographer has deigned to notice it.

> "Thus RUMLY floor'd, the kind Acestes ran,
> And pitying, rais'd from earth the game old man."
> VIRGIL'S ÆNEID, book v., *Translation by Thomas Moore.*

RUMBUMPTIOUS, haughty, pugilistic.

RUMBUSTIOUS, or RUMBUSTICAL, pompous, haughty, boisterous, careless of the comfort of others.

RUMGUMPTION, or GUMPTION, knowledge, capacity, capability, —hence, RUMGUMPTIOUS, knowing, wide-awake, forward, positive, pert, blunt.

RUM MIZZLERS, persons who are clever at making their escape, or getting out of a difficulty.

RUMPUS, a noise, disturbance, a "row."

RUMY, a good woman, or girl.—*Gipsey slang.* In the regular *Gipsey* language, ROMI, a woman, a wife, is the feminine of RO, a man; and in the *Robber's Language* of Spain (partly *Gipsey*), RUMI signifies a harlot.

RUN (good or bad), the success of a performance.—*Theatrical.*

RUN, to comprehend, &c.; "I don't RUN, to it," *i.e.*, I can't do it, or I don't understand, or I have not money enough.—*North.*

RUN, "to get the RUN upon any person," to have the upper hand, or be able to laugh at them. RUN DOWN, to abuse or backbite anyone.

RUNNING PATTERER, a street seller who runs or moves briskly along, calling aloud his wares.

RUNNING STATIONERS, hawkers of books, ballads, dying speeches, and newspapers. They formerly used to run with newspapers, blowing a horn, when they were also termed FLYING STATIONERS.

RUSH, "doing it on the RUSH," running away, or making off.

RUST, "to nab the RUST," to take offence. RUSTY, cross, ill-tempered, morose, one who cannot go through life like a person of easy and *polished* manners.

RUSTY GUTS, a blunt, rough old fellow. Corruption of RUSTICUS.

SACK, "to get the SACK," to be discharged by an employer.

SADDLE, an additional charge made by the manager to a performer upon his benefit night.—*Theatrical.*

SAD DOG, a merry fellow, a joker, a gay or "fast" man.

SAINT MONDAY, a holiday most religiously observed by journeymen shoemakers, and other mechanics. An Irishman observed that this saint's anniversary happened every week. —*North,* where it is termed COBBLERS' MONDAY.

SAL, a salary.—*Theatrical.*

SALAMANDERS, street acrobats, and jugglers who eat fire.

SALOOP, SALEP, or SALOP, a greasy, looking beverage, formerly sold on stalls at early morning, prepared from a powder made of the root of the *Orchis mascula,* or Red-handed Orchis. Within a few years coffee stands have superseded SALOOP stalls, but Charles Lamb, in one of his papers, has left some account of this drinkable, which he says was of all preparations the most grateful to the stomachs of young chimney-sweeps.

SALT, "its rather too SALT," said of an extravagant hotel bill.

SALT BOX, the condemned cell in Newgate.

SALTEE, a penny. Pence, &c., are thus reckoned :—

ONEY SALTEE, a penny, from the *Ital.,* UNO SOLDO.
DOOE SALTEE, twopence ... ... DUE SOLDI.
TRAY SALTEE, threepence ... ... TRE SOLDI.
QUARTERER SALTEE, fourpence ... QUATTRO SOLDI.
CHINKER SALTEE, fivepence ... ... CINQUE SOLDI.
SAY SALTEE, sixpence ... ... SEI SOLDI.
SAY ONEY SALTEE, or SETTER SALTEE, sevenpence ... ... SETTE SOLDI.
SAY DOOE SALTEE, or OTTER SALTEE, eightpence ... ... OTTO SOLDI.
SAY TRAY SALTEE, or NOBBA SALTEE, ninepence ... ... NOVE SOLDI
SAY QUARTERER SALTEE, or DACHA SALTEE, tenpence ... ... DIECI SOLDI.

SAY CHINKER SALTEE, or DACHA ONE SALTEE, elevenpence ... ... DIECI UNO SOLDI, &c.

ONEY BEONG, one shilling.

A BEONG SAY SALTEE, one shilling and sixpence.

DOOE BEONG SAY SALTEE, or MADZA CAROON, half-a-crown, or two shillings and sixpence.

_ This curious list of numerals in use among the London street folk is, strange as it may seem, derived from the *Lingua Franca*, or bastard *Italian*, of the Mediterranean seaports, of which other examples may be found in the pages of this Dictionary. SALTEE, the cant term used by the costermongers and others for a penny, is no other than the *Italian*, SOLDO (plural, SOLDI), and the numerals—as may be seen by the *Italian* equivalents—are a tolerably close imitation of the originals. After the number SIX, a curious variation occurs, which is peculiar to the London cant, seven being reckoned as SAY ONEY, *six-one*, SAY DOOE, *six-two* = 8, and so on. DACHA, I may remark, is perhaps from the *Greek*, DEKA (δέκα), ten, which, in the Constantinopolitan *Lingua Franca*, is likely enough to have been substituted for the *Italian*. MADZA, is clearly the *Italian* MEZZA. The origin of BEONG I have not been so fortunate as to discover, unless it be the *French*, BIEN, the application of which to a shilling is not so evident; but amongst costermongers and other street folk, it is quite immaterial what foreign tongue contributes to their secret language. Providing the terms are unknown to the police and the public generally, they care not a rushlight whether the polite French, the gay Spaniards, or the cloudy Germans helped to swell their vocabulary. The numbers of low foreigners, however, dragging out a miserable existence in our crowded neighbourhoods, organ grinders and image sellers, foreign seamen from the vessels in the river, and our own connection with Malta and the Ionian Isles, may explain, to a certain extent, the phenomenon of these Southern phrases in the mouths of costers and tramps.

SALT JUNK, navy salt beef.—*See* OLD HORSE.

SALVE, praise, flattery, chaff.

SAM, to "stand SAM," to pay for refreshment, or drink, to stand paymaster for anything. An *Americanism*, originating in the letters U.S. on the knapsacks of the United States soldiers, which letters were jocularly said to be the initials of *Uncle Sam* (the Government), who pays for all. In use in this country as early as 1827.

SANGUINARY JAMES, a sheep's head.—*See* BLOODY JEMMY.

SANK WORK, making soldiers' clothes. *Mayhew* says from the *Norman*, SANG, blood,—in allusion either to the soldier's calling, or the colour of his coat.

SAP, or SAPSCULL, a poor green simpleton, with no heart for work.

SAUCEBOX, a mouth, also a pert young person.

SAVELOY, a sausage of chopped beef smoked, a minor kind of POLONY.

SAVEY, to know; "do you SAVEY that?"—*French*, SAVEZ VOUS CELA? In the nigger and *Anglo Chinese patois*, this is SABBY, "me no SABBY." The Whampoa slang of this description is very extraordinary; from it we have got our word CASH!

SAW YOUR TIMBER, "be off!" equivalent to *cut your stick*. —*See* CUT.

SAWBONES, a surgeon.

SAWNEY, or SANDY, a Scotchman. Corruption of Alexander.

SAWNEY, a simpleton.

SAWNEY, bacon. SAWNEY HUNTER, one who steals bacon.

SCAB, a worthless person.—*Old*. *Shakespere* uses SCALD in a similar sense.

SCALDRUM DODGE, burning the body with a mixture of acids and gunpowder, so as to suit the hues and complexions of the accident to be deplored.

SCALY, shabby, or mean. *Shakespere* uses SCALD, an old word of reproach.

SCAMANDER, to wander about without a settled purpose;—possibly in allusion to the winding course of the Homeric river of that name.

SCAMMERED, drunk.

SCAMP, a graceless fellow, a rascal; formerly the cant term for plundering and thieving. A ROYAL-SCAMP was a highwayman, whilst a FOOT-SCAMP was an ordinary thief with nothing but his legs to trust to in case of an attempt at capture. Some have derived SCAMP from *qui ex campo exit*, viz., one who leaves the field, a deserter.

SCARPER, to run away.—*Spanish*, ESCAPAR, to escape, make off; *Italian*, SCAPPARE. "SCARPER with the feele of the donna of the cassey," to run away with the daughter of the landlady of the house; almost pure *Italian*, "*scappare colla figlia della donna della casa.*"

SCHISM-SHOP, a dissenters' meeting-house.—*University.*

SCHOFEL, bad money.—*See* SHOW-FULL.

SCHOOL, or MOB, two or more "patterers" working together in the streets.

SCHOOLING, a low gambling party.

SCHWASSLE BOX, the street performance of Punch and Judy. —*Household Words*, No. 183.

SCONCE, the head, judgment, sense.—*Dutch.*

SCORE, "to run up a SCORE at a public house," to obtain credit there until pay day, or a fixed time, when the debt must be WIPED OFF.

SCOT, a quantity of anything, a lot, a share.—*Anglo Saxon,* SCEAT, pronounced SHOT.

SCOT, temper, or passion,—from the irascible temperament of that nation; "oh! what a SCOT he was in," *i.e.*, what temper he showed,—especially if you allude to the following.

SCOTCH FIDDLE, the itch; "to play the SCOTCH FIDDLE," to work the index finger of the right hand like a fiddlestick between the index and middle finger of the left. This provokes a Scotchmen in the highest degree, it implying that he is afflicted with the itch.

SCOTCH GRAYS, lice. Our northern neighbours are calumniously reported, from their living on oatmeal, to be peculiarly liable to cutaneous eruptions and parasites.

SCOTCHES, the legs; also synonymous with NOTCHES.

SCOUT, a college valet, or waiter.—*Oxford.*—*See* GYP.

SCRAG, the neck.—*Old cant. Scotch,* CRAIG. Still used by butchers. Hence, SCRAG, to hang by the neck, and SCRAGGING, an execution,—also *old cant.*

SCRAN, pieces of meat, broken victuals. Formerly the reckoning at a public-house. SCRANNING, begging for broken victuals. Also, an *Irish* malediction of a mild sort, "Bad SCRAN to yer!"

SCRAPE, a difficulty; SCRAPE, low wit for a shave.

SCRAPE, cheap butter; "bread and SCRAPE," the bread and butter issued to school-boys—so called from the butter being laid on, and then *scraped* off again, for economy's sake.

SCRAPING CASTLE, a water-closet.

SCRATCH, a fight, contest, point in dispute; "coming up to the SCRATCH," going or preparing to fight—in reality, approaching the line usually chalked on the ground to divide the ring.—*Pugilistic.*

SCRATCH, "no great SCRATCH," of little worth.

SCRATCH, to strike a horse's name out of the list of runners in a particular race. "Tomboy was SCRATCHED for the Derby, at 10, a.m., on Wednesday," from which period all bets made in reference to him (with one exception) are void.—*See* P.P.—*Turf.*

SCRATCH-RACE (on the *Turf*), a race where any horse, aged, winner, or loser, can run with any weights; in fact, a race without restrictions. At *Cambridge* a boat-race, where the crews are drawn by lot.

SCREAMING, first-rate, splendid. Believed to have been first used in the *Adelphi* play-bills; "a SCREAMING farce," one calculated to make the audience scream with laughter. Now a general expression.

SCREEVE, a letter, a begging petition.

SCREEVE, to write, or devise; "to SCREEVE a fakement," to concoct, or write, a begging letter, or other impostor's document. From the *Dutch*, SCHRYVEN; *German*, SCHREIBEN; *French*, ECRIVANT (old form), to write.

SCREEVER, a man who draws with coloured chalks on the pavement figures of our Saviour crowned with thorns, specimens of elaborate writing, thunderstorms, ships on fire, &c. The men who attend these pavement chalkings, and receive halfpence and sixpences from the admirers of street art, are not always the draughtsmen. The artist, or SCREEVER, drew, perhaps, in half-a-dozen places that very morning, and rented the spots out to as many cadaverous looking men.

SCREW, an unsound, or broken-down horse, that requires both whip and spur to get him along.

SCREW, a key,—skeleton, or otherwise.

SCREW, a turnkey.

SCREW, a mean or stingy person.

SCREW, salary or wages.

SCREW, "to put on the SCREW," to limit one's credit, to be more exact and precise.

SCREW LOOSE, when friends become cold and distant towards each other, it is said there is a SCREW LOOSE betwixt them; said also when anything goes wrong with a person's credit or reputation.

SCREW, a small packet of tobacco.

SCREWED, intoxicated or drunk.

SCRIMMAGE, or SCRUMMAGE, a disturbance or row.—*Ancient.* Corruption of *skirmish?*

SCROBY, "to get SCROBY," to be whipped in prison before the justices.

SCROUGE, to crowd or squeeze.—*Wiltshire.*

SCRUFF, the back part of the neck seized by the adversary in an encounter.

SCRUMPTIOUS, nice, particular, beautiful.

SCUFTER, a policeman.—*North country.*

SCULL, or SKULL, the head or master of a college.—*University,* but nearly *obsolete;* the gallery, however, in St. Mary's (the University church), where the "Heads of Houses" sit in solemn state, is still nicknamed the GOLGOTHA by the undergraduates.

SCURF, a mean fellow.

SEALS, a religious slang term for converts.—*See* OWNED.

SEEDY, worn out, poverty stricken, used up, shabby. Metaphorical expression from the appearance of flowers when off bloom and running to *seed;* hence said of one who wears clothes until they crack and become shabby; "how SEEDY he looks," said of any man whose clothes are worn threadbare, with greasy facings, and hat brightened up by perspiration and continual polishing and wetting. When a man's coat begins to look worn out and shabby he is said to look SEEDY and ready for *cutting.* This term has been "on the streets" for nearly two centuries, and latterly has found its way into most dictionaries. Formerly slang, it is now a recognised word, and one of the most expressive in the English language. The French are always amused with it, they having no similar term.

SELL, to deceive, swindle, or play a practical joke upon a person. A sham is a SELL in street parlance. "SOLD again, and got the money," a costermonger cries after having successfully deceived somebody. *Shakespere* uses SELLING in a similar sense, viz., blinding or deceiving.

SELL, a deception, disappointment; also a lying joke.

SENSATION, a quartern of gin.

SERENE, all right; "it's all SERENE," a street phrase of very modern adoption, the burden of a song.

SERVE OUT, to punish, or be revenged on any one.

SETTER, sevenpence. *Italian*, SETTE.—*See* SALTEE.

SETTER, a person employed by the vendor at an auction to run the biddings up; to bid against *bonâ fide* bidders.

SETTLE, to kill, ruin, or effectually quiet a person.

SETTLED, transported.

SET TO, a sparring match, a fight; "a dead set," a determined stand, in argument or in movement.

SEVEN PENNORTH, transported for seven years.

SEWED-UP, done up, used up, intoxicated. *Dutch*, SEEUWT, sick.

SHACK, a "chevalier d'industrie."

SHACKLY, loose, rickety.—*Devonshire.*

SHAKE, a prostitute, a disreputable man or woman.—*North.*

SHAKE, to take away, to steal, or run off with anything; "what SHAKES, Bill?" "None," *i.e.*, no chance of committing a robbery.—*See the following.*

SHAKE, or SHAKES, a bad bargain is said to be "no great SHAKES;" "pretty fair SHAKES" is anything good or favourable.—*Byron.* In *America*, a fair SHAKE is a fair trade or a good bargain.

SHAKE LURK, a false paper carried by an impostor, giving an account of a "dreadful shipwreck."

SHAKER, a shirt.

SHAKESTER, or SHICKSTER, a prostitute. Amongst costermongers this term is invariably applied to *ladies*, or the wives of tradesmen, and females generally of the classes immediately above them.

SHAKY, said of a person of questionable health, integrity, or solvency; at the *University*, of one not likely to pass his examination.

SHALER, a girl.

SHALLOW, a flat basket used by costers.

SHALLOWS, "to go on the SHALLOWS," to go half naked.

SHALLOW-COVE, a begging rascal who goes about the country half naked,—with the most limited amount of rags upon his person, wearing neither shoes, stockings, nor hat.

SHALLOW-MOT, a ragged woman,—the frequent companion of the SHALLOW-COVE.

SHALLOW-SCREEVER, a man who sketches and draws on the pavement.—*See* SCREEVER.

SHAM ABRAHAM, to feign sickness.—*See* ABRAHAM.

SHANDY-GAFF, ale and ginger beer; perhaps SANG DE GOFF, the favourite mixture of one GOFF, a blacksmith.

SHANKS, legs.

SHANKS' NAG, "to ride SHANKS' NAG," to go on foot.

SHANT, a pot or quart; "SHANT of bivvy," a quart of beer.

SHAPES, "to cut up" or "show SHAPES," to exhibit pranks, or flightiness.

SHARP, or SHARPER, a cunning cheat, a rogue,—the opposite of FLAT.

SHARP'S-ALLEY BLOOD WORMS, beef sausages and black puddings. Sharp's-alley was very recently a noted slaughtering place near Smithfield.

SHARPING-OMEE, a policeman.

SHARK, a sharper, a swindler. *Bow-street* term in 1785, now in most dictionaries.—*Friesic* and *Danish*, SCHURK.—*See* LAND-SHARK.

SHAVE, a false alarm, a hoax, a sell. This was much used in the Crimea during the Russian campaign.

SHAVE, a narrow escape. At Cambridge, "just SHAVING through," or "making a SHAVE," is just escaping a "pluck" by coming out at the bottom of the list.

> "My terms are anything but dear,
> Then read with me, and never fear;
> The examiners we're sure to queer,
> And get through, if you make a SHAVE on't."
> *The Private Tutor.*

SHAVER, a sharp fellow; "a young" or "old SHAVER," a boy or man.—*Sea.*

SHEEN, bad money.—*Scotch.*

SHEEP'S EYES, "to make SHEEP'S EYES at a person," to cast amorous glances towards one on the sly:—

> "But he, the beast, was casting SHEEP'S EYES at her,
> Out of his bullock head."
> *Colman, Broad Grins*, p. 57.

SHEEP'S FOOT, an iron hammer used in a printing office, the end of the handle being made like a sheep's foot.

SHELF, "on the SHELF," not yet disposed of; young ladies are said to be so situated when they cannot meet with a husband; "on the SHELF," pawned.

SHELL OUT, to pay or count out money.

SHICE, nothing; "to do anything for SHICE," to get no payment. The term was first used by the Jews in the last century. *Grose* gives the phrase CHICE-AM-A-TRICE, which has a synonymous meaning. *Spanish*, CHICO, little; *Anglo Saxon*, CHICHE, niggardly.

SHICER, a mean man, a humbug, a "duffer,"—a person who is either worthless or will not work.

SHICKERY, shabby, bad.

SHICKSTER; a prostitute, a lady.—*See* SHAKESTER.

SHILLY SHALLY, to trifle or fritter away time; irresolute. Corruption of *Shall I, shall I?*

SHINDY, a row, or noise.

SHINE, a row, or disturbance.

SHINE, "to take the SHINE out of a person," to surpass or excel him.

SHINER, a looking-glass.

SHINERS, sovereigns, or money.

SHINEY RAG, "to win the SHINEY RAG," to be ruined,—said in gambling, when any one continues betting after "luck has set in against him."

SHIP-SHAPE, proper, in good order; sometimes the phrase is varied to "SHIP-SHAPE and *Bristol* fashion."—*Sea.*

SHIRTY, ill-tempered, or cross. When one person makes another in an ill humour he is said to have "got his SHIRT out."

SHITTEN-SATURDAY (corruption of SHUT-IN-SATURDAY), the Saturday between Good Friday and Easter Sunday, when our Lord's body was enclosed in the tomb.

SHIVERING JEMMY, the name given by street folk to any cadger who exposes himself, half naked, on a cold day, to excite pity and procure alms. The "game" is unpleasant, but exceedingly lucrative.

SHODDY, old cloth worked up into new; also, a term of derision applied to workmen in woollen factories.—*Yorkshire.*

SHOE, to free, or initiate a person,—a practice common in most trades to a new comer. The SHOEING consists in paying for beer, or other drink, which is drunk by the older hands. The cans emptied, and the bill paid, the stranger is considered properly SHOD.

SHOE LEATHER! a thief's warning cry, when he hears footsteps. This exclamation is used in the same spirit as Bruce's friend, who, when he suspected treachery towards him at King Edward's court, in 1306, sent him a purse and a pair of spurs, as a sign that he should use them in making his escape.

SHOES, "to die in one's SHOES," to be hung.

SHOOL, to saunter idly, become a vagabond, beg rather than work.—*Smollett's Roderick Random,* vol. i., p. 262.

SHOOT THE CAT, to vomit.

SHOOT THE MOON, to remove furniture from a house in the night, without paying the landlord.

SHOOT WITH THE LONG BOW, to tell lies, to exaggerate. Synonymous with THROWING THE HATCHET.

SHOP BOUNCER, or SHOP LIFTER, a person generally respectably attired, who, while being served with a small article at a shop, steals one of more value. *Shakespere* has the word LIFTER, a thief.

SHOPPING, purchasing at shops. Termed by *Todd* a slang word, but used by *Cowper* and *Byron.*

SHORT, when spirit is drunk without any admixture of water, it is said to be taken "short;" "summat SHORT," a dram. A similar phrase is used at the counters of banks; upon presenting a cheque, the clerk asks, "how will you take it?" *i.e.*, in gold, or in notes? Should it be desired to receive it in as small a compass as possible, the answer is, "SHORT."

SHORT COMMONS, short allowance of food.—*See* COMMONS.

SHOT, from the modern sense of the word to SHOOT,—a guess, a random conjecture; "to make a bad SHOT," to expose one's ignorance by making a wrong guess, or random answer without knowing whether it is right or wrong.

SHOT, from the once *English,* but now provincial word, to SHOOT, to subscribe, contribute in fair proportion;—a share, the same as SCOT, both being from the *Anglo Saxon* word, SCEAT; "to pay one's SHOT," *i.e.*, share of the reckoning, &c.

SHOT, "I wish I may be SHOT, if," &c., a common form of mild swearing.

SHOVE-HALFPENNY, a gambling street game.

SHOWFULL, or SCHOFELL, a Hansom cab,—said to have been from the name of the inventor.—*Led de hor qu.*

SHOW-FULL, or SCHOFUL, bad money. *Mayhew* thinks this word is from the *Danish,* SKUFFE, to shove, to deceive, cheat; *Saxon,* SCUFAN,—whence the *English,* SHOVE. The term, however, is possibly one of the many street words from the *Hebrew* (through the low Jews); SHEPHEL, in that language, signifying a *low* or debased estate. *Chaldee*, SHAPHAL.—*See* Psalm cxxxvi. 23, "in our *low estate*." A correspondent suggests another very probable derivation, from the *German*, SCHOFEL, trash, rubbish,—the *German* adjective, SCHOFELIG, being the nearest possible translation of our *shabby*.

SHOWFULL-PITCHER, a passer of counterfeit money.

SHOWFULL PITCHING, passing bad money.

SHOWFULL PULLET, a "gay" woman.

SHRIMP, a diminutive person.—*Chaucer*.

SHUNT, to throw or turn aside.—*Railway term*.

SHUT OF, or SHOT OF, rid of.

SHUT UP! be quiet, don't make a noise; to stop short, to make cease in a summary manner, to silence effectually. "Only the other day we heard of a preacher who, speaking of the scene with the doctors in the Temple, remarked that the Divine disputant completely SHUT THEM UP!"—*Athen.* 30th July, 1859. SHUT UP, utterly exhausted, done for.

SHY, a throw.

SHY, "to fight SHY of a person," to avoid his society either from dislike, fear, or any other reason. SHY has also the sense of flighty, unsteady, untrustworthy.

SHY, to fling; COCK-SHY, a game at fairs, consisting of throwing short sticks at trinkets set upon other sticks,—both name and practice derived from the old game of throwing or SHYING at live cocks.

SICES, or SIZES, a throw of *sixes* at dice.

SICK AS A HORSE, popular simile,—curious, because a horse never vomits.

SICKNER, or SICKENER, a dose too much of anything.

SIDE BOARDS, or STICK-UPS, shirt collars.

SIGHT, "to take a SIGHT at a person," a vulgar action employed by street boys to denote incredulity, or contempt for authority, by placing the thumb against the nose and closing all the fingers except the little one, which is agitated in token of derision.—*See* WALKER.

SIM, one of a Methodistical turn in religion; a low-church-man; originally a follower of the late Rev. Charles Simeon.—*Cambridge*.

SIMON, a sixpenny piece.

SIMON PURE, "the real SIMON PURE," the genuine article.

Those who have witnessed Mr. C. Mathews' performance in Mrs. Centlivre's admirable comedy of *A Bold Stroke for a Wife*, and the laughable coolness with which he, the *false* SIMON PURE, assuming the quaker dress and character of the REAL ONE, elbowed that worthy out of his expected entertainment, will at once perceive the origin of this phrase. —*See* act v., scene 1.

SING OUT, to call aloud.—*Sea.*

SING SMALL, to lessen one's boasting, and turn arrogance into humility.

SINKERS, bad money.

SINKS, a throw of fives at dice. *French*, CINQS.

SIR HARRY, a close stool.

SISERARA, a hard blow.—*Suffolk.* Moor derives it from the story of Sisera in the Old Testament, but it is more probably a corruption of CERTIORARI, a Chancery writ reciting a complaint of hard usage.

SIT UNDER, a term employed in Dissenters' meeting houses, to denote attendance on the ministry of any particular preacher.

SITTING PAD, sitting on the pavement in a begging position.

SIT-UPONS, trousers.—*See* INEXPRESSIBLES.

SIVVY, "'pon my SIVVY," *i.e.*, upon my soul or honour. Corruption of *asseveration*, like DAVY, which is an abridgment of *affidavit*.

SIXES AND SEVENS, articles in confusion are said to be all SIXES and SEVENS. The Deity is mentioned in the Towneley Mysteries as He that "sett all on seven," *i.e.*, set or appointed everything in seven days. A similar phrase at this early date implied confusion and disorder, and from these, *Halliwell* thinks, has been derived the phrase "to be at SIXES AND SEVENS." A Scotch correspondent, however, states that the phrase probably came from the workshop, and that amongst needle makers when the points and eyes are "heads and tails" ("heeds and thraws"), or in confusion, they are said to be SIXES AND SEVENS, because those numbers are the sizes most generally used, and in the course of manufacture have frequently to be distinguished.

SIXTY, "to go along like SIXTY," *i.e.*, at a good rate, briskly.

SIZE, to order extras over and above the usual commons at the dinner in college halls. Soup, pastry, &c., are SIZINGS, and are paid for at a certain specified rate *per* SIZE, or portion, to the college cook.—*Peculiar to Cambridge. Minsheu* says, "SIZE, a farthing which schollers in Cambridge have at the buttery, noted with the letter *s*."

SIZERS, or SIZARS, are certain poor scholars at Cambridge, annually elected, who get their dinners (including *sizings*) from what is left at the upper, or Fellows' table, free, or nearly so. They pay rent of rooms, and some other fees, on a lower scale than the "Pensioners" or ordinary students, and answer to the "battlers" and "servitors" at Oxford.

SIZINGS, *see* SIZE.

SKATES LURK, a begging impostor dressed as a sailor.

SKID, a sovereign. Fashionable slang.

SKIE, to throw upwards, to toss "coppers."—*See* ODD MAN.

SKILLY, broth served on board the hulks to convicts.—*Linc.*

SKILLIGOLEE, prison gruel, also sailors' soup of many ingredients.

SKIN, a purse.

SKIN, to abate, or lower the value of anything ; "thin SKINNED," sensitive, touchy.

SKIN-FLINT, an old popular simile for a "close-fisted," stingy person.

SKIPPER, the master of a vessel. *Dutch*, SCHIFFER, from *schiff* a ship ; sometimes used synonymous with "Governor."

SKIPPER, a barn.—*Ancient cant.*

SKIPPER IT, to sleep in the open air, or in a rough way.

SKIPPER-BIRDS, or KEYHOLE WHISTLERS, persons who sleep in barns or outhouses in preference to lodging-houses.

SKIT, a joke, a squib.

SKITTLES, a game similar to Ten Pins, which, when interdicted by the Government was altered to Nine Pins, or SKITTLES. They are set up in an alley and are *thrown at* (not bowled) with a round piece of hard wood, shaped like a small flat cheese. The costers consider themselves the best players in London.

SKROUGE, to push or squeeze.—*North.*

SKULL-THATCHERS, straw bonnet makers,—sometimes called "bonnet-BUILDERS."

SKY, a disagreeable person, an enemy.—*Westminster School.*

SKY-BLUE, London milk much diluted with water, or from which the cream has been too closely skimmed.

> "Hence, Suffolk dairy wives run mad for cream,
> And leave their milk with nothing but the name;
> Its name derision and reproach pursue,
> And strangers tell of three times skimmed—SKY-BLUE."
> *Bloomfield's Farmer's Boy.*

SKY-BLUE formerly meant gin.

SKY-LARK.—*See* LARK.

SKY PARLOUR, the garret.

SKY SCRAPER, a tall man; "are you cold up there, old SKY SCRAPER?" Properly a sea term; the light sails which some adventurous skippers set above the royals in calm latitudes are termed SKY-SCRAPERS and MOON-RAKERS.

SKY WANNOCKING, unsteady, frolicking.—*Norfolk.*

SLAMMOCK, a slattern or awkward person.—*West;* and *Norf.*

SLANG, low, vulgar, unwritten, or unauthorised language. *Gipsey,* SLANG, the secret language of the Gipseys, synonymous with GIBBERISH, another Gipsey word. This word is only to be found in the Dictionaries of *Webster* and *Ogilvie.* It was, perhaps, first recorded by *Grose,* in his *Dictionary of the Vulgar Tongue,* 1785. SLANG, since it has been adopted as an English word, generally implies vulgar language not known or recognised as CANT; and latterly, when applied to speech, has superseded the word FLASH.

SLANG, counterfeit or short weights and measures. A SLANG quart is a pint and a half. SLANG measures are lent out at 2d. per day. The term is used principally by costermongers.

SLANG, to cheat, to abuse in foul language.

SLANG, a travelling show.

SLANG, a watch chain.

SLANGY, flashy, vulgar; loud in dress, manner, and conversation.

SLANTINGDICULAR, oblique, awry,—as opposed to PERPENDICULAR.

SLAP, paint for the face, rouge.

SLAP, exactly, precisely; "SLAP in the wind's eye," *i.e.,* exactly to windward.

SLAP-UP, first-rate, excellent, very good.

SLAP-BANG, suddenly, violently.

SLAP-BANG SHOPS, low eating houses, where you have to pay down the ready money with a SLAP-BANG.—*Grose.*

SLAP-DASH, immediately, or quickly.

SLASH, a pocket in an overcoat.

SLASHER, a powerful roisterer, a pugilist; "the TIPTON SLASHER."

SLATE, to pelt with abuse, to beat, to "LICK;" or, in the language of the reviewers, to "cut up."

SLATE, "he has a SLATE loose," *i.e.*, he is slightly crazy.

SLAVEY, a maid servant.

SLEWED, drunk, or intoxicated.—*Sea term.* When a vessel changes the tack she, as it were, staggers, the sails flap, she gradually heels over, and the wind catching the waiting canvas, she glides off at another angle. The course pursued by an intoxicated, or SLEWED man, is supposed to be analagous to that of the ship.

SLICK, an *Americanism*, very prevalent in England since the publication of Judge Haliburton's facetious stories. As an *adjective*, SLICK means rapidly, effectually, utterly; as a *verb*, it has the force of "to despatch rapidly," turn off, get done with a thing.

SLICK A DEE, a pocket book.

SLING, to pass from one person to another.

SLIP, "to give the SLIP," to run away, or elude pursuit. *Shakespere* has "you *gave me the counterfeit*," in Romeo and Juliet. GIVING THE SLIP, however, is a *Sea phrase*, and refers to fastening an anchor and chain cable to a floating buoy, or water cask, until such a time arrives that is convenient to return and take them on board. In fastening the cable, the home end is *slipped* through the hawse pipe. Weighing anchor is a noisy task, so that giving it the SLIP infers to leave it in quietness.

SLIP, or LET SLIP; "to SLIP into a man," to give him a sound beating; "to LET SLIP at a cove," to rush violently upon him, and assault with vigour.

SLOG, or SLOGGER (its original form), to beat, baste, or wallop. *German*, SCHLAGEN; or, perhaps a vulgar corruption of SLAUGHTER. The pretended *Greek* derivation from σλογω, which *Punch* puts in the mouth of the schoolboy, in his impression of 4th May, 1859, is of course only intended to mystify grandmamma, there being no such word in the language.

SLOGGERS, *i.e.*, SLOW-GOERS, the second division of race-boats at *Cambridge*. At *Oxford* they are called TORPIDS.—*Univ.*

SLOGGING, a good beating.

SLOP, cheap, or ready made, as applied to clothing, is generally supposed to be a modern appropriation; but it was used in this sense in 1691, by *Maydman*, in his *Naval Speculations;* and by *Chaucer* two centuries before that. SLOPS properly signify sailors' working clothes.

SLOP, a policeman. Probably at first *back slang*, but now general.

SLOPE, to decamp, to run, or rather *slip* away. Originally from LOPE, to make off; the *s* probably became affixed as a portion of the preceding word, as in the case of "*let's lope*," let us run.—*Americanism.*

SLOPS, chests or packages of tea; "he shook a slum of SLOPS," *i.e.*, stole a chest of tea.

SLOUR, to lock, or fasten.

SLOUR'D, buttoned up; SLOUR'D HOXTER, an inside pocket buttoned up.

SLOWED, to be locked up—in prison.

SLUICERY, a gin shop or public house.

SLUM, a letter.

SLUM, a chest, or package.—*See* SLOPS.

SLUM, gammon; "up to SLUM," wide awake, knowing,

"And this, without more SLUM, began,
Over a flowing Pot-house can,
To settle, without botheration,
The rigs of this here tip-top nation."
Jack Randall's Diary, 1820.

SLUM THE GORGER, to cheat on the sly, to be an eye servant. SLUM in this sense is *old cant.*

SLUMMING, passing bad money.

SLUMS, or BACK SLUMS, dark retreats, low neighbourhoods; "the Westminster SLUMS," favourite haunts for thieves.

SLUSHY, a ship's cook.

SMACK SMOOTH, even, level with the surface, quickly.

SMALL BEER, "he does't think SMALL BEER of himself," *i.e.*, he has a great opinion of his own importance. SMALL COALS is also used in the same sense.

SMASH, to become bankrupt, or worthless; "to go all to SMASH;" to break, or "go to the dogs."

SMASH, to pass counterfeit money.

SMASHER, one who passes bad coin.

SMASHFEEDER, a Britannia metal spoon,—the best imitation shillings are made from this metal.

SMELLER, a blow on the nose, or a NOSER.

SMIGGINS, soup served to convicts on board the hulks.

SMISH, a shirt, or chemise. Corruption of the *Span.*—*See* MISH.

SMITHERS, or SMITHEREENS, "all to SMITHEREENS," all to smash. SMITHER, is a *Lincolnshire* word for a fragment.

SMOKE, to detect, or penetrate an artifice.

SMUDGE, to smear, obliterate, daub. Corruption of SMUTCH.—*Times*, 10th August, 1859.

SMUG, extremely neat, after the fashion, in order.

SMUG, to snatch another's property and run.

SMUGGINGS, snatchings, or purloinings,—shouted out by boys, when snatching the tops, or small play property, of other lads, and then running off at full speed.

> "Tops are in ; spin 'em agin.
> Tops are out ; SMUGGING about.'

SMUT, a copper boiler. Also, the "blacks" from a furnace.

SMUTTY, obscene,—vulgar as applied to conversation.

SNACK, booty, or share. Also, a light repast —*Old cant and Gipsey term.*

SNAFFLED, arrested, "pulled up,"—so termed from a kind of horse's bit, called a SNAFFLE. In *East Anglia*, to SNAFFLE is to talk foolishly.

SNAGGLE TEETH, uneven, and unpleasant looking dental operators.—*West.* SNAGS (*Americanism*), ends of sunken drift-wood sticking out of the water, on which river steamers are often wrecked.

SNAGGLING, angling after geese with a hook and line, the bait being a worm or snail. The goose swallows the bait, and is quietly landed and bagged.

SNAGGY, cross, crotchetty, malicious.

SNAM, to snatch, or rob from the person.

SNAPPS, share, portion; any articles or circumstances out of which money may be made; "looking out for SNAPPS," waiting for windfalls, or odd jobs.—*Old. Scotch*, CHITS,—term also used for "coppers," or halfpence.

SNEAKSMAN, a shoplifter ; a petty, cowardly thief.

SNEEZER, a snuff box ; a pocket-handkerchief.

SNEEZE LURKER, a thief who throws snuff in a person's face and then robs him.

SNID, a sixpence.—*Scotch.*

SNIGGER, "I'm SNIGGERED if you will," a mild form of swearing. Another form of this is JIGGERED.

SNIGGERING, laughing to oneself.—*East.*

SNIP, a tailor.

SNIPE, a long bill; also a term for attorneys,—a race remarkable for their propensity to long bills.

SNIPES, "a pair of SNIPES," a pair of scissors. They are occasionally made in the form of that bird.

SNITCHERS, persons who turn queen's evidence, or who tell tales. In *Scotland*, SNITCHERS signify handcuffs.

SNOB, a low, vulgar, or affected person. Supposed to be from the nickname usually applied to a Crispin, or a maker of shoes; but believed by a writer in *Notes and Queries* to be a contraction of the *Latin*, SINE OBOLO. A more probable derivation, however, has just been forwarded by an ingenious correspondent. He supposes that NOBS, *i.e.*, *Nobiles*, was appended in lists to the names of persons of gentle birth, whilst those who had not that distinction were marked down as S. NOB., *i.e.*, *sine nobilitate*, without marks of gentility,—thus reversing its meaning. Another "word-twister" remarks that, as at college sons of nobleman wrote after their names in the admission lists, *fil nob.*, son of a lord, and hence all young noblemen were called NOBS, and what they did NOBBY, so those who imitated them would be called *quasi-nobs*, "like a nob," which by a process of contraction would be shortened to *si-nob*, and then SNOB, one who pretends to be what he is not, and apes his betters. The short and expressive terms which many think fitly represent the three great estates of the realm, NOB, SNOB, and MOB, were all originally slang words. The last has safely passed through the vulgar ordeal of the streets, and found respectable quarters in the standard dictionaries.

SNOBBISH, stuck up, proud, make believe.

SNOB-STICK, a workman who refuses to join in strikes, or trade unions. Query, properly KNOB-STICK.

SNOOKS, an imaginary personage often brought forward as the answer to an idle question, or as the perpetrator of a senseless joke.

SNOOZE, or SNOODGE (vulgar pronunciation), to sleep or doze.

SNOT, a term of reproach applied to persons by the vulgar when vexed or annoyed. In a Westminster school vocabulary for boys, published in the last century, the term is curiously applied. Its proper meaning is the glandular mucus discharged through the nose.

SNOTTER, or WIPE-HAULER, a pickpocket who commits great depredations upon gentlemen's pocket-handkerchiefs.—*North.*

SNOTTINGER, a coarse word for a pocket-handkerchief. The German *schnupftuch* is, however, nearly as plain. A handkerchief was also anciently called a MUCKINGER, or MUCKENDER.

SNOTS, small bream, a slimy kind of flat fish.—*Norwich.*

SNOW, wet linen.

SNOW GATHERERS, or SNOW-DROPPERS, rogues who steal linen from hedges and drying grounds.

SNUFF, "up to SNUFF," knowing and sharp; "to take SNUFF," to be offended. *Shakespere* uses SNUFF in the sense of anger, or passion. SNUFFY, tipsy.

SNYDER, a tailor. *German*, SCHNEIDER.

SOAP, flattery.—*See* SOFT SOAP.

SOFT, foolish, inexperienced. An old term for bank notes.

SOFT-SOAP, or SOFT-SAWDER, flattery, ironical praise.

SOFT TACK, bread.—*Sea.*

SOLD, "SOLD again! and the money taken," gulled, deceived.—*Vide* SELL.

SOLD UP, or OUT, broken down, bankrupt.

SOLDIER, a red herring.

SON OF A GUN, a contemptuous title for a man. In the army it is sometimes applied to an artilleryman.

SOOT BAG, a reticule.

SOP, a soft or foolish man. Abbreviation of MILKSOP.

SOPH (abbreviation of SOPHISTER), a title peculiar to the University of *Cambridge.* Undergraduates are *junior* SOPHS before passing their "*Little Go,*" or first University examination,—*senior* SOPHS after that.

SOUND, to pump, or draw information from a person in an artful manner.

SOW, the receptacle into which the liquid iron is poured in a gun-foundry. The melted metal poured from it is termed PIG.—*Workmen's terms.*

SOW'S BABY, a pig; sixpence.

SPANK, a smack, or hard slap.

SPANK, to move along quickly; hence a fast horse or vessel is said to be "a SPANKER to go."

SPANKING, large, fine, or strong; *e.g.*, a SPANKING pace, a SPANKING breeze, a SPANKING fellow.

SPECKS, damaged oranges.

SPEEL, to run away, make off; "SPEEL the drum," to go off with stolen property.—*North.*

SPELL, "to SPELL for a thing," hanker after it, intimate a desire to possess it.

SPELLKEN, or SPEELKEN, a playhouse. *German*, SPIELEN. —*See* KEN.—*Don Juan.*

SPICK AND SPAN, applied to anything that is quite new and fresh.—*Hudibras.*

SPIFFED, slightly intoxicated.—*Scotch slang.*

SPIFFS, the percentage allowed by drapers to their young men when they effect a sale of old-fashioned or undesirable stock.

SPIFFY, spruce, well-dressed, *tout à la mode.*

SPIFLICATE, to confound, silence, or thrash.

SPILT, thrown from a horse or chaise.—*See* PURL.

SPIN, to reject from an examination.—*Army.*

SPIN-EM-ROUNDS, a street game consisting of a piece of brass, wood, or iron, balanced on a pin, and turned quickly around on a board, when the point, arrow shaped, stops at a number and decides the bet one way or the other. The contrivance very much resembles a sea compass, and was formerly the gambling accompaniment of London piemen. The apparatus then was erected on the tin lids of their pie cans, and the bets were ostensibly for pies, but more frequently for "coppers," when no policeman frowned upon the scene, and when two or three apprentices or porters happened to meet.

SPINIKEN, a workhouse.

SPIRT, or SPURT, "to put on a SPIRT," to make an increased exertion for a brief space, to attain one's end; a nervous effort.

SPITFIRE, a passionate person.

SPLENDIFEROUS, sumptuous, first-rate.

SPLICE, to marry; "and the two shall become one flesh."—*Sea.*

SPLICE THE MAIN BRACE, to take a drink.—*Sea.*

SPLIT, to inform against one's companions, to tell tales. "To SPLIT with a person," to cease acquaintanceship, to quarrel.

SPLODGER, a lout, an awkward countryman.

SPOFFY, a bustling busy-body is said to be SPOFFY.

SPONGE, "to throw up the SPONGE," to submit, give over the struggle,—from the practice of throwing up the SPONGE used to cleanse the combatants' faces, at a prize fight, as a signal that the "mill" is concluded.

SPOON, synonymous with SPOONEY. A SPOON has been defined to be "a thing that touches a lady's lips without kissing them."

SPOONEY, a weak-minded and foolish person, effeminate or fond; "to be SPOONEY on a girl," to be foolishly attached to one.

SPOONS, "when I was SPOONS with you," *i.e.*, when young, and in our courting days before marriage.—*Charles Mathews*, in the farce of *Everybody's Friend.*

SPORT, to exhibit, to wear, &c.,—a word which is made to do duty in a variety of senses, especially at the University. *See the Gradus ad Cantabrigiam.* "To SPORT a new tile;" "to SPORT an *Ægrotat*" (*i.e.*, a permission from the "Dons" to abstain from lectures, &c., on account of illness); "to SPORT ONE'S OAK," to shut the outer door and exclude the public, —especially *duns*, and boring acquaintances. Common also in the Inns of Court.—*See Notes and Queries*, 2nd series, vol. viii., p. 492, and *Gentleman's Magazine*, December, 1794.

SPORTING DOOR, the outer door of chambers, also called the OAK.—*See* under SPORT.—*University.*

SPOTTED, to be known or marked by the police.

SPOUT, "up the SPOUT," at the pawnbroker's; SPOUTING, pawning.—*See* POP for origin.

SPOUT, to preach, or make speeches; SPOUTER, a preacher or lecturer.

SPRAT, sixpence.

SPREAD, butter.

SPREAD, a lady's shawl. SPREAD, at the *East* end of London, a feast, or a TIGHTENER; at the *West* end a fashionable re-union, an entertainment, display of good things.

SPREE, a boisterous piece of merriment; "going on the SPREE," starting out with intent to have a frolic. *French*, ESPRIT. In the *Dutch* language, SPREEUW is a jester.

SPRINGER-UP, a tailor who sells low-priced ready made clothing, and gives starvation wages to the poor men and women who "make up" for him. The clothes are said to be SPRUNG-UP, or "blown together."

SPRY, active, strong, manly.—*Americanism.*

SPUDDY, a seller of bad potatoes. In *Scotland*, a SPUD is a raw potato; and roasted SPUDS are those cooked in the cinders with their jackets on.

SPUNGING-HOUSE, the sheriff's officer's house, where prisoners, when arrested for debt, are sometimes taken. As extortionate charges are made there for accommodation, the name is far from inappropriate.

SPUNK, spirit, *fire*, courage, mettle.

> "In that snug room, where any man of SPUNK
> Would find it a hard matter to get drunk."
> *Peter Pindar*, i., 245.

Common in *America*. For derivation see the following.

SPUNKS, lucifer matches.—*Herefordshire; Scotland.* SPUNK, says Urry, in his MS. notes to Ray, "is the excrescency of some tree, of which they make a sort of tinder to light their pipes with."

SPUNK-FENCER, a lucifer match seller.

SQUABBY, flat, short and thick.

SQUARE, honest; "on the SQUARE," *i.e.*, fair and strictly honest; "to turn SQUARE," to reform, and get one's living in an honest manner,—the opposite of CROSS.

SQUARE, "to be SQUARE with a man," to be *even* with him, or to be revenged; "to SQUARE up to a man," to offer to fight him. *Shakespere* uses SQUARE in the sense of to quarrel.

SQUARE COVE, an honest man.

SQUARE MOLL, an honest woman.

SQUARE RIGGED, well dressed.—*Sea.*

SQUARING HIS NIBS, giving a policeman money.

SQUEEZE, silk.

SQUIB, a temporary *jeu d'esprit*, which, like the firework of that denomination, sparkles, bounces, stinks, and vanishes.—*Grose.*

SQUINNY-EYED, squinting.—*Shakespere.*

SQUIRT, a doctor, or chemist.

STAFF NAKED, gin.

STAG, a shilling.

STAG, a term applied during the railway mania to a speculator without capital, who took "scrip" in "*Diddlesex Junction*," and other lines, *ejus et sui generis*, got the shares up to a premium, and then sold out. *Punch* represented the house of Hudson, "the Railway King," at Albert Gate, with a STAG on it, in allusion to this term.

STAG, to demand money, to "cadge."

STAG, to see, discover, or watch,—like a STAG at gaze; "STAG the push," look at the crowd. Also, to dun, or demand payment.

STAGGER, one who looks out, or watches.

STAGGERING BOB, an animal to whom the knife only just anticipates death from natural disease or accident,—said of meat on that account unfit for human food.

STALE, to evacuate urine.—*Stable term.*

STALL, to lodge, or put up at a public house. Also, to act a part.—*Theatrical.*

STALL, or STALL OFF, a dodge, a blind, or an excuse. STALL is *ancient cant.*

STALL OFF, to blind, excuse, hide, to screen a robbery during the perpetration of it by an accomplice.

STALL YOUR MUG, go away; spoken sharply by any one who wishes to get rid of a troublesome or inconvenient person.

STALLSMAN, an accomplice.

STAMPERS, shoes.—*Ancient cant.*

STAND, "to STAND treat," to pay for a friend's entertainment; to bear expense; to put up with treatment, good or ill; "this house STOOD me in £1,000," *i.e.*, cost that sum; "to STAND PAD," to beg on the curb with a small piece of paper pinned on the breast, inscribed "*I'm starving.*"

STANDING, the position at a street corner, or on the curb of a market street, regularly occupied by a costermonger, or street seller.

STANDING PATTERERS, men who take a stand on the curb of a public thoroughfare, and deliver prepared speeches to effect a sale of any articles they have to vend.—*See* PATTERER.

STANGEY, a tailor; a person under petticoat government,—derived from the custom of "*riding the* STANG," mentioned in Hudibras:—

> "It is a custom used of course
> Where the grey mare is the better horse."

STARK-NAKED (originally STRIP-ME-NAKED, *vide Randall's Diary*, 1820), raw gin.—*Bulwer's Paul Clifford.*

STARCHY, stuck-up, high-notioned, showily dressed, disdainful, cross.

STAR IT, to perform as the centre of attraction, with inferior subordinates to set off one's abilities.—*Theatrical.*

STAR THE GLAZE, to break the window or show glass of a jeweller or other tradesman, and take any valuable articles, and run away. Sometimes the glass is cut with a diamond, and a strip of leather fastened to the piece of glass cut out to keep it from falling in and making a noise. Another plan is to cut the sash.

START, "THE START," London,—the great starting point for beggars and tramps.

START, a proceeding of any kind; a rum START," an odd circumstance; "to get the START of a person," to anticipate, him, overreach him.

STASH, to cease doing anything, to refrain, be quiet, leave off; "STASH IT, there, you sir!" *i.e.*, be quiet, sir; to give over a lewd or intemperate course of life is termed STASHING IT.

STEEL, the house of correction in London, formerly named the *Bastile*, but since shortened to STEEL.

STEEL BAR DRIVERS, or FLINGERS, journeymen tailors.

STEMS, the legs.

STEP IT, to run away, or make off.

STICK, a derogatory expression for a person; "a rum" or "odd STICK," a curious man. More generally a "poor STICK."—*Provincial.*

STICK, "cut your STICK," be off, or go away; either simply equivalent to a recommendation to prepare a walking staff in readiness for a journey—in allusion to the Eastern custom of cutting a stick before setting out—or from the ancient mode of reckoning by notches or tallies on a stick. In Cornwall the peasantry tally sheaves of corn by cuts in a stick, reckoning by the score. CUT YOUR STICK in this sense may mean to make your mark and pass on—and so realise the meaning of the phrase "IN THE NICK (or notch) OF TIME." Sir J. Emerson Tennent, in *Notes and Queries* (December, 1859), considers the phrase equivalent to "cutting the connection," and suggests a possible origin in the prophets breaking the staves of "Beauty" and "Bands,"—*vide* Zech., xi., 10, 14.

STICK, to cheat; "he got STUCK," he was taken in; STICK, to

forget one's part in a performance—*Theatrical;* STICK ON, to overcharge or defraud; STICK UP FOR, to defend a person, especially when slandered in his absence; STICK UP TO, to persevere in courting or attacking, whether in fisty-cuffs or argument; "to STICK in one's gizzard," to rankle in one's heart; "to STICK TO a person," to adhere to one, be his friend through adverse circumstances.

STICKS, furniture, or household chattels; "pick up your STICKS and cut!" summary advice to a person to take himself and furniture away.—*Cumberland.*

STICKS, pistols.—*Nearly obsolete.*

STICK-UPS, or GILLS, shirt collars.

STICKINGS, bruised or damaged meat sold to sausage makers and penny pie shops.—*North.*

STICKY, wax.

STIFF, paper, a bill of acceptance, &c.; "how did you get it, STIFF or *hard?*" *i.e.*, did he pay you cash or give a bill?

STIFF FENCER, a street seller of writing paper.

STIFF 'UN, a corpse.—*Term used by undertakers.*

STILTON, "that's the STILTON," or "it is not the STILTON," *i.e.*, that is quite the thing, or that is not quite the thing; —polite rendering of "that is not the CHEESE," which see.

STINGO, strong liquor.—*Yorkshire.*

STINK, a disagreeable exposure.

STINKOMALEE, a name given to the then New London University by Theodore Hook. Some question about *Trincomalee* was agitated at the same time. It is still applied by the students of the old Universities, who regard it with disfavour from its admitting all denominations.

STIPE, a stipendiary magistrate.—*Provincial.*

STIR, a prison, a lock-up; "IN STIR," in jail. *Anglo Saxon,* STYR, correction, punishment.

STIR UP SUNDAY, the Sunday next before Advent, the collect for that day commencing with the words "Stir up." Schoolboys, growing excited at the prospect of the vacation, irreverently commemorate it by stirring up—pushing and poking each other. CRIB CRUST MONDAY and TUG BUTTON TUESDAY are distinguished by similar tricks; while on PAY-OFF WEDNESDAY they retaliate small grudges in a playful facetious way. Forby says, good housewives in Norfolk consider themselves reminded by the name to mix the ingredients for their Christmas mince pies.

STOCKDOLAGER, a heavy blow, a "finisher." *Italian*, STOCCADO, a fencing term.

STODGE, to surfeit, gorge, or clog with food.

STONE JUG, a prison.

STOOK, a pocket-handkerchief.

STOOK HAULER, or BUZZER, a thief who takes pocket-handkerchiefs.

STOP, a detective policeman.

STORY, a falsehood,—the soft synonyme for a *lie*, allowed in family circles and boarding-schools. A Puritanism that came in fashion with the tirade against romances, all novels and stories being considered as dangerous and false.

STOTOR, a heavy blow, a SETTLER.—*Old cant.*

STOW, to leave off, or have done; "STOW IT, the gorger's leary," leave off, the person is looking. *See* STASH, with which it is synonymous.—*Ancient cant.*

STOW FAKING! leave off there, be quiet! FAKING implying anything that may be going on.

STRAW. Married ladies are said to be "in THE STRAW" at their *accouchements*. The phrase is a coarse allusion to farm-yard animals in a similar condition.

STRAWING, *selling* straws in the streets (generally for a penny) and *giving* the purchaser a paper (indecent or political), or a gold (!) ring,—neither of which the patterer states he is allowed to sell.

STREAK, to decamp, run away.—*Saxon*. In *America* the phrase is "to make STREAKS," or "make TRACKS."

STREAKY, irritated, ill-tempered.

STREET PITCHERS, negro minstrels, ballad singers, long song men, men "working a board" on which have been painted various exciting scenes in some terrible drama, the details of which the STREET PITCHER is bawling out, and selling in a little book or broadsheet (price one penny); or any persons who make a stand in the streets, and sell articles for their living.

STRETCH, abbreviation of "STRETCH one's neck," to hang, be executed as a malefactor.—*Bulwer's Paul Clifford.*

STRETCH, twelve months,—generally used to intimate the time any one has been sentenced by the judge or magistrate. ONE STRETCH is to be imprisoned twelve months, TWO STRETCH is two years, THREE STRETCH is three years, and so on.

STRETCHER, a falsehood.

STRETCHER, a contrivance with handles, used by the police to carry off persons who are violent or drunk.

STRETCHER FENCER, one who sells braces.

STRETCHING MATCH, an execution.—*See* STRETCH.

STRIKE ME LUCKY! an expression used by the lower orders when making a bargain, derived from the old custom of striking hands together, leaving in that of the seller a LUCK PENNY as an earnest that the bargain is concluded. In Ireland, at cattle markets, &c., a penny, or other small coin, is always given by the buyer to the seller to ratify the bargain.—*Hudibras.* Anciently this was called a GOD'S PENNY.

> "With that he cast him a God's peny."—*Heir of Linne.*

The origin of the phrase being lost sight of, like that of many others, it is often corrupted now-a-days into STRIKE ME SILLY.

STRIKE THE JIGGER, to pick the lock, or break open the door.

STROMMEL, straw.—*Ancient cant.* Halliwell says that in Norfolk STRUMMEL is a name for hair.

STRONG, "to come it STRONG."—*See* COME.

STUCK-UP, "purse-proud"—a form of snobbishness very common in those who have risen in the world. Mr. Albert Smith has written some amusing papers on the *Natural History of* STUCK-UP *People.*

STUFF, money.

STUFF, to make false but plausible statements, to praise ironically, to make game of a person,—literally, to STUFF or CRAM him with gammon or falsehood.

STUMP, to go on foot.

STUMPED, bowled out, done for, bankrupt, poverty stricken.—*Cricketing term.*

STUMPS, legs, or feet.

STUMPY, money.

STUMP UP, to pay one's share, to pay the reckoning, to bring forth the money reluctantly.

STUN, to astonish.

STUNNER, a first-rate person or article.

STUNNERS, feelings of great astonishment; "it put the STUNNERS on me," it confounded me.

STUNNING, first-rate, very good. "STUNNING pears," shouts the coster, "only eight a penny."—*Vide Athenæum,* 26th

March, 1859. Sometimes amplified to STUNNING JOE BANKS ! when the expression is supposed to be in its most intense form. JOE BANKS was a noted character in the last generation. He was the proprietor of a public house in Dyott-street, Seven Dials, and afterwards, on the demolition of the Rookery, of another in Cranbourne alley. His houses became well-known from their being the resort of the worst characters, at the same time that the strictest decorum was always maintained in them. JOE BANKS also acquired a remarkable notoriety by acting as a medium betwixt thieves and their victims. Upon the proper payment to Joe, a watch or a snuff box would at any time be restored to its lawful owner—"no questions in any case being asked." The most daring depredators in London placed the fullest confidence in Joe, and it is believed (although the *Biographie Universelle* is quiet upon this point) that he never, in any instance, "sold" them. He was of the middle height, stout, and strongly made, and was always noted for a showy pin, and a remarkably STUNNING *neck-tie*. It was this peculiarity in the costume of Mr. Banks, coupled with those true and tried qualities as a friend, for which, as I have just remarked, he was famous, that led his customers to proclaim him as STUNNING JOE BANKS ! The Marquis of Douro, Colonel Chatterley, and men of their stamp, were accustomed to resort to a private room at his house, when too late or too early to gain admittance to the clubs or more aristocratic establishments.

STUNNED ON SKILLY, to be sent to prison and compelled to eat SKILLY, or SKILLIGOLEE.

STURABAN, a prison. *Gipsey*, DISTARABIN.

SUCK, a parasite, flatterer of the "nobs."—*University*.

SUCK, to pump, or draw information from a person.

SUCK-CASSA, a public-house.

SUCK THE MONKEY, to rob a cask of liquor by inserting a straw through a gimlet hole, and sucking a portion of the contents.

SUCK UP, "to SUCK UP to a person," to insinuate oneself into his good graces.

SUFFERER, a tailor.

SUIT, a watch and seals.

SULKY, a one-horse chaise, having only room for one person.

SUN IN THE EYES, to have too much drink.—*Dickens*.

SUP, abbreviation of *supernumerary*.—*Theatrical*.

SUPER, a watch; SUPER-SCREWING, stealing watches.

SURF, an actor who frequently pursues another calling.—*Theat.*

SWADDLER, a Wesleyan Methodist; a name originally given to members of that body by the Irish mob; said to have originated with an ignorant Romanist, to whom the words of the English Bible were a novelty, and who, hearing one of John Wesley's preachers mention the *swaddling clothes* of the Holy Infant, in a sermon on Christmas-day at Dublin, shouted out in derision, "*A swaddler! a swaddler!*" as if the whole story were the preacher's invention.—*Southey's Life of Wesley,* vol. ii., p. 109.

SWADDY, or COOLIE, a soldier. The former was originally applied to a discharged soldier, and perhaps came from SHODDY, of which soldiers' coats are made.

SWAG, a lot or plenty of anything, a portion or division of property. In Australia the term is used for the luggage carried by diggers: in India the word LOOT is used. *Scotch,* SWEG, or SWACK; *German,* SWEIG, a flock. *Old cant* for a shop.

SWAG, booty, or plundered property; "collar the SWAG," seize the booty.

SWAG-SHOP, a warehouse where "Brummagem" and general wares are sold,—fancy trinkets, plated goods, &c. Jews are the general proprietors, and the goods are excessively low priced, trashy, and showy. SWAG-SHOPS were formerly plunder depôts.—*Old cant.*

SWAGSMAN, one who carries the booty after a burglary.

SWANKEY, cheap beer.—*West.*

SWAP, to exchange. *Grose* says it is *Irish* cant, but the term is now included in most dictionaries as an allowed vulgarism.

SWEAT, to extract money from a person, to "bleed," to squander riches.—*Bulwer.*

SWEATER, common term for a "cutting" or "grinding" employer.

SWEEP, a low or shabby man.

SWEET, loving or fond; "how SWEET he was upon the moll," *i.e.*, what marked attention he paid the girl.

SWELL, a man of importance; a person with a showy, jaunty exterior; "a rank SWELL," a very "flashly" dressed person, a man who by excessive dress apes a higher position than he actually occupies. Anything is said to be SWELL or

SWELLISH that looks showy, or is many coloured, or is of a desirable quality. Dickens and Thackeray are termed great SWELLS in literature; so indeed are the first persons in the learned professions.

SWELL FENCER, a street salesman of needles.

SWELL HUNG IN CHAINS, said of a showy man in the habit of wearing much jewellery.

SWIG, to drink. *Saxon*, SWIGAN.

SWIG, a hearty drink.

SWIM, "a good SWIM." a good run of luck, a long time out of the policeman's clutches.—*Thieves' term.*

SWINDLER, although a recognised word in respectable dictionaries, commenced service as a slang term. It was used as such by the poor Londoners against the German Jews who set up in London about the year 1762, also by our soldiers in the German War about that time. SCHWINDEL, in *German*, signifies to cheat.

SWING, to be hanged.

SWINGING, large, huge.

SWIPES, sour or small beer. SWIPE, to drink—*Sea.*

SWIPEY (from SWIPES), intoxicated.

SWISHED, married.

SWIZZLE, small beer, drink.

SWOT, mathematics; also a mathematician; as a verb, to work hard for an examination, to be diligent in one's studies.—*Army.*

This word originated at the great slang manufactory for the army, the Royal Military College, Sandhurst, in the broad Scotch pronunciation of Dr. Wallace, one of the Professors, of the word *sweat.*—*See Notes and Queries*, vol. i., p. 369.

T, "to suit to a T," to fit to a nicety.—*Old.* Perhaps from the T-square of carpenters, by which the accuracy of work is tested.

TACKLE, clothes.—*Sea.*

TAFFY (corruption of *David*), a Welshman. Compare SAWNEY (from *Alexander*), a Scotchman.

TAG-RAG-AND-BOBTAIL, a mixed crowd of low people, mobility.

TAIL BUZZER, a thief who picks coat pockets.

TAKE, to succeed, or be patronised; "do you think the new

opera will TAKE?" "No, because the same company TOOK so badly under the old management;" "to TAKE ON," to grieve; *Shakespere* uses the word TAKING in this sense. To "TAKE UP for any one," to protect or defend a person; "to TAKE OFF," to mimic; "to TAKE heart," to have courage; "to TAKE down a peg or two," to humiliate, or tame; "to TAKE UP," to reprove; "to TAKE AFTER," to resemble; "to TAKE IN," to cheat or defraud, from the lodging-house keepers' advertisements, "single men TAKEN IN AND DONE FOR,"—an engagement which is as frequently performed in a bad as a good sense; "to TAKE THE FIELD, when said of a *General*, to commence operations against the enemy; when a *racing man* TAKES THE FIELD he stakes his money against the favourite.

TAKE BEEF, to run away.

TAKE IN, a cheating or swindling transaction,—sometimes termed "a DEAD TAKE IN." *Shakespere* has TAKE IN in the sense of conquering. To BE HAD, or TO BE SPOKE TO, were formerly synonymous phrases with TO BE TAKEN IN.

TALLY, five dozen bunches of turnips.

TAN, to beat or thrash; I'll TAN your hide, *i.e.*, give you a good beating.

TANNER, a sixpence. *Gipsey*, TAWNO, little, or *Latin*, TENER, slender?

TANNY, or TEENY, little. *Gipsey*, TAWNO, little.

TANTREMS, pranks, capers, or frolicking; from the *Tarantula* dance? See account of the involuntary phrensy and motions caused by the bite of the tarantula in Italy.—*Penny Cyclopædia*.

TAPE, gin,—term with female servants.

TAPER, to gradually give over, to run short.

TAP TUB, the *Morning Advertiser*.

TAT BOX, a dice box.

TATER, "s'elp my TATER," another street evasion of a profane oath, sometimes varied by "s'elp my GREENS."

TATLER, a watch; "nimming a TATLER," stealing a watch.

TATS, dice.

TATS, old rags; MILKY TATS, white rags.

TATTING, gathering old rags.

TAW, a large or principal marble; "I'll be one on your TAW," I will pay you out, or be even with you,—a simile taken from boys aiming always at winning the TAW when playing at marbles.

TEAGUELAND, Ireland.

TEETH, "he has cut his *eye* TEETH," *i.e.,* is old and cute enough.

TEETH-DRAWING, wrenching off knockers.

TEETOTALLER, a total abstainer from alcoholic drinks.

TEETOTALLY, amplification of TOTALLY.

TELL-ON, to tell about.

TENPENCE TO THE SHILLING, a vulgar phrase denoting a deficiency in intellect.

TESTER, sixpence. From TESTONE, a shilling in the reign of Henry VIII., but a sixpence in the time of Q. Elizabeth.—*Shakespere. French,* TESTE, or TETE, the head of the monarch on the coin.

TEVISS, a shilling.

THEATRE, a police court.

THICK, intimate, familiar. *Scotch,* CHIEF; "the two are very CHIEF now," *i.e.*, friendly.

THICK-UN, a sovereign; a crown piece, or five shillings.

THIMBLE, or YACK, a watch.

THIMBLE-RIG, a noted cheating game played at fairs and places of great public thronging, consisting of two or three thimbles rapidly and dexterously placed over a pea, when the THIMBLE-RIGGER, suddenly ceasing, asks you under which thimble the pea is to be found. If you are not a practised hand you will lose nine times out of ten any bet you may happen to make with him. The pea is sometimes concealed under his nail.

THIMBLE TWISTERS, thieves who rob persons of their watches.

THINSKINNED, over nice, petulant, apt to get a "raw."

THREE SHEETS IN THE WIND, unsteady from drink.—*Sea.*

THREE-UP, a gambling game played by costers. Three halfpennies are thrown up, and when they fall all "heads," or all "tails," it is a mark; and the man who gets the greatest number of marks out of a given amount—three, five, or more—wins. The costers are very quick and skilful at this game, and play fairly at it amongst themselves; but should a stranger join in they invariably unite to cheat him.

THRUMS, threepence.

THRUMMER, a threepenny bit.

THRUPS, threepence.

THUMPING, large, fine, or strong.

THUNDERER, the *Times* newspaper.

THUNDERING, large, extra-sized.

TIBBING OUT, going out of bounds.—*Charterhouse.*

TICK, credit, trust. *Johnson* says it is a corruption of *ticket,*—tradesmen's bills being formerly written on tickets or cards. ON TICK, therefore, is equivalent to *on ticket,* or on trust. In use 1668. Cuthbert Bede, in *Notes and Queries,* supplies me with an earlier date, from the *Gradus ad Cantabrigiam.*

> "No matter upon landing whether you have money or no—you may swim in twentie of their boats over the river UPON TICKET.—*Decker's Gul's Hornbook,* 1609.

TICKER, a watch.

TICKET, "that's the TICKET," *i.e.,* what was wanted, or what is best. Corruption of "that is not *etiquette,*" by adding, in vulgar pronunciation, *th* to the first *e* of etiquette; or, perhaps, from TICKET, a bill or invoice. This phrase is sometimes extended into "that's the TICKET FOR SOUP," in allusion to the card given to beggars for immediate relief at soup kitchens.—*See* TICK.

TIDY, tolerably, or pretty well; "how did you get on to-day?"—"Oh, TIDY."—*Saxon.*

TIED UP, given over, finished; also married, in allusion to the Hymenial knot, unless a jocose allusion be intended to the *halter* (altar).

TIFFIN, a breakfast, *dejeuner a la fourchette.*—*Anglo Indian slang.*

TIGER, a boy employed to wait on *gentlemen;* one who waits on ladies is a page.

TIGHT, close, stingy; hard up, short of cash; TIGHT, spruce, strong, active; "a TIGHT lad," a smart, active young fellow; TIGHT, drunk, or nearly so; "TIGHT laced," puritanical, over-precise. Money is said to be TIGHT, when the public, from want of confidence in the aspect of affairs, are not inclined to speculate.

TIGHTNER, a dinner, or hearty meal.

TIKE, or BUFFER LURKING, dog stealing.

TILE, a hat; a covering for the head.

> "I'm a gent, I'm a gent,
> In the Regent-street style,—
> Examine my vest,
> And look at my TILE."—*Popular Song.*

Sometimes used in another sense, "having a TILE loose," *i.e.*, being slightly crazy.—*See* PANTILE.

TIMBER MERCHANT, or SPUNK FENCER, a lucifer match seller.

TIME O' DAY, a dodge, the latest aspect of affairs; "that's your TIME O' DAY," *i.e.*, *Euge*, well done; to PUT A PERSON UP TO THE TIME O' DAY, let him know what is o' clock,—to instruct him in the knowledge needful for him.

TIN, money,—generally applied to silver.

TINGE, the percentage allowed by drapers and clothiers to their assistants, upon the sale of old-fashioned articles.—*See* SPIFFS.

TIN-POT, "he plays a TIN-POT game," *i.e.*, a low or shabby one. —*Billiards.*

TIP, a douceur; also to give, lend, or hand over anything to another person; "come, TIP up the tin," *i.e.*, hand up the money; "TIP the wink," to inform by winking; "TIP us your fin," *i.e.*, give me your hand; "TIP one's boom off," to make off, depart.—*Sea.* "To miss one's TIP," to fail in a scheme.—*Old cant.*

TIP THE DOUBLE, to "bolt," or run away from a creditor or officer. Sometimes TIP THE DOUBLE TO SHERRY, *i.e.*, to the sheriff.

TIP-TOP, first-rate, of the best kind.

TIPTOPPER, a "swell," or dressy man, a "*Gorger.*"

TIT, favourite name for a horse.

TIT FOR TAT, an equivalent.

TITIVATE, to put in order, or dress up.

TITLEY, drink.

TITTER, a girl.

'TIZER, the *Morning Advertiser*.

TIZZY, a sixpence. Corruption of TESTER.

TOASTING FORK, derisive term for a sword.

TOBY CONSARN, a highway expedition.

TOBY, a road; "high TOBY," the turnpike road. "High TOBY spice," robbery on horse-back.—*Don Juan*, canto xi., 19.

TODDLE, to walk as a child.

TO-DO (pronounced quickly, and as one word), a disturbance, trouble; "here's a pretty TO-DO," here is an unpleasant difficulty. This exactly tallies with the *French* word AFFAIRE (*a faire*).—*See Forby's Vocabulary of East Anglia.*

TOFFER, a well dressed, "gay" woman.

TOFFICKY, dressy, showy.

TOFT, a showy individual, a SWELL, a person who, according to a Yorkshireman's vocabulary, is UP-ISH.

TOG, a coat. *Latin*, TOGA.—*Ancient cant.*

TOG, to dress, or equip with an outfit; "TOGGED out to the nines," dressed in the first style.

TOGS, clothes; "Sunday TOGS," best clothes. One of the oldest cant words, in use in the time of Henry VIII.

TOGERY, clothes, harness, domestic paraphernalia of any kind.

TOKE, dry bread.

TOL LOL, or TOL-LOLISH, tolerable, or tolerably.

TOMMY.—*See* DICKEY.

TOMMY, bread,—generally a penny roll.

TOMMY, a truck, barter, the exchange of labour for goods, not money. Both term and practice general among English operatives for half-a century.

TOMMY-MASTER, one who pays his workmen in goods, or gives them tickets upon tradesmen, with whom he shares the profit.

TOMMY SHOP, where wages are generally paid to mechanics or others, who are expected to "take out" a portion of the money in goods.

TOM-TOM, a street instrument, a small kind of drum beaten with the fingers, somewhat like the ancient tabor; a performer on this instrument. It was imported, doubtless, with the *Nigger* melodies,—TOM-TOMS being a favourite instrument with the darkies.

TONGUED, talkative; "to TONGUE a person," *i.e.*, talk him down.

TOOL, "a poor TOOL," a bad hand at anything.

TOOL, to drive a mail coach.

TOOL, to pick pockets.

TOOLER, a pickpocket. MOLL-TOOLER, a female pickpocket.

TOOTH, "he has cut his eye TOOTH," *i.e.*, he is sharp enough, or old enough, to be so; "up in the TOOTH," far advanced in age,—said often of old maids. *Stable term* for aged horses which have lost the distinguishing mark in their teeth.

TOPHEAVY, drunk.

TOPPED, hung or executed.

TOP-SAWYER, the principal of a party, or profession. "A TOP-SAWYER, signifies a man that is a master genius in any profession. It is a piece of *Norfolk* slang, and took its rise from Norfolk being a great timber county, where the *top* sawyers get double the wages of those beneath them."—*Randall's Diary*, 1820.

TOPS, dying speeches and gallows broadsides.

TOPSY-TURVY, the bottom upwards. *Grose* gives an ingenious etymology of this once cant term, viz., "*top-side turf-ways*,"—turf being always laid the wrong side upwards.

TO-RIGHTS, excellent, very well, or good.

TORPIDS, the second-class race-boats at Oxford, answering to the Cambridge SLOGGERS.

TOSHERS, men who steal copper from ships' bottoms in the Thames.

TOSS, a measure of sprats.

TOUCHED, slightly intoxicated.

TOUCHER, "as near as a TOUCHER," as near as possible without actually touching.—*Coaching term*. The old jarveys, to show their skill, used to drive against things so close as absolutely to *touch*, yet without injury. This they called a TOUCHER, or, TOUCH AND GO, which was hence applied to anything which was within an ace of ruin.

TOUCHY, peevish, irritable. *Johnson* terms it a low word.

TOUT, to look out, or watch.—*Old cant*.

TOUTER, a looker out, one who watches for customers, a hotel runner.

TOWEL, to beat or whip. In *Warwickshire* an oaken stick is termed a TOWEL—whence, perhaps, the vulgar verb.

TOWELLING, a rubbing down with an *oaken* TOWEL, a beating.

TRACKS, "to make TRACKS," to run away.—*See* STREAK.

TRANSLATOR, a man who deals in old shoes or clothes, and refits them for cheap wear.

TRANSLATORS, second-hand boots mended and polished, and sold at a low price. Monmouth-street, Seven Dials, is a great market for TRANSLATORS.

TRANSMOGRIPHY, to alter or change.

TRAP, a "fast" term for a carriage of any kind. TRAPS, goods and chattels of any kind, but especially luggage and personal effects; in Australia, SWAG.

TRAP, "up to TRAP," knowing, wide awake,—synonymous with "up to SNUFF."

TRAP, a sheriff's officer.

TRAPESING, gadding or gossiping about in a slatternly way. —*North.*

TRAVELLER, name given by one tramp to another. "A TRAVELLER at her Majesty's expense," *i.e.*, a transported felon, a convict.

TREE, "up a TREE," in temporary difficulties,—out of the way. *American expression*, derived from RACCOON or BEAR-HUNTING. When Bruin is TREED, or is forced UP A TREE by the dogs, it means that then the tug of war begins.—*See* 'COON. Hence when an opponent is fairly run to bay, and can by no evasion get off, he is said to be TREED. These expressions originated with Colonel Crockett. In *Scotland* the phrase is "up a CLOSE," *i.e.*, a passage, out of the usual track, or removed from observation.

TRINE, to hang.—*Ancient cant.*

TROLLING, sauntering or idling.

TROLLY, or TROLLY-CARTS, term given by costermongers to a species of narrow cart, which can either be drawn by a donkey, or driven by hand.

TROTTER, a tailor's man who goes round for orders.—*University.*

TROTTER CASES, shoes.

TROTTERS, feet. Sheep's TROTTERS, boiled sheep's feet, a favourite street delicacy.

TRUCK, to exchange or barter.

TRUCK-GUTTED, pot-bellied, corpulent.—*Sea.*

TRUCKS, trowsers.

TRUMP, a good fellow; "a regular TRUMP," a jolly or good natured person,—in allusion to a TRUMP card; "TRUMPS may turn up," *i.e.*, fortune may yet favour me.

TUB THUMPING, preaching or speech making.

TUCK, a schoolboy's term for fruit, pastry, &c. TUCK IN, or TUCK OUT, a good meal.

TUFTS, fellow commoners, *i.e.*, wealthy students at the University, who pay higher fees, dine with the Dons, and are distinguished by golden TUFTS, or tassels, in their caps.

TUFT-HUNTER, a hanger on to persons of quality or wealth. Originally *University slang*, but now general.

TUMBLE, to comprehend or understand. A coster was asked what he thought of *Macbeth*,—"the witches and the fighting was all very well, but the other moves I couldn't TUMBLE to exactly; few on us can TUMBLE to the jaw-breakers; they licks us, they do."

TURF, horse racing, and betting thereon; "on the TURF," one who occupies himself with race course business; said also of a street-walker, nymph of the pavé.

TURKEY-MERCHANTS, dealers in plundered or contraband silk. Poulterers are sometimes termed TURKEY MERCHANTS, in remembrance of Horne Tooke's answer to the boys at Eton, who wished in an aristocratic way to know who *his* father was,—a TURKEY MERCHANT, replied Tooke;—his father was a poulterer. TURKEY MERCHANT, also, was formerly slang for a driver of turkeys or geese to market.

TURNED OVER, to be stopped and searched by the police.

TURNED UP, acquitted by the magistrate or judge for want of evidence.

TURNER OUT, a coiner of bad money.

TURN OUT, personal show or appearance; a man with a showy carriage and horses is said to have a good TURN OUT.

TURNOVER, an apprentice who finishes with a second master the indentures he commenced with the first.

TURNPIKE-SAILORS, beggars who go about dressed as sailors.

TURN UP, a street fight; a sudden leaving, or making off.

TURN UP, to quit, change, abscond, or abandon; "Ned has TURNED UP," *i.e.* run away; "I intend TURNING IT UP," *i.e.* leaving my present abode or altering my course of life. Also to happen; let's wait, and see what will TURN UP.

TUSHEROON, a crown piece, five shillings.

TUSSLE, a pull, struggle, fight, or argument. *Johnson* and *Webster* call it a vulgar word.

TUSSLE, to struggle, or argue.

TWELVER, a shilling.

TWIG, style, *à-la-mode;* "get your strummel faked in TWIG," *i.e.*, have your hair dressed in style; PRIME TWIG, in good order and high spirits.—*Pugilistic.*

TWIG, "to hop the TWIG," to decamp, "cut one's stick," to die.

TWIG, to understand, detect, or observe.

TWIST, brandy and gin mixed.

TWIST, appetite; "Will 's got a capital TWIST,"

TWITCHETTY, nervous, fidgetty.

TWITTER, "all in a TWITTER," in a fright, or fidgetty state.

TWO-HANDED, awkward.

TWOPENNY, the head; "tuck in your TWOPENNY," bend down your head.

TWOPENNY-HOPS, low dancing rooms, the price of admission to which was formerly—and not infrequently now—two pence. The clog hornpipe. the pipe dance, flash jigs, and hornpipes in fetters, *à la* Jack Sheppard. are the favourite movements, all entered into with great spirit and "joyous, laborious capering."—*Mayhew.*

TYBURN COLLAR, the fringe of beard worn under the chin.—*See* NEWGATE COLLAR.

TYE, or TIE, a neckerchief. Proper hosier's term now, but slang thirty years ago, and as early as 1718. Called also, SQUEEZE.

UNBETTY, to unlock.—*See* BETTY.

UNCLE, the pawnbroker.—*See* MY UNCLE.

UNDER THE ROSE.—*See* ROSE.

UNICORN, a style of driving with two wheelers abreast, and one leader,—termed in the *United States*, a SPIKE TEAM. TANDEM is one wheeler and one leader. RANDOM, three horses in line.

UNUTTERABLES, trousers —*See* INEXPRESSIBLES.

UNWHISPERABLES, trousers.

UP, "to be UP to a thing or two," to be knowing, or understanding; "to put a man UP to a move," to teach him a trick; "it's all UP with him," *i.e.*, it is all over with him, often pronounced U.P., naming the two letters separately; "UP a tree," see TREE; "UP to TRAP," "UP to SNUFF," wide awake. acquainted with the last new move; "UP to one's GOSSIP," to be a match for one who is trying to take you in;—"UP to SLUM," proficient in roguery, capable of committing a theft successfully.

UPPER BENJAMIN, a great coat.

UPPER STOREY, or UPPER LOFT, a person's head; "his UPPER STOREY is unfurnished," *i.e.*, he does not know very much.

UPPISH, proud, arrogant.

USED UP, broken-hearted, bankrupt, fatigued.

VAMOS, or VAMOUS, to go, or be off. *Spanish*, VAMOS, "let us go!" Probably NAMUS. or NAMOUS the costermonger's word, was from this, although it is generally considered back slang.

VAMPS, old stockings. From VAMP, to piece.

VARDO, to look; "VARDO the cassey," look at the house. VARDO formerly was *old cant* for a wagon.

VARMENT, "you young VARMENT, you!" you bad, or naughty boy. Corruption of *vermin*.

VELVET, the tongue.

VERTICAL-CARE-GRINDER, the treadmill.

VIC., the Victoria Theatre, London,—patronised principally by costermongers and low people; also the street abbreviation of the Christian name of her Majesty the Queen.

VILLAGE, or THE VILLAGE, *i.e.*, London.—*Sporting.*

VILLE, or VILE, a town or village,—pronounced *phial*, or *vial*.—*French.*

VINNIED, mildewed, or sour.—*Devonshire.*

VOKER, to talk; "can you VOKER Romany?" can you speak the canting language.—*Latin*, VOCARE; *Spanish*, VOCEAR.

WABBLE, to move from side to side, to roll about. *Johnson* terms it a "low, barbarous word."

WALKER! or HOOKEY WALKER! an ejaculation of incredulity, said when a person is telling a story which you know to be all gammon, or false. The *Saturday Reviewer's* explanation of the phrase is this:—"Years ago, there was a person named *Walker*, an aquiline-nosed Jew, who exhibited an orrery, which he called by the erudite name of *Eidouranion.* He was also a popular lecturer on astronomy, and often invited his pupils, telescope in hand, to *take a sight* at the moon and stars. The lecturer's phrase struck his school-boy auditory, who frequently "took a sight" with that gesture of outstretched arm, and adjustment to nose and eye, which was the first garnish of the popular saying. The next step was to assume phrase and gesture as the outward and visible mode of knowingness in general." A correspondent, however, denies this, and states that HOOKEY WALKER was a magistrate of dreaded acuteness and incredulity, whose hooked nose gave the title of BEAK to all his successors; and, moreover, that the gesture of applying the thumb to the nose and agitating the little finger, as an expression of "Don't you wish you may get it?" is considerably older than the story in the *Saturday Review* would seem to indicate. There is a third explanation of HOOKEY WALKER in *Notes and Queries*, iv., 425.

WALK INTO, to overcome, to demolish; "I'll WALK INTO his affections" *i.e.*, I will scold or thrash him. The word

DRIVE (which see) is used in an equally curious sense in slang speech.

WALK OVER, a re-election without opposition.—*Parliamentary*, but derived from the *Turf*, where a horse—which has no rivals entered—WALKS OVER the course, and wins without exertion.

WALK-THE-BARBER, to lead a girl astray.

WALK YOUR CHALKS, be off, or run away,—spoken sharply by any one who wishes to get rid of you.—*See* CHALKS.

WALL-FLOWER, a person who goes to a ball, and looks on without dancing, either from choice or not being able to obtain a partner.

WALL-FLOWERS, left-off and "regenerated" clothes, exposed for sale in Monmouth-street.

WALLOP, to beat, or thrash. Mr. John Gough Nichols derives this word from an ancestor of the Earl of Portsmouth, one Sir John Wallop, Knight of the Garter, who, in King Henry VIII.'s time, distinguished himself by WALLOPING the French; but it is more probably connected with WEAL, a livid swelling in the skin, after a blow.—*See* POT-WALLOPER.

WALLOPING, a beating or thrashing; sometimes in an adjective sense, as big, or very large.

WAPPING, or WHOPPING, of a large size, great.

WARM, rich, or well off.

WARM, to thrash, or beat; "I'll WARM your jacket."

WASH, "it won't WASH," *i.e.*, will not stand investigation, is not genuine, can't be believed.

WATCHMAKER, a pickpocket, or stealer of watches.

WATCH AND SEALS, a sheep's head and pluck.

WATER-BEWITCHED, very weak tea, the third brew (or the first at some houses), grog much diluted.

WATER OF LIFE, gin.

WATERMAN, a light blue silk handkerchief. The Oxford and Cambridge boats' crews always wear these—light blue for Cambridge, and a darker shade for Oxford.

WATTLES, ears.

WAXY, cross, ill-tempered.

WEDGE, silver.—*Old cant*.

WEDGE-FEEDER, silver spoon.

WEED, a cigar; *the* WEED, tobacco generally.

WELL, to pocket, or place as in a well.

WENCH, provincial and old-fashioned term for a girl, derived from WINK. In *America*, negro girls only are termed WENCHES.

WEST CENTRAL, a water-closet, the initials being the same as those of the London Postal District. It is said that for this reason very delicate people refuse to obey Rowland Hill's instructions in this particular.

WET, a drink, a "drain."

WET, to drink. Low people generally ask an acquaintance to WET any recently purchased article, *i.e.*, to stand treat on the occasion; "WET your whistle," *i.e.*, take a drink; "WET the other eye," *i.e.*, take another glass.

WET QUAKER, a drunkard of that sect; a man who pretends to be religious, and is a dram drinker on the sly.

WHACK, a share or lot; "give me my WHACK," give me my share. *Scotch*, SWEG, or SWACK.

WHACK, to beat; WHACK, or WHACKING, a blow or thrashing.

WHACKING, large, fine, or strong.

WHALE, "very like a WHALE in a teacup," said of anything that is very improbable; taken from a speech of Polonius in *Hamlet*.

WHEEDLE, to entice by soft words. "This word cannot be found to derive itself from any other, and therefore is looked upon as wholly invented by the CANTERS."—*Triumph of Wit*, 1705.

WHERRET, or WORRIT, to scold, trouble, or annoy.—*Old English*.

WHIDDLE, to enter into a parley, or hesitate with many words, &c.; to inform, or discover.

WHIDS, words.—*Old Gipsey cant*.

WHIM-WAM, an alliterative term, synonymous with *fiddle-faddle*, *riff-raff*, &c., denoting nonsense, rubbish, &c.

WHIP, to "WHIP anything *up*," to take it up quickly; from the method of hoisting heavy goods or horses on board ship by a WHIP, or running tackle, from the yard-arm. Generally used to express anything dishonestly taken—*L'Estrange* and *Johnson*.

WHIP JACK, a sham shipwrecked sailor, called also a TURNPIKE SAILOR.

WHIPPER-SNAPPER, a waspish, diminutive person.

WHIPPING THE CAT, when an operative works at a private house by the day. Term used amongst tailors and carpenters.

WHISKER. There is a curious slang phrase connected with this word. When an improbable story is told, the remark is, "the mother of that was a WHISKER," meaning it is a lie.

WHISTLE, "as clean as a WHISTLE," neatly, or "SLICKLY done," as an American would say; "to WET ONE'S WHISTLE," to take a drink. This is a very old term. *Chaucer* says of the Miller of Trumpington's wife (*Canterbury Tales*, 4153)—

> "So was hir joly WHISTAL well Y-WET;"

"to WHISTLE FOR ANYTHING," to stand small chance of getting it, from the nautical custom of *whistling* for a wind in a calm, which of course comes none the sooner for it.

WHITE FEATHER, "to show the WHITE FEATHER," to evince cowardice. In the times when great attention was paid to the breeding of game-cocks, a white feather in the tail was considered a proof of cross-breeding.

WHITE LIE, a harmless lie, one told to reconcile people at variance; "mistress is not at home, sir," is a WHITE LIE often told by servants.

WHITE LIVER'D, or LIVER FACED, cowardly, much afraid, very mean.

WHITE PROP, a diamond pin.

WHITE SATIN, gin,—term amongst women.

WHITE TAPE, gin,—term used principally by female servants.

WHITE WINE, the fashionable term for gin.

> "Jack Randall then impatient rose,
> And said, 'Tom's speech were just as fine
> If he would call that first of GO's
> By that genteeler name—WHITE WINE.'"
> *Randall's Diary*, 1820.

WHITECHAPEL, or WESTMINSTER BROUGHAM, a costermonger's donkey-barrow.

WHITECHAPEL, the "upper-cut," or strike.—*Pugilistic.*

WHITEWASH, when a person has taken the benefit of the Insolvent Act he is said to have been WHITEWASHED.

WHOP, to beat, or hide. Corruption of WHIP; sometimes spelled WAP.

WHOP-STRAW, cant name for a countryman; *Johnny* WHOP-STRAW, in allusion to threshing.

WHOPPER, a big one, a lie.

WIDDLE, to shine.—*See* OLIVER.

WIDE-AWAKE, a broad-brimmed felt, or stuff hat,—so called because it never had a *nap*, and never wants one.

WIDO, wide awake, no fool.

WIFE, a fetter fixed to one leg.—*Prison.*

WIFFLE-WOFFLES, in the dumps, sorrow, stomach ache.

WIGGING, a rebuke *before comrades.* If the head of a firm calls a clerk into the parlour, and rebukes him, it is an *earwigging;* if done before the other clerks, it is a WIGGING.

WILD, a village.—*Tramps' term.*—*See* VILE.

WILD, vexed, cross, passionate. In the United States the word *mad* is supplemented with a vulgar meaning similar to our Cockneyism, WILD; and to make a man MAD on the other side of the Atlantic is to vex him, or "rile" his temper —not to render him a raving maniac, or a fit subject for Bedlam.

WILD OATS, youthful pranks.

WIND, "to raise the WIND," to procure money; "to slip one's WIND," coarse expression meaning to die.

WIND, "I'll WIND your cotton," *i.e.*, I will give you some trouble. The Byzantine General, Narses, used the same kind of threat to the Greek Empress,—"I will spin such a thread that they shall not be able to unravel."

WINDED-SETTLED, transported for life.

WINDOWS, the eyes, or "peepers."

WINEY, intoxicated.

WINKIN, "he went off like WINKIN," *i.e.*, very quickly.

WINKS, periwinkles.

WINN, a penny.—*Ancient cant.*

WIPE, a pocket handkerchief.—*Old cant.*

WIPE, a blow.

WIPE, to strike; "he fetcht me a WIPE over the knuckles," he struck me on the knuckles; "to WIPE a person down," to flatter or pacify a person; to WIPE off a score, to pay one's debts, in allusion to the slate or chalk methods of account keeping; "to WIPE a person's eye," to shoot game which he has missed—*Sporting term;* hence to obtain an advantage by superior activity.

WIRE, a thief with long fingers, expert at picking ladies' pockets.

WOBBLESHOP, where beer is sold without a license.

WOODEN SPOON, the last junior optime who takes a University degree; denoting one who is only fit to stay at home, and stir porridge.—*Cambridge.*

WOODEN WEDGE, the last name in the classical honours list

at Cambridge. The last in mathematical honours had long been known as the WOODEN SPOON; but when the classical Tripos was instituted, in 1824, it was debated among the undergraduates what *sobriquet* should be given to the last on the examination list. Curiously enough, the name that year which happened to be last was WEDGEWOOD (a distinguished Wrangler). Hence the title.

WOOL, courage, pluck; "you are not half-WOOLLED," term of reproach from one thief to another.

WOOLBIRD, a lamb; "wing of a WOOLBIRD," a shoulder of lamb.

WOOL-GATHERING, said of any person's wits when they are wandering, or in a reverie.—*Florio.*

WOOL-HOLE, the workhouse.

WORK, to plan, or lay down and execute any course of action, to perform anything; "to WORK the BULLS," *i.e.*, to get rid of false crown pieces; "to WORK the ORACLE," to succeed by manœuvring, to concert a wily plan, to victimise,—a possible reference to the stratagems and bribes used to corrupt the *Delphic oracle*, and cause it to deliver a favourable response. "To WORK a street or neighbourhood," trying at each house to sell all one can, or so bawling that every housewife may know what you have to sell. The general plan is to drive a donkey barrow a short distance, and then stop and cry. The term implies thoroughness; to "WORK a street well" is a common saying with a coster.

WORM, *see* PUMP.

WORMING, removing the beard of an oyster or muscle.

W. P., or WARMING PAN. A clergyman who holds a living *pro tempore*, under a bond of resignation, is styled a W. P., or WARMING PAN rector, because he keeps the place warm for his successor.—*Clerical slang.*

WRINKLE, an idea, or fancy; an additional piece of knowledge which is supposed to be made by a WRINKLE *à posteriori.*

WRITE, "to WRITE ONE'S NAME on a joint," to have the first cut at anything,—leaving sensible traces of one's presence on it.

YACK, a watch; to "*church* a YACK," to take it out of its case to avoid detection.

YARD OF CLAY, a long, old-fashioned tobacco pipe, also called a *churchwarden.*

YARMOUTH CAPON, a bloater, or red herring.—*Old.*—*Ray's Proverbs.*

YARN, a long story, or tale; "a tough YARN," a tale hard to be believed; "spin a YARN," tell a tale.—*Sea.*

YAY-NAY, "a poor YAY-NAY" fellow, one who has no conversational power, and can only answer *yea* or *nay* to a question.

YELLOW BELLY, a native of the Fens of Lincolnshire, or the Isle of Ely,—in allusion to the frogs and a yellow-bellied eel caught there; they are also said to be *web-footed.*

YELLOW-BOY, a sovereign, or any gold coin.

YELLOW-GLOAK, a jealous man.

YELLOW-JACK, the yellow fever prevalent in the West Indies.

YELLOW-MAN, a yellow silk handkerchief.

YOKEL, a countryman.—*West.*

YOKUFF, a chest, or large box.

YORKSHIRE, "to YORKSHIRE," or "come YORKSHIRE over any person," is to cheat or BITE them.—*North.*

YORKSHIRE ESTATES, "I will do it when I come into my YORKSHIRE ESTATES,"—meaning if I ever have the money or the means. The phrase is said to have originated with *Dr. Johnson.*

YOUNKER, in street language, a lad or a boy. Term in general use amongst costermongers, cabmen, and old-fashioned people. *Barnefield's Affectionate Shepherd,* 1594, has the phrase, "a seemelie YOUNKER." *Danish* and *Friesic,* JONKER. In the *Navy,* a naval cadet is usually termed a YOUNKER.

YOUR-NIBS, yourself.

ZIPH, LANGUAGE OF, a way of disguising English in use among the students at *Winchester College.* Compare MEDICAL GREEK.

ZOUNDS, a sudden exclamation,—abbreviation of *God's wounds.*

SOME ACCOUNT OF THE

BACK SLANG,

THE SECRET LANGUAGE OF COSTERMONGERS.

THE costermongers of London number between thirty and forty thousand. Like other low tribes, they boast a language, or secret tongue, in which they hide their earnings, movements, and other private affairs. This costers' speech, as Mayhew remarks, offers no new fact, or approach to a fact, for philologists; it is not very remarkable for originality of construction; neither is it spiced with low humour, as other cant. But the costermongers boast that it is known only to themselves; that it is far beyond the Irish, and puzzles the Jews.

The main principle of this language is spelling the words backwards,—or rather, pronouncing them rudely backwards. Sometimes, for the sake of harmony, an extra syllable is prefixed, or annexed; and, occasionally, the word is given quite a different turn in rendering it backwards, from what an uninitiated person would have expected. One coster told Mayhew that he often gave the end of a word "a new turn, just as if he chorussed it with a tol-de-rol." Besides, the coster has his own idea of the *proper* way of spelling words, and is not to be convinced but by an overwhelming show of learning, —and frequently not then, for he is a very headstrong fellow. By the time a coster has spelt an ordinary word of two or three syllables in the proper way, and then spelt it backwards, it has become a tangled knot that no etymologist could unravel. The word GENERALISE, for instance, is considered to be "shilling" spelt backwards. Sometimes Slang and Cant words are introduced, and even these, when imagined to be tolerably well known, are pronounced backwards. Other terms, such as GEN, a shilling, and FLATCH, a halfpenny, help to confuse the outsider.

After a time, this back language, or BACK-SLANG, as it is called by the costermongers themselves, comes to be regarded by the rising generation of street sellers as a distinct and regular mode of speech. They never refer words, by inverting them, to their originals; and the YENEPS and ES-CLOPS, and NAMOWS, are looked upon as proper, but secret terms. "But it is a curious fact, that lads who become costermongers' boys, without previous association with the class, acquire a very ready command of the language, and this though they are not only unable to spell, but 'don't know a letter in a book.*'" They soon obtain a considerable stock vocabulary, so that they converse rather from the memory than the understanding. Amongst the senior costermongers, and those who pride themselves on their proficiency in BACK-SLANG, a conversation is often sustained for a whole evening, especially if any "flatties" are present whom they wish to astonish or confuse. The women use it sparingly, but the girls are generally well acquainted with it.

The addition of an *s*, I should state, always forms the plural, so that this is another source of complication. For instance, *woman* in the BACK-SLANG, is NAMOW, and NAMUS, or NAMOWS, is *women*, not NEMOW. The explorer, then, in undoing the BACK-SLANG, and turning the word NAMUS once more into English, would have *suman*,—a novel and very extraordinary rendering of *women*. Where a word is refractory in submitting to a back rendering, as in the case of *pound*, letters are made to change positions for the sake of harmony; thus, we have DUNOP, a pound, instead of *dnuop* which nobody could pleasantly pronounce. This will remind the reader of the Jews' "*old clo! old clo!*" instead of *old clothes*, *old clothes*, which would tire even the patience of a Jew to repeat all day.

* *Mayhew*, vol. i., p. 24.

This singular BACK tongue has been in vogue about twenty-five years. It is, as before stated, soon acquired, and is principally used by the costermongers (as the specimen Glossary will show), for communicating the secrets of their street tradings, the cost and profit of the goods, and for keeping their natural enemies, the police, in the dark. COOL THE ESCLOP (look at the police) is often said amongst them, when one of the constabulary makes his appearance.

Perhaps on no subject is the costermonger so particular as on money matters. All costs and profits he thinks should be kept profoundly secret. The Back Slang, therefore, gives the various small amounts very minutely.

FLATCH, halfpenny.
YENEP, penny.
OWT-YENEPS, twopence.
ERTH-YENEPS, threepence.
ROUF-YENEPS, fourpence.
EVIF, or EWIF-YENEPS, fivepence.
EXIS-YENEPS, sixpence.
NEVIS-YENEPS, sevenpence.
TEAICH, or THEG-YENEPS, eightpence.
ENIN-YENEPS, ninepence,
NET-YENEPS. tenpence.
NEVELÉ-YENEPS, elevenpence.
EVLÉNET-YENNEPS, twelvepence.
GEN, or GENERALIZE, one shilling, or twelvepence.
YENEP-FLATCH, three halfpence.

OWT-YENEP-FLATCH, twopence halfpenny,
&c. &c. &c.
GEN, or ENO-GEN, one shilling.
OWT-GENS, two shillings.
ERTH-GENS, three shillings.

The GENS continue in the same sequence as the YENEPS above, excepting THEG-GENS, 8s., which is usually rendered THEG-GUY,—a deviation with ample precedents in all civilised tongues.

YENORK, a crown piece, or five shillings.
FLATCH-YENORK, half a-crown.

Beyond this amount the costermonger reckons after an intricate and complicated mode. Fifteen shillings would be ERTH-EVIF-GENS, or, literally, three times 5s.; seventeen shillings would be ERTH-YENORK-FLATCH, or three crowns and a half; or, by another mode of reckoning, ERTH-EVIF-GENS FLATCH-YENORK, *i.e.*, three times 5s., and half-a-crown.

DUNOP, a pound.

Further than which the costermonger seldom goes in money reckoning.

In the following Glossary only those words are given which costermongers principally use,—the terms connected with street traffic, the names of the different coins, vegetables, fruit and fish, technicalities of police courts, &c.

The reader might naturally think that a system of speech so simple as the BACK-SLANG would require no Glossary; but he will quickly perceive, from the specimens given, that a great many words in frequent use in a BACK sense, have become so twisted as to require a little glossarial explanation.

GLOSSARY

OF THE

BACK SLANG.

BIRK, a "crib,"—house.

COOL, to look.

COOL HIM, look at him. A phrase frequently used when one costermonger warns another of the approach of a policeman.

DAB, bad.

DABHENO, one bad, or a bad market.—*See* DOOGHENO.

DAB TROS, a bad sort.

DA-ERB, bread.

DEB, or DAB, a bed; "I'm on to the DEB," I'm going to bed.

DILLO-NAMO, an old woman.

DLOG, gold.

DOOG, good.

DOOGHENO, literally "one-good," or "good-one," but implying generally a good market.

DOOGHENO HIT, one good hit. A coster remarks to a "mate," *Jack made a* DOOGHENO HIT *this morning*," implying that he did well at market, or sold out with good profit.

DUNOP, a pound.

ERTH, three.

EARTH* GENS, three shillings.

EARTH SITH-NOMS, three months.

EARTH YANNOPS, or YENEPS, threepence.

EDGABAC, cabbage.

* My informant preferred EARTH to ERTH,—for the reason, he said, "that it looked more sensible!"

EDGENARO, an orange.

E-FINK, knife.

EKAME, a "make," or swindle.

EKOM, a "moke," or donkey.

ELRIG, a girl.

ENIF, fine.

ENIN GENS, nine shillings.

ENIN YENEP, ninepence.

ENIN YANNOPS, or YENEPS, ninepence.

ENO, one.

ERIF, fire.

ERTH GENS, three shillings.

ERTH-PU, three-up, a street game.

ERTH SITH-NOMS, three months,—a term of imprisonment unfortunately very familiar to the lower orders.

ERTH-YENEPS, threepence.

ESCLOP, the police.

ES-ROPH, or ES-ROCH, a horse.

EVIF-YENEPS, five pence.

EVLENET-GENS, twelve shillings.

EVLENET SITH-NOMS, twelve months.

EWIF-GENS, a crown, or five shillings.

EWIF-YENEPS, fivepence.

EXIS GENS, six shillings.

EXIS-EWIF-GENS, six times five shillings, *i.e.*, 30s. All moneys may be reckoned in this manner, either with YENEPS or GENS.

EXIS-EVIF YENEPS, elevenpence,—literally, "sixpence and fivepence = elevenpence." This mode of reckoning, distinct from the preceding, is also common amongst those who use the back slang.

EXIS SITH-NOMS, six months.

EXIS-YENEPS, sixpence.

FI-HEATH, a thief.

FLATCH, a half, or halfpenny.

FLATCH KEN-NURD, half drunk.

FLATCH YENEP, a halfpenny.

FLATCH-YENORK, half a-crown.

GEN, twelvepence, or one shilling. Possibly an abbreviation of ARGENT, cant term for silver.—See following.

GENERALIZE, a shilling, generally shortened to GEN.

GEN-NET, or NET GENS, ten shillings.

HEL-BAT, a table.

HELPA, an apple.

KENNETSEENO, stinking.

KENNURD, drunk.

KEW, a week.

KEWS, or SKEW, weeks.

KIRB, a brick.

KOOL, to look.

LAWT, tall.

LEVEN, in back slang, is sometimes allowed to stand for *eleven*, for the reason that it is a number which seldom occurs. An article is either 10d. or 1s.

LUR-AC-HAM, mackarel.

MOTTAB, bottom.

MUR, rum.

NALE, or NAEL, lean.

NAM, a man.

NAMESCLOP, a policeman.

NAMOW, a woman; DILLO NAMOW, an old woman.

NEERGS, greens.

NETENIN GENS, nineteen shillings.

NEETEWIF GENS, fifteen shillings.

NEETEXIS, or NETEXIS GENS, sixteen shillings.

NETNEVIS GENS, seventeen shillings.

NET-THEG GENS, eighteen shillings.

NEETRITH GENS, thirteen shillings.

NEETROUF GENS, fourteen shillings.

NET-GEN, ten shillings, or half a sovereign.

NET-YENEPS, tenpence.

NEVELE GENS, eleven shillings.

NEVELE YENEPS, elevenpence,—generally LEVEN YENEPS.

NEVIS GENS, seven shillings.

NEVIS STRETCH, seven years' transportation, or imprisonment.—*See* STRETCH, in the *Slang Dictionary*.

NEVIS YENEPS, sevenpence.
NIRE, rain.
NIG, gin.
NI-OG OT TAKRAM, going to market.
NITRAPH, a farthing.
NOL, long.
NOOM, the moon.
NOS-RAP, a parson.
OCCABOT, tobacco; "tib of OCCABOT," bit of tobacco.
ON, no.
ON DOOG, no good.
OWT GENS, two shillings.
OWT YENEPS, twopence.
PAC, a cap.
PINURT POTS, turnip tops.
POT, top.
RAPE, a pear.
REEB, beer.
REV-LIS, silver.
ROUF-EFIL, for life,—sentence of punishment.
ROUF-GENS, four shillings.
ROUF-YENEPS, fourpence.
RUTAT, or RATTAT, a "tatur," or potato.
SAY, yes.
SEE O, shoes.
SELOPAS, apples.
SHIF, fish.
SIR-ETCH, cherries.
SITH-NOM, a month.
SLAOC, coals.
SLOP, a policeman.—*See Dictionary of Slang and Cant Words.*
SNEERG, greens.
SOUSH, a house.
SPINSRAP, parsnips.
SRES-WORT, trowsers.
STARPS, sprats.
STOOB, boots.

STORRAC, carrots.
STUN, nuts.
STUNLAWS, walnuts.
SWRET-SIO, oysters.
TACH, a hat.
TAF, or TAFFY, fat.
THEG, or TEAICH GENS, eight shillings.
TEAICH-GUY, eight shillings,—a slight deviation from the numerical arrangement of GENS.
TENIP, a pint.
THEG YENEPS, eightpence.
TIB, a bit, or piece.
TOAC, or TOG, a coat. TOG is the *old cant* term.—See *Dictionary of Slang, &c.*
TOAC-TISAW, a waistcoat.
TOL, lot, stock, or share.
TOP O' REEB, a pot of beer.
TOP-YOB, a pot boy.
TORRAC, a carrot.
TRACK (or TRAG), a quart.
TROSSENO, literally, "one sort," but the costermongers use it to imply anything that is bad.
WAR-RAB, a barrow.
WEDGE, a Jew.
YAD, a day; YADS, days.
YADNAB, brandy.
YENEP, a penny.
YENEP-A-TIME, penny each time,—term in betting.
YENEP-FLATCH, three halfpence,—all the halfpence and pennies continue in the same sequence.
YAP-POO, pay up.
YEKNOD, or JERK-NOD, a donkey.
YENORK, a crown.
YOB, a boy.
ZEB, best.

SOME ACCOUNT OF THE

RHYMING SLANG,

THE SECRET LANGUAGE OF

CHAUNTERS AND PATTERERS.

THERE exists in London a singular tribe of men, known amongst the "fraternity of vagabonds" as Chaunters and Patterers. Both classes are great talkers. The first sing or chaunt through the public thoroughfares ballads—political and humorous—carols, dying speeches, and the various other kinds of gallows and street literature. The second deliver street orations on grease-removing compounds, plating powders, high polishing blacking, and the thousand and one wonderful pennyworths that are retailed to gaping mobs from a London kerb stone.

They are quite a distinct tribe from the costermongers; indeed, amongst tramps, they term themselves the "harristocrats of the streets," and boast that they live by their intellects. Like the costermongers, however, they have a secret tongue or Cant speech, known only to each other. This Cant, which has nothing to do with that spoken by the costermongers, is known in Seven Dials and elsewhere as the RHYMING SLANG, *or the substitution of words and sentences which rhyme with other words intended to be kept secret.* The chaunter's Cant, therefore, partakes of his calling, and he transforms and uses up into a rough speech the various odds and ends of old songs, ballads, and street nick-names, which are found suitable to his purpose. Unlike nearly all other systems of Cant, the rhyming Slang is not founded upon allegory; unless we except a few rude similes, thus—I'M AFLOAT is the rhyming Cant for *boat*, SORROWFUL TALE is equivalent to *three months in jail,* ARTFUL DODGER signifies a *lodger*, and a SNAKE IN THE GRASS stands for a *looking-glass*—a meaning that would delight a fat Chinaman, or a collector of Oriental proverbs. But, as in the case of the costers' speech and the old gipsey-vagabond Cant, the chaunters and patterers so interlard this rhyming Slang with their general remarks, while their ordinary language is so smothered and subdued, that, unless when they are professionally engaged and talking of their wares, they might almost pass for foreigners.

From the inquiries I have made of various patterers and "paper workers," I learn that the rhyming Slang was introduced about twelve or fifteen years ago. Numbering this class of oratorical and bawling wanderers at twenty thousand, scattered over Great Britain, including London and the large provincial towns, we thus see the number of English vagabonds who converse in rhyme and talk poetry, although their habitations and mode of life constitute a very unpleasant Arcadia. These nomadic poets, like the other talkers of Cant or secret languages, are stamped with the vagabond's mark, and are continually on the move. The married men mostly have lodgings in London, and come and go as occasion may require. A few never quit London streets, but the greater number tramp to all the large provincial fairs, and prefer the MONKERY (country) to town life. Some transact their business in a systematic way, sending a post-office order to the Seven Dials printer, for a fresh supply of ballads or penny books, or to the SWAG SHOP, as the case may be, for trinkets and gewgaws, to be sent on by rail to a given town by the time they shall arrive there.

When any dreadful murder, colliery explosion, or frightful railway accident has happened in a country district, three or four chaunters are generally on the spot in a day or two after the occurrence, vending and bawling "*A True and Faithful Account*," &c., which "true and faithful account" was concocted purely in the imaginations of the successors of Catnach and Tommy Pitts,* behind the counters of their printing shops in Seven Dials. And but few fairs are held in any part of England without the patterer being punctually at his post, with his nostrums, or real gold rings (with the story of the wager laid by the gentleman—see FAWNEY BOUNCING, in the Dictionary), or save-alls for candlesticks, or paste which, when applied to the strop, makes the dullest razor keen enough to hack broom handles and sticks, and after that to have quite enough sharpness left for splitting hairs, or shaving them off the back of one of the clod-hoppers' hands, looking on in amazement. And CHEAP JOHN, too, with his coarse jokes, and no end of six-bladed knives, and pocket-books, containing information for everybody, with pockets to hold money, and a pencil to write with in the bargain, and a van stuffed with the cheap productions of Sheffield and "Brummagem,"—he, too, is a patterer of the highest order, and visits fairs, and can hold a conversation in the rhyming Slang.

Such is a rough description of the men who speak this jargon; and simple and ridiculous as the vulgar scheme of a rhyming Slang may appear, it must always be regarded as a curious fact in linguistic history. In order that the reader's patience may not be too much taxed, only a

* The famous printers and publishers of sheet songs and last dying speeches thirty years ago.

selection of rhyming words has been given in the Glossary,—and these for the most part, as in the case of the back Slang, are the terms of everyday life, as used by this order of tramps and hucksters.

It must not be supposed, however, that the chaunter or patterer confines himself entirely to this Slang when conveying secret intelligence. On the contrary, although he speaks not a "leash of languages," yet is he master of the beggars' Cant, and is thoroughly "up" in street Slang. The following letter, written by a chaunter to a gentleman who took an interest in his welfare, will show his capabilities in this line.

Dear Friend,*

Excuse the liberty, since i saw you last i

* The writer, a street chaunter of ballads and last dying speeches, alludes in his letter to two celebrated criminals, Thos Drory, the murderer of Jael Denny, and Sarah Chesham, who poisoned her husband, accounts of whose Trials and "Horrid Deeds" he had been selling. I give a glossary of the cant words:

Thickun, a crownpiece.
Dowry of Parny, a lot of rain.
Stumped, bankrupt.
Coopered, spoilt.
Bossman, a farmer.
*** Drory was a farmer.
Patter, trial.
Tops, last dying speeches.
Dies, ib.
Croaks, ib.
Burick, a woman.
Topped, hung.
Sturaban, a prison.
Quid, a sovereign.
James, ib.
Clye, a pocket.
Carser, a house or residence.
Speel on the Drum, to be off to the country.
All Square, all right, or quite well.

have not earned a thickun, we have had such a Dowry of Parny that it completely stumped or Coopered Drory the Bossmans Patter therefore i am broke up and not having another friend but you i wish to know if you would lend me the price of 2 Gross of Tops, Dies, or Croaks, which is 7 shillings, of the above mentioned worthy and Sarah Chesham the Essex Burick for the Poisoning job, they are both to be topped at Springfield Sturaban on Tuesday next. i hope you will oblige me if you can for it will be the means of putting a Quid or a James in my Clye. i will call at your Carser on Sunday Evening next for an answer, for i want to Speel on the Drum as soon as possible. hoping you and the family are All Square,

I remain Your obedient Servant,

———

GLOSSARY

OF THE

RHYMING SLANG.

ABRAHAM'S WILLING, a shilling.
ALACOMPAIN, rain.
ALL AFLOAT, a coat.
ANY RACKET, a penny faggot.
APPLES AND PEARS, stairs.
ARTFUL DODGER, a lodger.
ARTICHOKE RIPE, smoke a pipe.
BABY PAPS, caps.
BARNET FAIR, hair.
BATTLE OF THE NILE, a tile—vulgar term for a hat.
BEN FLAKE, a steak.
BILLY BUTTON, mutton.
BIRCH BROOM, a room.
BIRD LIME, time.
BOB, MY PAL, a gal,—vulgar pronunciation of *girl*.
BONNETS SO BLUE, Irish stew.
BOTTLE OF SPRUCE, a deuce,—slang for twopence.
BOWL THE HOOP, soup.
BRIAN O'LINN, gin.
BROWN BESS, yes—the affirmative.
BROWN JOE, no—the negative.
BULL AND COW, a row.
BUSHY PARK, a lark.
BUTTER FLAP, a cap.

CAIN AND ABEL, a table.

CAMDEN TOWN, a brown,—vulgar term for a halfpenny.

CASTLE RAG, a flag,—slang term for fourpence.

CAT AND MOUSE, a house.

CHALK FARM, the arm.

CHARING CROSS, a horse.

CHARLEY LANCASTER, a handkercher,—vulgar pronunciation of handkerchief.

CHARLEY PRESCOTT, waistcoat.

CHERRY RIPE, a pipe.

CHEVY CHASE, the face.

CHUMP (or CHUNK) OF WOOD, no good.

COW AND CALF, to laugh.

COVENT GARDEN, a farden,—Cockney pronunciation of farthing.

COWS AND KISSES, mistress or missus—referring to the ladies.

CURRANTS AND PLUMS, thrums,—slang for threepence.

DAISY RECROOTS (so spelt by my informant of Seven Dials; he means, doubtless, *recruits*), a pair of boots.

DAN TUCKER, butter.

DING DONG, a song.

DRY LAND, you understand.

DUKE OF YORK, take a walk.

EAST AND SOUTH, a mouth.

EAT A FIG, to "crack a crib," to break into a house, or commit a burglary.

EGYPTIAN HALL, a ball.

ELEPHANT'S TRUNK, drunk.

EPSOM RACES, a pair of braces.

EVERTON TOFFEE, coffee.

FANNY BLAIR, the hair.

FILLET OF VEAL, the treadwheel, house of correction.

FINGER AND THUMB, rum.

FLAG UNFURLED, a man of the world.

FLEA AND LOUSE, a bad house.

FLOUNDER AND DAB (two kinds of flat fish), a cab.

FLY MY KITE, a light.

FROG AND TOAD, the main road.
GARDEN GATE, a magistrate.
GERMAN FLUTES, a pair of boots.
GIRL AND BOY, a saveloy,—a penny sausage.
GLORIOUS SINNER, a dinner.
GODDESS DIANA (pronounced DIANER), a tanner,—sixpence.
GOOSEBERRY PUDDING (*vulgo* PUDDEN), a woman.
HANG BLUFF, snuff.
HOD OF MORTAR, a pot of porter.
HOUNSLOW HEATH, teeth.
I DESIRE, a fire.
I'M AFLOAT, a boat.
ISLE OF FRANCE, a dance.
ISABELLA (vulgar pronunciation, ISABELLER), an umbrella.
I SUPPOSE, the nose.
JACK DANDY, brandy.
JACK RANDALL (a noted pugilist), a candle.
JENNY LINDER, a winder,—vulgar pronunciation of window.
JOE SAVAGE, a cabbage.
LATH AND PLASTER, a master.
LEAN AND LURCH, a church.
LEAN AND FAT, a hat.
LINENDRAPER, paper.
LIVE EELS, fields.
LOAD OF HAY, a day.
LONG ACRE, a baker.
LONG ACRE, a newspaper. See the preceding.
LORD JOHN RUSSELL, a bustle.
LORD LOVEL, a shovel.
LUMP OF COKE, a bloak,—slang term for a man.
LUMP OF LEAD, the head.
MACARONI, a pony.
MAIDS A DAWNING (I suppose my informant means *maids adorning*), the morning.
MAIDSTONE JAILOR, a tailor.
MINCE PIES, the eyes.
MOTHER AND DAUGHTER, water.

MUFFIN BAKER, a Quaker.
NAVIGATORS, taturs,—vulgar pronunciation of potatoes.
NAVIGATOR SCOT, baked potatoes all hot.
NEEDLE AND THREAD, bread.
NEVER FEAR, a pint of beer.
NIGHT AND DAY, go to the play.
NOSE AND CHIN, a winn,—*ancient cant* for a penny.
NOSE-MY, backy,—vulgar pronunciation of tobacco.
OATS AND BARLEY, Charley.
OATS AND CHAFF, a footpath.
ORINOKO (pronounced ORINOKER), a poker.
OVER THE STILE, sent for trial.
PADDY QUICK, thick; or, a stick.
PEN AND INK, a stink.
PITCH AND FILL, Bill,—vulgar shortening for William.
PLATE OF MEAT, a street.
PLOUGH THE DEEP, to go to sleep.
PUDDINGS AND PIES, the eyes.
READ OF TRIPE (?), transported for life.
READ AND WRITE, to fight.
READ AND WRITE, flight.—See preceding.
RIVER LEA, tea.
ROGUE AND VILLAIN, a shillin,—common pronunciation of shilling.
RORY O'MORE, the floor.
ROUND THE HOUSES, trouses,—vulgar pronunciation of trousers.
SALMON TROUT, the mouth.
SCOTCH PEG, a leg.
SHIP IN FULL SAIL, a pot of ale.
SIR WALTER SCOTT, a pot,—of beer.
SLOOP OF WAR, a whore.
SNAKE IN THE GRASS, a looking glass.
SORROWFUL TALE, three months in jail.
SPLIT ASUNDER, a costermonger.
SPLIT PEA, tea.
SPORT AND WIN, Jim.
STEAM PACKET, a jacket.

ST. MARTINS-LE-GRAND, the hand.
STOP THIEF, beef.
SUGAR AND HONEY, money.
SUGAR CANDY, brandy.
TAKE A FRIGHT, night.
THREE QUARTERS OF A PECK, the neck,—in writing, expressed by the simple "¾."
THROW ME IN THE DIRT, a shirt.
TOMMY O'RANN, scran,—vulgar term for food.
TOM TRIPE, a pipe.
TOM RIGHT, night.
TOP JINT (vulgar pronunciation of joint), a pint,—of beer.
TOP OF ROME, home.
TURTLE DOVES, a pair of gloves.
TWO FOOT RULE, a fool.
WIND DO TWIRL, a fine girl.

THE

BIBLIOGRAPHY

OF

SLANG, CANT, AND VULGAR LANGUAGE;

OR A

LIST OF THE BOOKS WHICH HAVE BEEN CONSULTED IN COMPILING THIS WORK,

COMPRISING NEARLY EVERY KNOWN TREATISE UPON THE SUBJECT.

SLANG has a literary history, the same as authorised language. More than one hundred works have treated upon the subject in one form or another,—a few devoting but a chapter, whilst many have given up their entire pages to expounding its history and use. Old Harman, a worthy man, who interested himself in suppressing and exposing vagabondism in the days of good Queen Bess, was the first to write upon the subject. Decker followed fifty years afterwards, but helped himself, evidently, to his predecessor's labours. Shakespere, Beaumont and Fletcher, Ben Jonson, and Brome, each employed beggars' Cant as part of the machinery of their plays. Then came Head (who wrote "The English Rogue," in 1680) with a glossary of Cant words "used by the Gipseys." But it was only a reprint of what Decker had given sixty years before. About this time authorised dictionaries began to insert vulgar words, labelling them "Cant." The Jack Sheppards and Dick Turpins of the early and middle part of the last century made Cant popular, and many small works were published upon the subject. But it was Grose, burly, facetious Grose, who, in the year 1785, collected the scattered glossaries of Cant and secret words, and formed one large work, adding to it all the vulgar words and Slang terms used in his own day. I am aware that the indelicacy and extreme vulgarity of the work renders it a disgrace to its compiler, still we must admit that it is by far the most important work which has ever appeared on street or popular language; indeed, from its pages every succeeding work has, up to the present time, drawn its contents. The great fault of Grose's book consists in the author not contenting himself with Slang and Cant terms, but the inserting of every "smutty" and offensive word that could be raked out of the gutters of the streets. However, Harman and Grose are, after all, the only authors who have as yet treated the subject in an original manner, or have written on it from personal inquiry.

AINSWORTH'S (William Harrison) Novels and Ballads. *London*, V. D.

Some of this author's novels, such as Rookwood and Jack Sheppard, abound in cant words, placed in the mouths of the highwaymen. The author's ballads (especially "Nix my dolly pals fake away,") have long been popular favourites.

ANDREWS' (George) Dictionary of the Slang and Cant Languages, Ancient and Modern, 12mo. *London*, 1809

A sixpenny pamphlet, with a coloured frontispiece representing a beggar's carnival.

A NEW DICTIONARY OF THE JAUNTING CREW, 12mo. N. D.

Mentioned by John Bee in the Introduction to his Sportsman's Slang Dictionary.

ASH'S (John, LL.D.) New and Complete Dictionary of the English Language, 2 vols. 8vo. 1775

Contains a great number of cant words and phrases.

BACCHUS AND VENUS; or, a Select Collection of near 200 of the most Witty and Diverting Songs and Catches in Love and Gallantry, with Songs in the Canting Dialect, with a DICTIONARY, *explaining all Burlesque and Canting Terms*, 12mo. 1738

Prefixed is a curious woodcut frontispiece of a *Boozing Ken*. This work is scarce, and much prized by collectors. The Canting Dictionary appeared before, about 1710, with the initials B. E. on the title. It also came out afterwards, in the year 1751, under the title of the *Scoundrel's Dictionary*,—a mere reprint of the two former impressions.

BAILEY'S (Nath.) Etymological English Dictionary, 2 vols, 8vo 1737

Contains a great many cant and vulgar words;—indeed, Bailey does not appear to have been very particular what words he inserted, so long as they were actually in use. A *Collection of Ancient and Modern Cant Words* appears as an appendix to vol. ii. of this edition (3rd).

BANG-UP DICTIONARY, or the Lounger and Sportsman's Vade Mecum, containing a copious and correct Glossary of the Language of the Whips, illustrated by a great variety of original and curious Anecdotes, 8vo. 1812

A vulgar performance, consisting of pilferings from Grose, and made-up words with meanings of a degraded character.

BARTLETT'S Dictionary of Americanisms; a Glossary of Words and Phrases colloquially used in the United States, 8vo. *New York*, 1859

It is a curious fact connected with slang that a great number of vulgar words common in England are equally common in the

United States; and when we remember that America began to people two centuries ago, and that these colloquialisms must have crossed the sea with the first emigrants, we can form some idea of the antiquity of popular or street language. Many words, owing to the caprices of fashion or society, have wholly disappeared in the parent country, whilst in the colonies they are yet heard. The words SKINK, to serve drink in company, and the old term MICHING or MEECHING, skulking or playing truant, for instance, are still in use in the United States, although nearly, if not quite, obsolete here.

BEAUMONT and FLETCHER'S Comedy of *The Beggar's Bush*, 4to, 1661, or any edition.

Contains numerous cant words.

BEE'S (Jon.) Dictionary of the Turf, the Ring, the Chase, the Pit, the Bon Ton, and the Varieties of Life, forming the completest and most authentic Lexicon Balatronicum hitherto offered to the notice of the Sporting World, by Jon. Bee [*i.e.* John Badcock], Esq., Editor of the Fancy, Fancy Gazette, Living Picture of London, and the like of that, 12mo. 1823

This author published books on Stable Economy under the name of Hinds. He was the sporting rival of Pierce Egan. Professor Wilson, in an amusing article in *Blackwood's Magazine*, reviewed this work.

BEE'S (Jon.) Living Picture of London for 1828, and Stranger's Guide through the Streets of the Metropolis; shewing the Frauds, the Arts, Snares, and Wiles of all descriptions of Rogues that everywhere abound, 12mo. 1828

Professes to be a guide to society, high and low, in London, and to give an insight into the language of the streets.

BEE'S (Jon.) Sportsman's Slang, a New Dictionary of Terms used in the affairs of the Turf, the Ring, the Chase, and the Cockpit; with those of Bon Ton and the Varieties of Life, forming a *Lexicon Balatronicum et Macaronicum, &c.*, 12mo, *plate.* *For the Author*, 1825

The same as the preceding, only with an altered title. Both wretched performances, filled with forced and low wit.

BLACKGUARDIANA; or, Dictionary of Rogues, Bawds, &c., 8vo, WITH PORTRAITS [by *James Caulfield*]. 1795

This work, with a long and very vulgar title, is nothing but a reprint of *Grose*, with a few anecdotes of pirates, odd persons, &c., and some curious portraits inserted. It was concocted by Caulfield as a speculation, and published at *one guinea* per copy; and, owing to the remarkable title, and the notification at the bottom, that "only a few copies were printed," soon became scarce. For philological purposes it is not worth so much as any edition of Grose.

BOXIANA, or Sketches of Modern Pugilism, by Pierce Egan (an account of the prize ring), 3 vols, 8vo. 1820

Gives more particularly the cant terms of pugilism, but contains numerous (what were then styled) "flash" words.

BRANDON. Poverty, Mendicity, and Crime; or, the Facts, Examinations, &c., upon which the Report was founded, presented to the House of Lords by W. A. Miles, Esq., to which is added a *Dictionary of the Flash or Cant Language, known to every Thief and Beggar*, edited by H. Brandon, Esq., 8vo. 1839

A very wretched performance.

BROME'S (Rich.) Joviall Crew; or the Merry Beggars. Presented in a Comedie at the Cockpit, in Drury Lane, in the Year (4to.) 1652

Contains many cant words similar to those given by Decker,—from whose works they were doubtless obtained.

BROWN'S (Rev. Hugh Stowell) Lecture on Manliness, 12mo. 1857

Contains a few modern slang words.

BRYDGES' (Sir Egerton) British Bibliographer, 4 vols, 8vo. 1810—14

Vol ii., page 521, gives a list of cant words.

BULWER'S (Sir Edward Lytton) Paul Clifford. V. D.

Contains numerous cant words.

BULWER'S (Sir Edward Lytton) Pelham. V. D.

Contains a few cant terms.

BUTLER'S Hudibras, with Dr. Grey's Annotations, 3 vols, 8vo. 1819

Abounding in colloquial terms and phrases.

CAMBRIDGE. Gradus ad Cantabrigiam; or a Dictionary of Terms, Academical and Colloquial, or Cant, which are used at the University, *with Illustrations*, 12mo. *Camb.*, 1803

CANTING ACADEMY; or Villanies Discovered, wherein are shewn the Mysterious and Villanous Practices of that Wicked Crew—Hectors, Trapanners, Gilts, &c., with several new Catches and Songs; also Compleat Canting Dictionary, 12mo., *frontispiece*. 1674

Compiled by Richard Head.

CANTING; a Poem, interspersed with Tales and additional Scraps, post 8vo. 1814

A few words may be gleaned from this rather dull poem.

CANTING DICTIONARY; comprehending all the Terms, Antient and Modern, used in the several Tribes of Gypsies, Beggars, Shoplifters, Highwaymen, Foot Pads, and all other Clans of Cheats and Villains, with Proverbs, Phrases, Figurative Speeches, &c., to which is added a complete Collection of Songs in the Canting Dialect, 12mo. 1725

The title is by far the most interesting part of the work. A mere make-up of earlier attempts.

CAREW. Life and Adventures of Bamfylde Moore Carew, the King of the Beggars, *with Canting Dictionary, portrait*, 8vo. 1791

There are numerous editions of this singular biography. The Canting Dictionary is nothing more than a filch from earlier books.

CHARACTERISMS, or the Modern Age Displayed; being an attempt to expose the Pretended Virtues of Both Sexes, 12mo (part i., Ladies; part ii., Gentlemen), *E. Owen*. 1750

An anonymous work, from which some curious matter may be obtained.

CONYBEARE'S (Dean) Essay on Church Parties, reprinted from the *Edinburgh Review*, No. CC., October, 1853, 12mo. 1858

Several curious instances of religious or pulpit slang are given in this exceedingly interesting little volume.

COTTON'S (Charles) Genuine Poetical Works, 12mo. 1771

Scarronides, or Virgil Travestie, being the first and fourth Books of Virgil's Æneis, in English burlesque, 8vo, 1672, and other works by this author, contain numerous vulgar words now known as slang.

DECKER'S (Thomas) The Bellman of London; bringing to light the most notorious villanies that are now practised in the Kingdome, 4to, black letter. *London*, 1608

Watt says this is the first book which professes to give an account of the canting language of thieves and vagabonds. But this is wrong, as will have been seen from the remarks on Harman, who collected the words of the vagabond crew half a century before.

DECKER'S (Thomas) Lanthorne and Candle-light, or the Bellman's Second Night's Walke, in which he brings to light a brood of more strange villanies than ever were to this year discovered, 4to. *London*, 1608-9

This is a continuation of the former work, and contains the *Canter's Dictionary*, and has a frontispiece of the London Watchman with his staff broken.

DECKER'S (Thomas) Gulls Hornbook, 4to. 1609

"This work affords a greater insight into the fashionable follies and vulgar habits of Q. Elizabeth's day than perhaps any other extant."

DECKER'S (Thomas) O per se O, or a new Cryer of Lanthorne and Candle-light, an Addition of the Bellman's Second Night's Walke, 4to, black letter. 1612

A lively description of London. Contains a Canter's Dictionary, every word in which appears to have been taken from Harman without acknowledgment. This is the first work that gives the Canting Song, a verse of which is inserted at page 20 of the Introduction. This Canting Song was afterwards inserted in nearly all Dictionaries of Cant.

DECKER'S (Thomas) Villanies discovered by Lanthorne and Candle-light, and the Helpe of a new Cryer called O per se O, 4to. 1616

"With Canting Songs neuer before printed."

DECKER'S (Thomas) English Villanies, eight several times prest to Death by the Printers, but still reviving again, are now the eighth time (as at the first) discovered by Lanthorne and Candle-light, &c., 4to. 1648

The eighth edition of the "*Lanthorne and Candle-light.*"

DICTIONARY of all the Cant and Flash Languages, both Ancient and Modern, 18mo. *Bailey*, 1790

DICTIONARY of all the Cant and Flash Languages, 12mo. *London*, 1797

DICTIONARY of the Canting Crew (Ancient and Modern), of Gypsies, Beggars, Thieves, &c., 12mo. N. D. [1700]

DICTIONNAIRE des Halle, 12mo. *Bruxelles*, 1696

This curious Slang Dictionary sold in the Stanley sale for £4 16s.

DUCANGE ANGLICUS.—The Vulgar Tongue: comprising Two Glossaries of Slang, Cant, and Flash Words and Phrases used in London at the present day, 12mo. 1857

A silly and childish performance, full of blunders and contradictions. A second edition appeared during the past year.

DUNCOMBE'S Flash Dictionary of the Cant Words, Queer Sayings, and Crack Terms now in use in Flash Cribb Society, 32mo, *coloured print.* 1820

DUNTON'S Ladies Dictionary, 8vo. *London*, 1694

Contains a few cant words.

EGAN. Grose's Classical Dictionary of the Vulgar Tongue, with the addition of numerous Slang Phrases, edited by Pierce Egan, 8vo. 1823

The best edition of Grose, with many additions, including a Life of this celebrated antiquarian.

EGAN'S (Pierce) Life in London, 2 vols, thick 8vo, *with coloured plates by Geo. Cruikshank, representing high and low life*. 18—

Contains numerous cant, slang, sporting, and vulgar words, supposed by the author to form the basis of conversation in life, high and low, in London.

ELWYN'S (Alfred L.) Glossary of supposed *Americanisms*—Vulgar and Slang Words used in the United States, small 8vo. 1859

GENTLEMAN'S MAGAZINE, 8vo. N.D.

"In a very early volume of this parent magazine were given a few pages, by way of sample, of a Slang Vocabulary, then termed Cant. If, as we suspect, this part of the Magazine fell to the share of Dr. Johnson, who was then its editor, we have to lament that he did not proceed with the design."—*John Bee, in the Introduction to his Slang Dictionary*, 1825.

GENTLEMAN'S MAGAZINE, vol. xcii., p. 520.

Mention made of slang.

GLOSSARIES of County Dialects. V.D.

Many of these will repay examination, as they contain cant and slang words, wrongly inserted as provincial or old terms.

GOLDEN CABINET (The) of Secrets opened for Youth's delightful Pastime, in 7 parts, the last being the "City and Country Jester;" with a Canting Dictionary, by Dr. Surman, 12mo. *London*, N.D. (1730)

Contains some curious woodcuts.

GREENE'S (Robert) Notable Discovery of Coosnage, now daily practised by sundry lewd persons called Conie-catchers and Crosse biters. Plainly laying open those pernitious sleights that hath brought many ignorant men to confusion. Writen for the general benefit of all Gentlemen, Citizens, Aprentices, Country Farmers, and Yeomen, that may hap to fall into the company of such coosening companions. With a delightful discourse of the coosnage of Colliers, 4to, *with woodcuts*. *Printed by John Wolfe*, 1591

The *first edition*. A copy of another edition, supposed to be *unique*, is dated 1592. It was sold at the Heber sale.

GREENE'S (Robert) Groundworke of Conny-Catching, the manner of their PEDLERS' FRENCH, and the meanes to understand the same, with the cunning slights of the Conterfeit Cranke. Done by a Justice of the Peace of great Authoritie, 4to, *with woodcuts*. 1592

Usually enumerated among Greene's works, but it is only a reprint, with variations, of *Harman's Caveat*, and of which Rowland complains in his Martin Markall. The *second* and *third* parts of this curious work were published in the same year. Two other very rare volumes by Greene were published—*The Defence of Cony-Catching*, 4to, in 1592, and THE BLACK BOOKES MESSENGER, in 1595. They both treat on the same subjects.

GROSE'S (Francis, generally styled *Captain*) Classical Dictionary of the Vulgar Tongue, 8vo. 178

The much sought after FIRST EDITION, but containing nothing, as far as I have examined, which is not to be found in the *second* and *third* editions. As respects indecency, I find all the editions equally disgraceful. The Museum copy of the *First Edition* is, I suspect, Grose's own copy, as it contains numerous manuscript additions which afterwards went to form the second edition. Excepting the obscenities, it is really an extraordinary book, and displays great industry, if we cannot speak much of its morality. It is the well from which all the other authors—Duncombe, Caulfield, Clarke, Egan, &c. &c.—drew their vulgar outpourings, without in the least purifying what they had stolen.

HAGGART. Life of David Haggart, alias John Wilson, alias Barney M'Coul, written by himself while under sentence of Death, *curious frontispiece of the Prisoner in Irons*, intermixed with all the Slang and Cant Words of the Day, to which is added a Glossary of the same, 12mo. 1821

HALL'S (B. H.) Collection of College Words and Customs, 12mo. *Cambridge* (*U. S.*), 1856

Very complete. The illustrations are excellent.

HALLIWELL'S Archaic Dictionary, 2 vols, 8vo. 1855

An invaluable work, giving the cant words used by Decker, Brome, and a few of those mentioned by Grose.

HARLEQUIN Jack Shepherd, with a Night Scene in Grotesque Characters, 8vo. (*About* 1736)

Contains Songs in the *Canting* dialect.

HARMAN'S (Thomas, Esq.) Caveat or Warening for Common Cursetors, vulgarely called Vagabones, set forth for the utilitie and profit of his naturall countrey, augmented and inlarged by the first author thereof; whereunto is added the tale of the second taking of the counterfeit Crank, with the true report of his behaviour and also his punishment for his so dissembling, most marvellous to the hearer or reader thereof, newly imprinted, 4to.
Imprinted at London, by H. Middleton, 1573

Contains the earliest Dictionary of the Cant language. Four editions were printed— William Griffith.. 1566
.... 1567
.... 1567
Henry Middleton, 1573

What *Grose's Dictionary of the Vulgar Tongue* was to the authors of the earlier part of the present century, Harman's was to the Deckers, and Bromes, and Heads of the seventeenth.

HARRISON'S (William) Description of the Island of Britain (prefixed to Holinshed's Chronicle, 2 vols, folio. 1577

Contains an account of English vagabonds.

HAZLITT'S (William) Table Talk, 12mo (vol. ii. contains a chapter on *Familiar Style,* with a notice on *Slang Terms.*) V. D.

HEAD'S (Richard) English Rogue, described in the Life of Meriton Latroon, a Witty Extravagant, 4 vols., 12mo. *Frans. Kirkman,* 1671-80

Contains a list of cant words, evidently copied from Decker.

HELL UPON EARTH, or the most pleasant and delectable History of Whittington's Colledge, otherwise vulgarly called Newgate, 12mo. 1703

HENLEY'S (John, *better known as* ORATOR HENLEY) Various Sermons and Orations. 1719-53

Contain numerous vulgarisms and slang phrases.

[HITCHING'S (Charles, *formerly City Marshal, now a Prisoner in Newgate*)] Regulator; or, a Discovery of the Thieves, Thief-Takers, and Locks, alias Receivers of Stolen Goods in and about the City of London, also an Account of all the FLASH WORDS *now in vogue amongst the Thieves, &c.,* 8vo., VERY RARE, *with a curious woodcut.* 1718

A violent attack upon Jonathan Wild.

HOUSEHOLD WORDS, No. 183, September 24.

Gives an interesting but badly digested article on slang; many of the examples are wrong.

JOHNSON'S (Dr. Samuel) Dictionary (the earlier editions). V.D.

Contains a great number of words italicised as *cant,* low, or barbarous.

JONSON'S (Ben.) Bartholomew Fair, ii., 6.

Several cant words are placed in the mouths of the characters.

JONSON'S (Ben.) Masque of the Gipsies Metamorphosed, 4to. 16—

Contains numerous cant words.

KENT'S (E.) Modern Flash Dictionary, containing all the Cant Words, Slang Terms, and Flash Phrases now in Vogue, 18mo., *coloured frontispiece.* 1825

L'ESTRANGE'S (Sir Roger) Works (principally translations). V. D.

Abound in vulgar and slang phrases.

LEXICON Balatronicum; a Dictionary of Buckish Slang, University Wit, and Pickpocket Eloquence, by a Member of the Whip Club, assisted by Hell-fire Dick, 8vo. 1811

One of the many reprints of *Grose's* second edition, put forth under a fresh, and what was then considered more attractive title. It was given out in advertisements, &c., as a piece of puff, that it was edited by a Dr. H. Clarke, but it contains scarcely a line more than Grose.

LIBER VAGATORUM: Der Betler Orden, 4to.

The first edition of this book appears to have been printed at Augsburg, by Erhard Öglin, or Ocellus, about 1514,—a small quarto of twelve leaves. It was frequently reprinted at other places in Germany; and in 1528 there appeared an edition at Wittemberg, with a preface by Martin Luther, who says that the "Rotwelsche Sprach," the cant language of the beggars, comes from the Jews, as it contains many Hebrew words, as anyone who understands that language may perceive. This book is divided into three parts, or sections; the first gives a special account of the several orders of the "Fraternity of Vagabonds;" the second, sundry "*notabilia*" relating to the different classes of beggars previously described; and the third consists of a "Rotwelsche Vocabulary," or "Canting Dictionary." There is a long notice of the "Liber Vagatorum" in the "Wiemarisches Jahrbuch," 10te, Band, 1856. Mayhew, in his "London Labour," states that many of our cant words are derived from the Jew fences. It is singular that a similar statement should have been made by Martin Luther more than three centuries before.

LIFE IN ST. GEORGE'S FIELDS, or the Rambles and Adventures of Disconsolate William, Esq., and his Surrey Friend, Flash Dick, with Songs and a FLASH DICTIONARY, 8vo. 1821

MAGINN (Dr.) wrote Slang Songs in *Blackwood's Magazine*. 1827

MAYHEW'S (Henry) London Labour and London Poor, 3 vols, 8vo. 1851

An invaluable work to the inquirer into popular or street language.

MAYHEW'S (Henry) Great World of London, 8vo. 1857

An unfinished work, but containing several examples of the use and application of cant and slang words.

MIDDLETON (Thomas) and DECKER'S (Thomas) Roaring Girl; or Moll Cut Purse, 4to. 1611

The conversation in one scene is entirely in the so-called Pedlar's French. It is given in *Dodsley's Old Plays*.

MODERN FLASH DICTIONARY, 48mo. 1825

The smallest slang dictionary ever printed.

MONCRIEFF'S Tom and Jerry, or Life in London, a Farce in Three Acts, 12mo. 1820

An excellent exponent of the false and forced "high life" which was so popular during the minority of George IV. The farce had a run of a hundred nights, or more, and was a general favourite for years. It abounds in cant, and the language of "gig," as it was then often termed.

MORNINGS AT BOW STREET, by T. Wright, 12mo, *with Illustrations by George Cruikshank.* *Tegg,* 1838

In this work a few etymologies of slang words are attempted.

NEW CANTING DICTIONARY, 12mo. N. D.

A copy of this work is described in *Rodd's Catalogue of Elegant Literature*, 1845, part iv., No. 2128, with manuscript notes and additions in the autograph of Isaac Reed, price £1 8s.

NEW DICTIONARY of the Terms, Ancient and Modern, of the Canting Crew in its several tribes of Gypsies, Beggars, Thieves, Cheats, &c., with an addition of some *Proverbs, Phrases, Figurative Speeches, &c.*, by B. E. GENT, 12mo. N. D. [1710]

Afterwards issued under the title of *Bacchus and Venus*, 1737, and in 1754 as the *Scoundrel's Dictionary*.

NEW DICTIONARY of all the Cant and Flash Languages used by every class of offenders, from a Lully Prigger to a High Tober Gloak, small 8vo., pp. 62. 179—

Mentioned by John Bee.

NOTES AND QUERIES. The invaluable Index to this most useful periodical may be consulted with advantage by the seeker after etymologies of slang and cant words.

PARKER. High and Low Life, A View of Society in, being the Adventures in England, Ireland, &c., of Mr. G. Parker, a *Stage Itinerant*, 2 vols in 1, thick 12mo. *Printed for the Author*, 1781

A curious work, containing many cant words, with 100 orders of rogues and swindlers.

PARKER'S (Geo.) Life's Painter of Variegated Characters, with a Dictionary of Cant Language and Flash Songs, to which is added a Dissertation on Freemasonry, *portrait*, 8vo. 1789

PEGGE'S (Samuel) Anecdotes of the English Language, chiefly regarding the Local Dialect of London and Environs, 8vo. 1803—41

PERRY'S (William) London Guide and Stranger's Safeguard, against Cheats, Swindlers, and Pickpockets, by a Gentleman who has made the Police of the Metropolis an object of enquiry twenty-two years (no wonder when the author was in prison a good portion of that time!) 1818

Contains a dictionary of slang and cant words.

PHILLIPS' New World of Words, folio. 1696

PICKERING'S (F.) Vocabulary, or Collection of Words and Phrases which have been supposed to be peculiar to the United States of America, to which is prefixed an Essay on the present state of the English Language in the United States, 8vo. *Boston,* 1816

The remark made upon *Bartlett's Americanisms* applies equally to this work.

PICTURE OF THE FANCY, 12mo. 18—

Contains numerous slang terms.

POTTER'S (H. T., of *Clay, Worcestershire*) New Dictionary of all the Cant and Flash Languages, both ancient and modern, 8vo, pp. 62. 1790

POULTER. The Discoveries of John Poulter, alias Baxter, 8vo, 48 pages. (1770?)

At pages 42, 43, there is an explanation of the "Language of Thieves, commonly called Cant."

PRISON BREAKER, The, or the Adventures of John Shepherd, a Farce, 8vo. *London,* 1725

Contains a canting song, &c.

PUNCH, or the London Charivari,

Often points out slang, vulgar, or abused words. It also, occasionally, employs them in jokes, or sketches of character.

QUARTERLY REVIEW, vol. x., p. 528.

Gives a paper on Americanisms and slang phrases.

RANDALL'S (Jack, *the pugilist,* formerly of the "*Hole in the Wall,*" Chancery-lane) Diary of Proceedings at the House of Call for Genius, edited by Mr. Breakwindow, to which are added several of Mr. B.'s minor pieces, 12mo. 1820

Believed to have been written by Thomas Moore. The verses are mostly parodies of popular authors, and abound in the slang of pugilism, and the phraseology of the fast life of the period.

RANDALL (Jack) A Few Selections from his Scrap Book; to which are added Poems on the late Fight for the Championship, 12mo. 1822

Frequently quoted by Moore in *Tom Crib's Memorial.*

SCOUNDREL'S DICTIONARY, or an Explanation of the Cant Words used by Thieves, Housebreakers, Street-robbers, and Pickpockets about Town, with some curious dissertations on the Art of Wheedling, &c., *the whole printed from a copy taken on one of their gang, in the late scuffle between the watchmen and a party of them on Clerkenwell green*, 8vo. 1754

A reprint of *Bacchus and Venus*, 1737.

SHARP (Jeremy) The Life of an English Rogue, 12mo. 1740

Includes a "Vocabulary of the Gypsies' Cant."

SHERWOOD'S Gazetteer of Georgia, U.S., 8vo.

Contains a glossary of words, slang and vulgar, peculiar to the Southern States.

SMITH'S (Capt.) Compleat History of the Lives and Robberies of the most Notorious Highwaymen, Foot-pads, Shop-lifts, and Cheats, of both Sexes, in and about London and Westminster, 12mo, vol. i. 1719

This volume contains "THE THIEVES NEW CANTING DICTIONARY OF THE WORDS, PROVERBS, &c., USED BY THIEVES."

SMITH (Capt. Alexander) The Thieves Grammar, 12mo., p. 28. 17—

A copy of this work is in the collection formed by Prince Lucien Bonaparte.

SMITH'S (Capt.) Thieves Dictionary, 12mo. 1724

SNOWDEN'S Magistrate's Assistant, and Constable's Guide, thick small 8vo. 1852

Gives a description of the various orders of cadgers, beggars, and swindlers, together with a *Glossary of the Flash Language.*

SPORTSMAN'S DICTIONARY, 4to. 17—

By an anonymous author. Contains some low sporting terms.

STANLEYE'S Remedy, or the Way how to Reform Wandring Beggers, Thieves, etc., wherein is shewed that Sodomes Sin of Idlenes is the Poverty and the Misery of this Kingdome, 4to. 1646

This work has an engraving on wood which is said to be the veritable original of Jim Crow.

SWIFT'S coarser pieces abound in vulgarities and slang expressions.

THE TRIUMPH OF WIT, or Ingenuity display'd in its Perfection, being the Newest and most Useful Academy, Songs, Art of Love, *and the Mystery and Art of Canting, with Poems, Songs, &c., in the Canting Language*, 16mo. *J. Clarke*, 1735

What is generally termed a shilling *Chap Book.*

THE TRIUMPH OF WIT, or the Canting Dictionary, being the Newest and most Useful Academy, containing the Mystery and Art of Canting, with the original and present management thereof, and the ends to which it serves and is employed, illustrated with Poems, Songs, and various Intrigues in the Canting Language, with the Explanations, &c., 12mo. *Dublin*, N. D.

A Chap Book of 32 pages, *circa* 1760.

THOMAS (I.) My Thought Book, 8vo. 1825

Contains a chapter on slang.

THE WHOLE ART OF THIEVING and Defrauding Discovered: being a Caution to all Housekeepers, Shopkeepers, Salesmen, and others, to guard against Robbers of both Sexes, and the best Methods to prevent their Villanies; to which is added an Explanation of most of the cant terms in the Thieving Language, 8vo, pp. 46. 1786

TOM CRIB'S Memorial to Congress, with a Preface, Notes, and Appendix *by one of the Fancy* [Tom Moore, the poet], 12mo. 1819

A humorous poem, abounding in slang and pugilistic terms, with a burlesque essay on the classic origin of slang.

VACABONDES, The Fraternatye of, as well of ruflyng Vacabones, as of beggerly, of Women as of Men, of Gyrles as of Boyes, with their proper Names and Qualities, with a Description of the Crafty Company of Cousoners and Shifters, also the XXV. Orders of Knaves; otherwyse called a Quartern of Knaves, confirmed by Cocke Lorell, 8vo. *Imprinted at London by John Awdeley, dwellyng in little Britayne streete without Aldersgate.* 1575

It is stated in *Ames' Typog. Antiq.*, vol. ii., p. 885, that an edition bearing the date 1565 is in existence, and that the compiler was no other than old John Audley, the printer, himself. This conjecture, however, is very doubtful. As stated by Watt, it is more than probable that it was written by Harman, or was taken from his works, in MS. or print.

VAUX'S (Count de, *a swindler and a pickpocket*) Life, written by himself, 2 vols., 12mo, *to which is added a Canting Dictionary.* 1819

These Memoirs were suppressed on account of the scandalous passages contained in them.

WEBSTER'S (Noah) Letter to the Hon. John Pickering, on the Subject of his Vocabulary, or Collection of Words and Phrases supposed to be peculiar to the United States, 8vo, pp. 69. *Boston,* 1817

WILD (Jonathan) History of the Lives and Actions of Jonathan Wild, Thieftaker, Joseph Blake, *alias* Blue skin, Footpad, and John Sheppard, Housebreaker; together with A CANTING DICTIONARY BY JONATHAN WILD, *woodcuts,* 12mo. 1750

WILSON (Professor) contributed various Slang pieces to *Blackwood's Magazine;* including a Review of Bee's Dictionary.

WITHERSPOON'S (Dr., of America) Essays on Americanisms, Perversions of Language in the United States, *Cant* phrases, &c., 8vo., in the 4th vol. of his Works. *Philadelphia,* 1801

The earliest work on American vulgarisms. Originally published in a series of Essays, entitled the *Druid,* which appeared in a periodical in 1761.

LIST OF ABBREVIATIONS, &c.

A.N.—Anglo-Norman.

Ancient, or *Ancient English*—Whenever these terms are employed, it is meant to signify that the words to which they are attached were in respectable use in or previous to the reign of Elizabeth.—See *Old*.

Ancient Cant—In use as a *cant* word in or previous to the reign of Elizabeth.

A.S.—Anglo-Saxon.

Beds.—Bedfordshire.

Cor.—A corruption.

East.—Used in the Eastern Counties.

Eng.—English.

Fren.—French.

Ger.—German.

Glouc.—Gloucestershire.

Hants.—Hampshire.

Ital.—Italian.

L. F.—Lingua Franca, or Bastard Italian.

Lat.—Latin.

Linc.—Lincolnshire.

Midx.—Middlesex.

N. D.—No date.

Norf.—Norfolk.

Old, or *Old English*—In general use as a respectable word in or previous to the reign of Charles the Second.—See *Ancient*.

Old Cant—In use as a cant word in or previous to the reign of Charles II.

Oxon.—Oxfordshire.

Prov.—Provincial.

Pug.—Pugilistic.

Sal., or *Salop*—Shropshire.

Sax.—Saxon, or Anglo-Saxon.

Scot.—Scotch.

Sea—Used principally by Sailors.

Shaks.—Shakspeare.

Som.—Somerset.

Span.—Spanish.

Suf.—Suffolk.

Theat.—Theatrical.

Teut.—Teutonic.

V. D.—Various dates.

West.—Used in the Western Counties.

Wilts.—Wiltshire.

Worc.—Worcestershire.

Yorks.—Yorkshire.

"There is a certain amount of interest in preserving the origin of slang words as a record of existing manners, and of those strange popular sayings which have a rapid and almost universal popularity, and then fade away as rapidly. The combinations of language in cant are often curious. The London Antiquary informs us that the cant for a public house at the present day is *suck cassa*,—pure Saxon and pure Spanish."—*Saturday Review.*

"This is by far the most complete work upon a curious subject which has yet been compiled—a dictionary of more than three thousand words in current use in our streets and alleys, lanes and by-ways, from which the learned lexicographers have turned aside with contempt."—*Critic.*

"This new Dictionary of our English cant and slang is *full*, and may be received as an amusing and suggestive little book of common knowledge into any household. Indecency has been omitted from its pages."—*Examiner.*

"The 'London Antiquary' has certainly taken up a very curious and interesting branch of linguistic research."—*Notes and Queries.*

"An instructive as well as amusing work. The author may be congratulated upon the successful issue of his labours in the field of vagabond and unrecognised speech."—*Titan* in an article of *ten pages.*

"An amusing work, and a most useful and valuable contribution to the study of words. It is absolutely necessary to all those who in fast life would "mind their P's and Q's," as well as to the readers of our newspaper and periodical literature."—*Montrose Review.*

"We do not wonder that of so quaint and entertaining a compilation a new edition should so soon have been demanded."—*Globe.*

"Contains a good deal of curious historical and anecdotical information, and is altogether a well got up, well edited, and amusing little volume."—*Shipping Gazette.*

"Evinces a great amount of industry."—*Morning Star.*

Beautifully printed, 12mo., cloth, 3s. 6d.,

THE CHOICEST HUMOROUS POETRY OF THE AGE.

The Biglow Papers. By James Russell LOWELL. (Alluded to by John Bright in the House of Commons.)

WITH AN ILLUSTRATION BY GEORGE CRUIKSHANK.

*** *This Edition has been Edited with additional Notes explanatory of the persons and subjects mentioned therein.*

"The rhymes are as startling and felicitous as any in 'Hudibras.' 'Sam Slick is a mere pretender in comparison."—*Blackwood's Magazine.*

"The fun of the 'Biglow Papers' is quite equal to the fun of the 'Ingoldsby Legends.' This is the real doggerel, the Rabelaiesque of poetry."—*Fraser.*

☞ There is an edition of this work extant, hastily got up after my own was announced, edited by Mr. Hughes, the author of *Tom Brown's School Days.* It gives an introduction, long and occasionally amusing, but of not the least value in explaining to the *English* reader the peculiarities of the work. The *Globe* pointed out this sad defect in reviewing the present edition:—"The copy beside us," remarks the writer, "is apparently edited and published by Mr. Hotten, who gives a preface—which has the rare merit of explaining exactly what the ordinary English reader requires to know of satirical political poems, written in the Yankee dialect, touching the Mexican war, and the extension of the slave states—and of attempting to explain nothing else."—*Globe*, Dec. 8, 1859.

Now ready, SECOND EDITION, fcap. 8vo, neatly printed, price 1s.,

Macaulay; the Historian, Statesman,

and ESSAYIST: Anecdotes of his Life and Literary Labours, with some Account of his Early and Unknown Writings.

, Also, a fine paper Edition, cloth, neat, with a PHOTOGRAPHIC PORTRAIT (*the only one known to have been taken*) by MAULL and POLYBLANK, price 2s. 6d.

☞ Includes Anecdotes of SYDNEY SMITH, MOORE, ROGERS, and LORD JEFFREY; and gives numerous examples of Lord Macaulay's extraordinary memory and great powers of conversation.

"A brilliant sketch of the great historian, containing particulars of his youthful compositions, which are new and deeply interesting."—*Herald.*

"We regard the little work before us as a very opportune publication. The author has brought together such a mass of facts, sketches, and anecdotes, illustrative of the character and mind of Lord Macaulay, that the book is very valuable as supplying, in a small compass, a faithful and vivid account of the great historian."—*Bradford Review.*

"An interesting account of a man who was an ornament to our nation. Of the extraordinary capacity and availability of his memory many wonderful stories are told.—*Evangelical Repository.*

"This work is well timed. Here we really have all that is known concerning the great man. The little book brings together with much dexterity and success very various and very scattered materials. We have been peculiarly interested in the details of the late illustrious Baron's youthful productions. Never before has Wordswo-th's famous couplet, "The boy is father of the man," received so vivid illustration. It is earnestly to be hoped that the whole of these early papers, and his inedited speeches and addresses written and spoken in the flush of his powers, and with all the wealth of illustration that so distinguished him, shall be collected. Why not at once by the writer of the present brilliant sketch? We know not who he is, but he is a man of no common powers. He has evidently, too, put his heart into his book. It thrills and throbs with reverent love towards the man. We like exceedingly his fresh, generous, glowing style; and not less his genial, gossipy way of telling the many anecdotes with which his pages sparkle."—*Advertiser.*

"Valuable from the original matter and anecdotes it gives concerning Macaulay's youthful productions."—*Leader.*

"We hear Mr. Hotten's little book on Macaulay is a success. Ten thousand copies sold within a few days!"—*Critic.*

Now ready, NEW AND POPULAR EDITION, neatly printed, fcap. 8vo, pp. 336, price 2s. 6d.,

Anecdotes of the Green Room and

STAGE; or Leaves from an Actor's Note-Book, at Home and Abroad, by GEORGE VANDENHOFF.

☞ Mr. Vandenhoff, who earned for himself, both in the Old and New Worlds, the title of THE CLASSIC ACTOR, has retired from the Stage. His reminiscences are extremely interesting, and include Original Anecdotes of the Keans (father and son), the two Kembles, Macready, Cooke, Liston, Farren, Elliston, Braham and his Sons, Phelps, Buckstone, Webster, Chas. Mathews: Siddons, Vestris, Helen Faucit, Mrs. Nisbett, Miss Cushman, Miss O'Neil, Mrs. Glover, Mrs. Chas. Kean, Rachel, Ristori, and many other dramatic celebrities.

Now ready, post 8vo, cloth, 3s. 6d.,

Rubbing the Gilt Off: a West End Book

for All Readers. By JOHN HOLLINGSHEAD, Author of "Under Bow Bells, a City Book for All Readers."

WITH A HUMOROUS ILLUSTRATION.

CONTENTS.

The Humiliation of Fogmoor.
A Pet of the Law.
Navy Dry Rot.
How to Make a Madman.
Nine Kings.
An Official Scarecrow.
A Model Theatre.
The Suffering Sinecurist.
A National Christmas Bill.
The Social Reformer.
Mudfog on Colonies.
Diplomatic World.
The Man behind my Chair.
Wanted, a Court Guide.

"Clever and sagacious writing."—*Athenæum.*

"As a collection of papers which, through all their whimsical fancies, develope a political system with an earnestness and a consistency that are rare, we can cordially recommend Mr. Hollingshead's book."—*Leader and Saturday Analyst.*

"Mr. Hollingshead has lost nothing of his dramatic power."—*Critic.*

"The stories are no less interesting and amusing than instructive."—*Morning Star.*

"Mr. Hollingshead has considerably widened his range of humorous illustration, still keeping, however, to the field of political economy."—*Daily News.*

Now ready, fcap. 8vo, cloth, price 3s. 6d., beautifully printed,

Gog and Magog; or, the History of the

Guildhall Giants. With Some Account of the Giants which Guard English and Continental Cities. By F. W. FAIRHOLT, F.S.A.

WITH ILLUSTRATIONS ON WOOD BY THE AUTHOR, COLOURED AND PLAIN.

*** The critiques which have appeared upon this amusing little work have been uniformly favourable. The *Athenæum* pronounces it a perfect model of successful antiquarian exposition, readable from the first line to the last. The *Art Journal* devotes a considerable space to the little work, and congratulates the author upon his success. The *Leader* contributes two full columns of eulogy. The *Builder* directs its readers to purchase it. The *Critic* says, in a long article, that it thoroughly explains who these old Giants were, the position they occupied in popular mythology, the origin of their names, and a score of other matters, all of much interest in throwing a light upon fabulous portions of our history.

Nearly ready, beautifully printed, fcap. 8vo, price 3s. 6d.

The Choicest Jests of English Wits;

from the Rude Jokes of the Ancient Jesters, to the refined and impromptu Witticisms of Theodore Hook and Douglas Jerrold. Including the Cream of Joe Miller: comprising the best Sayings, Façetions and Merry, which have contributed to give to our country the name of Merry England.

Nearly ready, beautifully printed, on fine paper, fcap. 8vo, pp. 350, price 5s.,

The History of Playing Cards, and the

VARIOUS GAMES connected with them, from the Earliest Ages; with some Account of Card Conjuring, and Old-Fashioned Tricks.

ILLUSTRATED WITH FORTY CURIOUS WOODCUTS ON TINTED PAPER.

This most amusing work, introducing the reader to a curious chapter of our social history, gives an interesting account, replete with anecdotes, of the most popular and widely known pastime which has ever been invented by man for his amusement. A morei nstructive and entertaining book could not be taken in hand for a pleasant hour's reading.

Two Vols. royal 8vo, handsomely printed, £2 8s.

Ancient Songs, Ballads, and Dance

TUNES of the Olden Time, illustrative of the National Music of England, with Introductions to the different Reigns, and Notices of the Airs from Writers of the Sixteenth Century; also a Short Account of the Minstrels, by W. CHAPPELL, F.S.A.

This interesting work forms the largest and most complete collection of Ancient British Ballads and Songs ever published. The words are from the original old copies, and the addition of the Old Tunes to which they were formerly sung is an interesting and most curious feature. Several facsimiles adorn the work.

Preparing for publication, fcap. 8vo, beautifully printed,

Old English Ballads, relating to New

England, the Plantations, and other Parts of North America; with Ancient Poetical Squibs on the Puritans and the Quakers who emigrated there; now first collected from the original excessively rare Broadsides sold in the streets at the time, and edited with Explanatory Notes. *Illustrated with facsimiles of the very singular woodcuts which adorn the original Songs and Ballads.*

Preparing for publication, beautifully printed, post 8vo, half morocco, Roxburghe style,

Garland of Pepysian Ballads, Historical,

ROMANTIC, and HUMOROUS, some illustrating Shakespere, edited by EDWARD F. RIMBAULT, Esq., LL.D.

It is well known that the unfortunate regulation imposed by Pepys, the celebrated diarist, that his Manuscripts and Books should never be examined save in the presence of a Fellow of the College at Cambridge where they are preserved, has hitherto alone prevented the collecting and publishing some of the more interesting of these world-renowned Ballads and Songs. The difficulty, however, has been surmounted by Dr. Rimbault, aided by the authorities of Magdalene College; and the lovers of our charming old popular poetry will be glad to know that a *Garland* of these Balladian ditties is in course of publication. The work will be preceded by an Introduction on Ballad Lore, Ballad Writers, and Ballad Printers, giving some new and interesting particulars gathered from "old bookes," and other sources, hitherto unexplored The publisher would state that the work will be beautifully printed by Whittingham, and that it will be adorned by a curious woodcut facsimile frontispiece.

Nearly ready, in small 4to, half morocco, very neat,

An hitherto unknown Poem, written by John Bunyan, whilst confined in Bedford Jail, for the Support of his Family, entitled,

Profitable Meditations, Fitted to Man's

DIFFERENT CONDITION: in a Conference between Christ and a Sinner. By JOHN BUNYAN, Servant to the Lord Jesus Christ.

London: Printed for Francis Smith at the Sign of the Elephant and Castle without Temple Bar, 1661

This very interesting, though melancholy literary memorial of the Author of the celebrated Pilgrim's Progress, will be choicely reprinted by Whittingham, from the only known copy lately discovered by the publisher. It will be edited, with an Introduction by George Offor, Esq. The impression will be limited.

Now ready, price 5s.

Magna Charta. An Exact Facsimile of

the Original Document, preserved in the British Museum, very carefully drawn, and printed on fine plate paper, nearly 3 feet long by 2 feet wide, with the ARMS AND SEALS OF THE BARONS ELABORATELY EMBLAZONED IN GOLD AND COLOURS. A.D. 1215

COPIED BY EXPRESS PERMISSION, and the only *correct* drawing of the Great Charter *ever taken*. This important memorial of the liberties and rights of Englishmen is admirably adapted for framing, and would hang with propriety from the walls of every house in the country. As a guarantee to the purchaser that the facsimile is exact, the publisher need only state that Sir Frederick Madden has permitted copies to hang for public inspection upon the walls of the Manuscript Department in the British Museum. It was executed by Mr. Harrison, under whose auspices the splendid work on the Knights of the Garter was produced some years ago.

Printed by TAYLOR & GREENING, Graystoke-place, Fetter-lane, London, E.C.